Studies on the Chinese Economy

General Editors: **Peter Nolan**, Sinyi Professor of Chinese Management, Judge Institute of Management Studies, University of Cambridge, and Fellow of Jesus College, Cambridge, England; and **Dong Fureng**, Professor, Chinese Academy of Social Sciences, Beijing, China

This series analyses issues in China's current economic development, and sheds light upon that process by examining China's economic history. It contains a wide range of books on the Chinese economy past and present, and includes not only studies written by leading Western authorities, but also translations of the most important works on the Chinese economy produced within China. It intends to make a major contribution towards understanding this immensely important part of the world economy.

Titles include:

Thomas Chan, Noel Tracy and Zhu Wenhui
CHINA'S EXPORT MIRACLE

Sarah Cook, Shujie Yao and Juzhong Zhuang (*editors*)
THE CHINESE ECONOMY UNDER TRANSITION

Xu Dixin and Wu Chengming (*editors*)
CHINESE CAPITALISM, 1522–1840

Christopher Findlay and Andrew Watson (*editors*)
FOOD SECURITY AND ECONOMIC REFORM

Samuel P. S. Ho and Y. Y. Kueh
SUSTAINABLE ECONOMIC DEVELOPMENT IN SOUTH CHINA

Kali P. Kalirajan and Yanrui Wu (*editors*)
PRODUCTIVITY AND GROWTH IN CHINESE AGRICULTURE

Bozhong Li
AGRICULTURAL DEVELOPMENT IN JIANGNAN, 1620–1850

Alfred H. Y. Lin
THE RURAL ECONOMY OF GUANGDONG, 1870–1937

Dic Lo
MARKET AND INSTITUTIONAL REGULATION IN CHINESE INDUSTRIALIZATION

Jun Ma
THE CHINESE ECONOMY IN THE 1990s

Guo Rongxing
HOW THE CHINESE ECONOMY WORKS

Sally Sargeson
REWORKING CHINA'S PROLETARIAT

Ng Sek Hong and Malcolm Warner
CHINA'S TRADE UNIONS AND MANAGEMENT

Terence Tsai
CORPORATE ENVIRONMENTALISM IN CHINA AND TAIWAN

Michael Twohey
AUTHORITY AND WELFARE IN CHINA

Carl E. Walter and Fraser J. T. Howie
'TO GET RICH IS GLORIOUS!'
China's Stock Markets in the '80s and '90s

Michael Warner
CHANGING WORKPLACE RELATIONS IN THE CHINESE ECONOMY

Wang Xiao-qiang
CHINA'S PRICE AND ENTERPRISE REFORM

Xiaoping Xu
CHINA'S FINANCIAL SYSTEM UNDER TRANSITION

Yanni Yan
INTERNATIONAL JOINT VENTURES IN CHINA

Godfrey Yeung
FOREIGN INVESTMENT AND SOCIO-ECONOMIC DEVELOPMENT IN CHINA
The Case of Dongguan

Wei-Wei Zhang
TRANSFORMING CHINA

Xiao-guang Zhang
CHINA'S TRADE PATTERNS AND INTERNATIONAL COMPARATIVE
ADVANTAGE

Studies on the Chinese Economy
Series Standing Order ISBN 0–333–71502–0
(*outside North America only*)

You can receive future titles in this series as they are published by placing a standing order.
Please contact your bookseller or, in case of difficulty, write to us at the address below with
your name and address, the title of the series and the ISBN quoted above.

Customer Services Department, Macmillan Distribution Ltd, Houndmills, Basingstoke,
Hampshire RG21 6XS, England

'To Get Rich is Glorious!'

China's Stock Markets in the '80s and '90s

Carl E. Walter
Managing Director
China International Capital Corporation (CICC)
Beijing
China

and

Fraser J. T. Howie
Vice President in the Sales and Trading Department
China International Capital Corporation (CICC)
Beijing
China

First published 2001 by
PALGRAVE
Houndmills, Basingstoke, Hampshire RG21 6XS and
175 Fifth Avenue, New York, N.Y. 10010
Companies and representatives throughout the world

PALGRAVE is the new global academic imprint of
St. Martin's Press LLC Scholarly and Reference Division and
Palgrave Publishers Ltd (formerly Macmillan Press Ltd).

ISBN 0–333–92025–2

This book is printed on paper suitable for recycling and made from fully managed and sustained forest sources.

A catalogue record for this book is available from the British Library.

Library of Congress Cataloging-in-Publication Data
Walter, Carl E.
    "To get rich is glorious!" : China's stock markets in the '80s and '90s / Carl E. Walter and Fraser J.T. Howie.
        p. cm.
    Includes bibliographical references and index.
    ISBN 0–333–92025–2
    1. Stock exchanges—China. 2. Stocks—China. 3. Securities––China. 4. Industries—China—Finance. 5. Capitalism—China.
    I. Title: China's stock markets in the '80s and '90s. II. Howie, Fraser J.T. III. Title.
    HG5782 .W3453 2000
    332.64'251'09048—dc21
                                                                00–052457

10   9   8   7   6   5   4   3   2
10   09   08   07   06   05   04   03   02

Printed and bound in Great Britain by
Antony Rowe Ltd, Chippenham, Wiltshire

To
Our families and friends

Contents

List of Figures and Charts

Figures

Charts

List of Tables

Preface

Much is written about the various efforts aimed at reforming China's state-owned enterprises. But in all this literature the Chinese government's determined effort to use the equity capital markets as a tool of enterprise reform has been virtually ignored. The fact is that during the past decade this has been, and will continue to be, the principal thrust with regard to the reform of state-owned enterprises. On-again, off-again noises about bankruptcy, M&A solutions, and asset management companies are only side shows in the process.

China's companies have been offering securities to investors, both domestic and foreign, since 1984 and have listed their shares on international stock exchanges since 1992. By late 1999 there were over 1000 companies which had successfully listed shares. All of this amounts to a Big Deal in the international (and domestic) financial community where most market knowledge resides. Even so, little of China's experience has been explored systematically in English (and not much more in Chinese). This book is aimed at filling the gap by approaching China's securities reforms from both historical and technical angles and tracking their development through the end of 1999.

We do not intend this to be a handbook and believe that even those with a casual interest in the country will learn much about how China operates. Seeing where China and its companies have come from and what problems they face now should provide the reader a feeling of where things are going in the longer run. The securities markets everywhere produce colorful characters and outrageous scandals and China has been no exception to this. Although one of us has been involved in China's securities industry since 1992 and has seen plenty of 'color', our intent here is to provide a systematic record of events, showing how things happen and drawing a few conclusions. The colorful book will have to come later. This book is also not about privatization in China since this is not what is happening. It is about what happened to the policy of state enterprise reform through corporatization. By corporatizing state enterprises, the government began with the simple aim of increasing their operating efficiency. But some of these enterprises proceeded to sell shares to the public raising badly needed funds in the process. This transformed the entire reform.

It is a bit difficult not to be jaded about all this given the official spin put on the reforms. As a senior official in the now defunct, but once all powerful, State Committee for Restructuring of the Economic Systems put it in 1989, 'The purpose of the share system is the share system and not to issue shares to the public.' This official was an idealist or was, perhaps, protesting too much. If people were willing to pay money for pieces of paper evidencing minority ownership in an overall minority ownership of an enterprise notionally owned by the 'State', why shouldn't the actual owners of the enterprise, the management, satisfy their demands? Of course, this is what happened with great rapidity and the genie of the market was out of the bottle.

But that is not all that has happened. It seems that international investors were equally, if not more, interested in participating in what by 1992 was becoming a China boom. Over the ensuing eight years Chinese companies, the government and, indeed, the entire economy have become dependent for capital on the whims of the international investor community. As the recent market craze for 'New Economy' hi-tech companies clearly illustrates, what is hot in the West suddenly becomes hot in China, driving the government and its policy process before it. And equally so, if the global markets are cold, no Chinese company will succeed in selling its shares, no matter how 'good' the government may think the deal is. Markets do not fit well inside of plans. The global securities markets are visibly setting the government's domestic agenda to a degree that is no less significant for having gone unremarked. Money knows no language barriers.

The international impact is not just a matter of money, it is also a matter of values. As major Chinese companies seek the support of international investors, they have been, at times, forcibly reminded that there may be strings attached. The huge international money managers have their own constituency, the groups and organizations which have entrusted funds for them to manage. And as, for example, the surprising riots in Seattle against the vision of the World Trade Organization suggest, the Chinese government, its companies and their Western sponsors can likewise ill afford to disregard the ideologies and ideals found in Western democracies. China may strive to continue as the Middle Kingdom, but what it is in the 'middle' of has changed and is continuing to change with a speed and a far reaching influence never seen before in world history. If, as the Chinese say 'History is a mirror', it is important to understand the origins and the subsequent development of this new force in China's economy. Doing so, we believe, provides a clear insight into where China is going in the years ahead and provides the basis for a strengthened optimism.

Through the assistance of one of our colleagues, Mr Yang Changpo, we were given reason to satisfy our curiosity by developing a report on China's securities markets for the Asian Development Bank. Unfortunately, the report while only partially completed proved to be so interesting and information outside of China so completely lacking that we decided a full-blown overview might be welcomed. An on-line search for English materials on the Chinese stock markets revealed numerous statistical studies of Chinese stock volatilities and only a handful of patchwork commentaries. These we believed were either too sophisticated or too journalistic, lacking the basic overview that might be of more general interest. There was only one book, Yao Chengxi's excellent *Stock Market and Futures Market in the PRC*, which looks at these markets in 1995 from a lawyer's viewpoint. We felt that our view as market participants might also be of interest. Since one of us had been an investment banker in China since 1992 and had direct personal experience and the other an equity trader in Hong Kong, it seemed to us we had the right skill set to tackle the problem.

We apologize in advance if the chapters on Chinese shares are rather arcane, but then the variety of Chinese equities is exceedingly arcane to begin with, but important, nonetheless, to appreciate. These ingenious shares types are the means the government used to ring fence the market and inhibit outright privatization which seems to have been proceeding helter-skelter in Guangdong during the 1980s. The book is also not particularly accurate, although we have certainly tried to track down accurate market statistics and other information to the best of our ability. But when the Shenzhen exchange, Qianlong Data Systems and Wind Information Systems all widely disagree, what can you do? We have stuck with the exchanges in each case. We feel sure that the overall climate, trends and general details of China's unique experiment with stocks through the end of 1999 are accurately portrayed. We eagerly await, however, the books we hope will be written by some of the early shapers of China's stock markets who most assuredly have something to say. In the meantime, if this book stimulates interest, a variety of related Internet websites are provided in the Bibliography so that Chinese A share day traders in New York or even Edinburgh can keep on top of the action.

We would like to express our deep appreciation to CICC's Chief Executive Officer, Ms Elaine LaRoche, for her interest and support, to Mr Yang Changpo for sparking the idea, as well as to various other colleagues at Morgan Stanley, CICC and elsewhere who steered us in the right direction from time to time. We also thank Vladimijr Attard who provided useful data on convertibles and Helen Hua Haiyue who proved the master of the Wind Information System from which we accumulated so much market data. To Professor Peter Nolan of The Judge Institute at Cambridge University we would like to express our heartfelt thanks for bringing the project to fruition. A portion of the royalties derived from this book will be donated to the Project Hope school now being sponsored by CICC and built in Hebei. Finally, we thank our families whose support and forbearance during the long evenings, weekends and holidays we worked on this project is so much appreciated and could not be done without.

We are quite certain we have made mistakes or errors of omission for which we alone are responsible. Our hope is that this work will prove useful to all those who are involved with China and provide at least the basis for the research and analysis many of our friends and colleagues will do over the next few years as China's securities markets become truly open to outside participation.

Beijing
January 2000

List of Abbreviations

CB	convertible bond
CGB	Chinese government bonds
CICC	China International Capital Corporation
CSRC	Chinese Securities Regulatory Commission
FMC	Fund Management Company
GDP	gross domestic product
IPO	initial public offering
JV	joint venture
M&A	mergers and acquisitions
MOF	Ministry of Finance
MOFERT	Ministry of Foreign Economic Relations and Trade
MOFTEC	Ministry of Foreign Trade and Economic Cooperation
NAV	net asset value
NETS	National Electronic Trading System
NYSE	New York Stock Exchange
OTC	over the counter trading
PBOC	People's Bank of China
P/E	price/earnings ratio
PRC	People's Republic of China
RMB	Renminbi
SAEC	State Administration for Exchange Control
SAMB	State Asset Management Bureau
SC	State Council
SCRES	State Committee for the Restructuring of the Economic Systems
SCSC	State Council Securities Committee
SEHK	Stock Exchange of Hong Kong
SLMB	State Land Management Bureau
SOE	state owned enterprise
SOET	State Council Office of Economics and Trade
SPC	State Planning Commission
SPCB	State Price Control Bureau
SSCCRC	Shanghai Securities Central Clearing and Registration Company
SSE	Shanghai Stock Exchange
SSSC	Shenzhen Securities Settlement Company

ST	special treatment (listed companies)
STAQ	Securities Trading Automated Quotations System
SZSE	Shenzhen Stock Exchange
TVE	Township and Village Enterprise
WTO	World Trade Organization

1
'To Get Rich is Glorious!'

In October 1992 a Chinese automobile company completed the initial public offering (IPO) of its shares on the New York Stock Exchange, becoming the first Chinese company in history to list on an international market. Wholly unexpected and wildly received by investors, this small transaction dramatically focused global attention on events unfolding in China. Although only US$80 million, this IPO marked the emergence of China on the global capital markets. Its domestic impact was even larger, however, since it presaged massive changes in the operating environment of China's state-owned industrial sector. These changes were driven by new State policies which promoted corporate structures limited by shares wherein the shares themselves could be sold to non-state investors and listed and traded on domestic and international stock exchanges. Although the Chinese Premier at the time believed such changes represented little more than the traditional joint venture ('JV') financings, the revival of domestic stock exchanges and the listing of Chinese companies internationally symbolized a dramatic and highly visible break with past political and economic arrangements and was recognized as such by Chinese and non-Chinese alike. The 1990s have since witnessed the elaboration of this policy line to the point that the demands and requirements of the securities markets have become a major influence on State economic policy.

But if Deng Xiaoping had never gone to see Guangdong himself in early 1992, China's experiment with State enterprise corporatization and public listing might have remained at the half-baked stage of the late 1980s and early 1990s. Amidst the political paralysis stemming from the June 4 crisis, only Deng could have provided cover to those who wanted to promote equity shares and stock markets in the midst of a still solidly Soviet-style planned economy. His open-minded

1

comment on securities and stock markets is still cited repeatedly in all manner of books. In response to a question raised in Shenzhen he said, 'Are such things as securities and stock markets good or not? Are they dangerous? Do these things exist only in capitalist systems or can socialist ones use them too? It is permitted to try them out, but it must be done in a determined fashion'.[1]

His comment was clearly heard throughout China's still nascent securities industry and, by extension, those parts of the bureaucracy which had an interest in the 'shareholding system'. And his positive attitude touched off an explosion of activity, not just domestically, but internationally as well as the world's investors suddenly 'discovered' China's potential. China fever extended not only to the private markets, from which direct investment poured in as if there were no limit, it also included the international public equity and debt capital markets. For the first time international money managers found themselves looking at the opportunity to buy the shares and fixed income securities of China's state-owned enterprises. Having looked, they liked what they saw and took hold of the chance with both hands as if whatever piece of China they had grabbed was pure gold. In short, against the background of the Soviet Union's collapse and the technological triumph of the Gulf War, there was a nearly universal belief that Deng had now removed the final barrier to capitalism in China and everyone, Chinese and foreigner alike, was going to get rich by participating in the development of the country's vast, untapped market. This belief was not limited only to foreigners. Across China ordinary Chinese took to heart Deng's claim that 'To get rich is glorious'. Without question, China had changed overnight.

Perhaps if Deng had remained in vigorous health for a few more years this promise would have been taken to its expected conclusion much sooner. Instead, and despite great progress earlier in the decade, at the turn of the century China remains mired in a deflationary spiral caused by a crisis of confidence in what is equivocally called a 'socialist market economy', but which is most assuredly neither. Caught in the middle of a transition to something resembling Western capitalism, the country appears directionless, the government gridlocked and its leaders seeking a solution from the World Trade Organization as if from a *deus ex machina*. On the other hand, anything other than a tinkering approach may be too much to expect from a country as complex and with such deep-rooted traditions as China.

The evolution of China's shares and stock markets fully reflect this 'tinkering' reality as well as that of Soviet-style central planning. Even so, China's securities markets have come a long way from those days in the early 1980s when farmers in the Pearl River Delta put their money together to capitalize by means of the 'shareholding co-operative system' what later became known as 'Township and Village Enterprises'. Now at the turn of the century in Shenzhen, the birthplace of equity shares, and Shanghai, the once and future Hong Kong, gleaming, fully automated securities exchanges stand making a national market in equity and fixed income securities for over 30 million Chinese retail and institutional investors. The shares of nearly 1000 Chinese companies change hands each day with a total market capitalization of approximately US$350 billion, still small when compared to the United States, but large enough to rank China as the second or third largest market in non-Japan Asia. Without question, this is a great achievement, made all the more so by the fact that these markets coexist uncomfortably within what is still predominantly a state owned and planned economy.

These are what might be called equity markets 'with Chinese characteristics'. Securities markets in any other country in the world evolved in market economies in support of and benefiting from the capital raising efforts of privately owned companies. In such markets equity securities from an investor's viewpoint represent a right, both of ownership and economic benefit, in a company and from the company viewpoint, an obligation. In China the objective of securities markets is to create greater operating efficiencies in state owned enterprises that

Chart 1.1: Comparative market capitalizations, non-Japan Asia (6 August 1999)

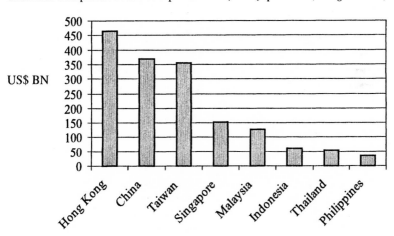

Source: Bloomberg and Shanghai and Shenzhen Market Statistics

continue to be controlled absolutely by the State. It is, therefore, entirely unclear just what securities do, in fact, represent other than the opportunity to perhaps profit from trading and to receive a dividend. As for the companies, there seems as yet to be no sense of obligation to minority shareholders, but only to the state if at all. In China the markets are operated by the state, regulated by the state, legislated by the state, raise funds for the benefit of the state by selling shares in enterprises owned by the state. No doubt there is some conflict of interest in all this; in the entire system the only things which do not belong to the state are the actual money, or capital, put up by predominantly individual investors and the market itself. These, however, are the very heart of the system that have created a dynamic that is without question driving the rest before it.

Despite the many advances over the past ten years, in the overall context of China's economy the securities markets remain relatively small, most especially the primary market, which at about US$9 billion in 1998 is a fraction of total bank deposits of over US$700 billion or of total state fixed asset investment of US$400 billion.[2] More interestingly, the primary market is also only a fraction of foreign direct investment which has been running at around US$40 billion per year. On the other hand, the total market capitalization of domestically listed A share companies of about US$300 billion is rather larger and it is this figure which is compared to other Asian markets in Chart 1.1. The only problem is that this figure is at best only notional. Some 70 per cent of China's equity market capitalization is represented by the value of legally nontradable shares owned directly or indirectly by the State. The remaining 30 per cent represents what might in other circumstances be called publicly owned shares freely tradable in the secondary market. The approximately US$90 billion market value of these shares, however, is based on the expectation that the other 70 per cent will remain nontradable in the long term, if not in perpetuity. Such an expectation is founded on the State's declaration at the outset of the market experiment that it must maintain absolute majority ownership in the companies listed. Should this position alter, or be perceived to alter, the possibility of huge volumes of new shares coming on the market could destroy current market values leading to a crash with its attendant unforeseeable consequences, both economic and otherwise. But this is only one consequence of the way China's stock markets have evolved.

This evolution traces its beginning to the early 1980s when a quasi-shareholding structure was spontaneously created to capitalize what became known as Township and Village Enterprises ('TVEs'). In 1983 a Shenzhen TVE named Baoan County United Investment Company became the first Chinese enterprise to issue shares to the public follow-ing the establishment of the PRC in 1949. The following year Beijing Tianqiao Department Store became the first state owned enterprise ever to reorganize itself as a shareholding company, but it was beaten to the public market by a Shanghai SOE, Shanghai Feile Acoustics Company, which actually sold shares to the public later in the year. All such issues were in effect private placements given the lack of a formal market and market regulator.

These and other scattered reorganizations and transactions were the early frontrunners of a trend given added momentum in 1984 by the Communist Party's momentous passage of 'The decision on the reform of the economic system', which promoted the broad development of a mixed economy including co-operative and individual enterprises. The next development came in 1986 when Shenzhen produced the first regulations standardizing the process through which enterprises could be reorganized as shareholding companies. This effort led directly to the first major public offering of shares by the Shenzhen Development Bank in 1987. This offering, however, was well undersubscribed and in the end had to be bought by the arranging underwriters so as to avoid total failure. Quite clearly no one knew what stocks were at this point.

Chart 1.2: The relative size of China's equity markets (31 Dec. 1998)

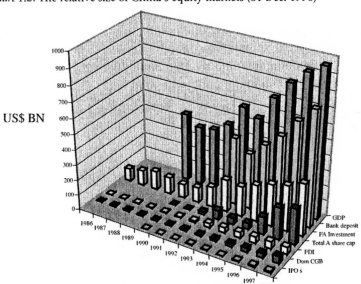

Source: *China Statistical Yearbook* and Wind Information System

This period of spontaneous experimentation with corporate forms and securities was entirely unregulated, promoted by local governments and largely unnoticed by Beijing until, almost as an afterthought, the People's Bank of China ('PBOC') was given responsibility for the industry in 1986 as part of a more elaborate set of new regulations governing the commercial banking sector. From that point on, until its displacement by the Chinese Securities Regulatory Commission ('CSRC') in 1992, the PBOC or, more properly, its local branches were active participants in the process of what might be called 'corporatization' as contrasted to privatization.

Corporatization refers to the reorganization of an indiscriminate body of state assets into a corporate legal entity. Under state planning and 'ownership by the whole people' enterprises and factories had no independent legal existence, they were part and parcel of the State from which they were virtually indivisible. The state's objective in the shareholding experiment was to enhance the efficiency of state enterprises by clarifying the responsibilities and authority of enterprise management via the corporatization process. Privatization refers to the sell off of state assets to non-state owners. This has never been what China's equity markets have been about, although this was not necessarily clear during the 1980s.[3]

On looking back, what was especially hopeful about this period and in particular the events in Shenzhen, was its freedom from state planning and political jargon. State owned and other enterprises reorganized, issued and sold shares to investors to raise funds. Notwithstanding the fact that investor categories were largely different arms of the state and enterprise employees (with the exception of Shenzhen where foreign investors were also active), there was nothing dogmatic about share types, investor restrictions and trading limitations. Although there were no formal securities markets until 1986, when the first OTC counter officially opened in Shanghai, shares could nonetheless be freely transferred. The fact, however, was that they were not.

It seems surprising but the reality was that after more than 30 years of central planning and state ownership, there was no understanding of what exactly an equity share was. The issuers saw them as similar to bonds only, instead of interest, equity securities paid a variable dividend. So at the start shares were seen by investors as valuable only for the dividends paid and, consequently, people bought them to hold for the cash flow. There was no awareness that they might appreciate (or, for that matter, depreciate) in value and so yield up a capital gain (or loss). But all this changed in early 1989 when the Shenzhen Development Bank announced its dividend plan for the 1988 financial year.

This announcement marked a major turning point in China's equity markets. The bank was exceedingly generous to its investors awarding them with a cash dividend of RMB7 per share, a two for one stock dividend, and a one for one stock split. In the blink of an eye, investors who had bought the bank's shares in 1988 for about RMB20 per share now enjoyed a profit several times their original investment. With this example, investors did not need a market guru to tell them that shares were worth (potentially) more than their value suggested. The rush was on and the bank's shares, as well as the few other shares available, soared in OTC trading. In the case of the bank, its shares skyrocketed from a year end price of RMB40 to RMB120 just before June 4 and ended the year at RMB90, the June interruption notwithstanding. In the late 1980s these sums were very big money.

Armed with this new understanding of equities China's investors set off a period of 'share fever' which was centered on Shenzhen and then gradually extended during 1990 to Shanghai, as prices in Shenzhen escalated while those in Shanghai were still unappreciated by the local populace. Interest became so hot that the black market flourished. In the end, government authorities were forced to take measures to cool the markets, even going so far in Shenzhen as to post billboards saying 'Investors Beware! Shares Can Lose Value!' More serious measures included daily price movement limits and increased transaction taxes and ownership transfer stamp duties. These measures eventually took hold leading to a market collapse in late 1990. But never mind, investors had learned the lesson of equity investing: stocks can appreciate and with this the speculative habit.

At the same time, Beijing had also learned something about the equity experiment: if it was not managed properly it could lead to social unrest, the bogey of all Chinese governments. There was a flurry of activity in late 1988 and early 1989 aimed first at documenting the extent of the market and then developing regulatory measures which would have further promoted the market's development. Final drafts had even been submitted in spring 1989 to the State Council for approval. The drafts, however, were shelved by the political fallout from the Tiananmen events. What did emerge in May 1990 came with the State Council announcement of restrictions on the shareholding experiment, including its limitation to the state sector and the designation of Shenzhen and Shanghai as the only officially recognized OTC trading markets. This limitation of the corporatization effort to the state sector alone marked a major reversal of 1980s practice and its effects have been felt in more recent years.

The focus of OTC trading in Shenzhen and Shanghai was the public part of a formal decision made at the same time to proceed with the establishment of the Shanghai and Shenzhen securities exchanges. The intent was to provide a formal venue for securities trading in two administrative areas presumably well under the control of the central government. The prospect of having socially sensitive securities trading facilities located throughout the country, much less Beijing, was unacceptable to the government at this point. In the event, the Shanghai exchange opened in December 1990 and Shenzhen shortly after in 1991. This great advance, however, was by no means the government's stamp of approval on the experiment, it was an effort to exert control – June 4 was barely a year in the past.

On the eve of Deng's historic Southern Trip and just after the opening of the Shanghai and Shenzhen exchanges, what kind of shares representing what sort of interest in what sort of enterprise were being traded? After all, there was no securities legislation, no body of corporate law, and no accounting system which even remotely resembled that used in the West. Ten years later, however, China is renowned, less for its companies, than for its extravagant variety of shares with such confusing names as state shares, legal person shares, overseas legal person shares, social legal person shares, internal staff shares and so on, not to mention A, B, H, N and S shares and Red and Pink Chips, and this list is by no means complete. What happened? The answer is relatively straightforward. Prior to 1992 the market was small, unregulated and without the required legislation necessary to develop further. The local government approach towards equity shares, moreover, was quite non-ideological, particularly in Shenzhen which was strongly influenced by Hong Kong. Shares were shares and anyone could invest in and trade them including foreigners and any sort of enterprise could reorganize and issue them.

With Deng's approving comments in early 1992, however, there poured forth all the provisional measures and other regulations which had been drafted in 1989 including China's first stab at a corporate law, the Standard Opinion. The thrust of these measures was to impose a standard framework on shareholding companies and the shares which they offered to investors. There is no question that such regulations were necessary if the experiment was to develop further. On the other hand, the regulations were imbued with the spirit of state planning, state control and state interest. This is best seen in the very definition of shares which proceeded based on who owned them rather than on the particular economic rights they might represent in a company. Thus, if an agency of the government owned the shares, the shares were state shares, if a state enterprise with legal person status owned them, they were legal person shares and so on. Shares were given names based on the relationship of the particular owner to the state and it is absolutely amazing how many permutations of this relationship came to light over the next few years. Similarly, shares listed overseas became known for the market on which they were listed, hence, H shares for those listed in Hong Kong and so on. For simplicity's sake, shares acquired for cash which can be freely traded on the market are the Alphabet Shares, while shares otherwise acquired and nontradable are some sort of State shares. The reality is, however, that all shares domestic and international are Renminbi shares with the same rights, same obligations and, theoretically, the same price; the Chinese have just placed certain of them in certain boxes for control purposes.

The greatest problem created by this approach, however, is that all such shares as are owned by the state, either directly or indirectly, are by legal definition tradable but in practical reality nontradable. Thus, all shares were not created equal. Why this was so is best illustrated by Article 4 of China's 1994 Company Law which states, 'The ownership rights to the state-owned assets of a company [limited by shares] belongs to the State'. This is an incredible assertion in a law whose very purpose is to give legal form to companies limited by shares. Something behind the mentality that feels the need to express this direct ownership and control over tangible assets is best explained by reference to the financial makeup of enterprises under central planning which is provided in Chapter 2. As this discussion shows, the formal birth of China's equity markets in 1992 was heavily marked by the country's heritage of state planning. The impact of this heritage, particularly as it relates to China's segmented share structure, is analyzed in Chapter 3.

Shenzhen made its second major contribution to market development in August 1992. Tens of thousands of would be investors had lined up overnight to obtain the forms necessary to subscribe to a share offering only to discover that all such forms had already been fully distributed 'internally'. Major riots ensued. The importance of what became known as the '810 Incident' was the displacement of the PBOC as market regulator and the formation of a new specialized body, the Chinese Securities Regulatory Commission (CSRC). The need for such a specialized body had always been an object of dispute since the goal of the corporatization process was primarily reorganizing enterprises, a matter internal to the state itself. Or as the State Committee for the Reform of the Economic Systems, put it in 1989, 'The purpose of the share system is the share system and not to issue shares to the public'. On the other hand, enterprises needed financing which the state could not fully provide and the state needed to manage the process so that investors stayed quiet. Practical reality won out over the original objective. The 810 Incident demonstrated that the PBOC was incapable of acting as regulator and the decision was taken to establish the CSRC. Such an independent body authorized to regulate both the primary and secondary securities markets provided a much needed focus to the effort and created a bureaucracy whose self interest lay in further market development.

This decision had a second and perhaps even more important ramification. Together with the CSRC announcement the State Council made public the designation of nine enterprises as candidates for listing on the Stock Exchange of Hong Kong. These two announcements came less than a week after the surprise PBOC sponsored listing of the first Chinese company overseas and on the New York Stock Exchange at that. Together these events put China on the map of international financial investors and gave rise to a China fever in the international capital markets which put Shenzhen and Shanghai in the shade.

Necessarily this meant that the CSRC spent an inordinate amount of time at its inception dealing with the issues of listing Chinese SOEs overseas. The commission's original staff was well prepared to do so since it consisted of a body of professionals many of whom had been educated, trained and spent time in Hong Kong and the United States. Moreover, its Chairman, Liu Hongru, had been the leader of the team which had negotiated the Chinese listings with the Hong Kong exchange. This association with overseas listings, however, tainted the CSRC and made its institutionalization even more difficult. On the one hand, the PBOC and other bureaucracies which stood to lose power, continued to resist the CSRC notwithstanding an extraordinary effort by the State Council to clarify the scope of authority of all entities involved. On the other hand, the two stock exchanges, which were controlled by their respective municipal governments, kept up a continuous criticism of the CSRC for supporting the listing of China's presumably best companies overseas instead of supporting the development of the domestic markets. This led eventually to Liu Hongru's resignation in late 1994 and the dispersal of most of the commission's international staff over the following year. The CSRC thus became a traditional Chinese organ of the bureaucracy.

Despite this, or perhaps because of it, the CSRC gradually gained authority over the markets, a process which was marked by three stages:

(1) 1992–93 marked the establishment and consolidation of authority over the securities and future markets and extension of investigatory and enforcement powers; (2) 1996 marked the CSRC's assumption of full control over the two securities exchanges; and (3) 1998 the CSRC became a full ministry-level organization empowered by the 1999 Securities Law. Along the way many of the remnants of the earlier period of market experimentation were done away with, the best examples being a variety of securities exchanges operated by the PBOC, local governments and other bodies leaving Shanghai and Shenzhen as China's two national exchanges. This background and the functions of the two exchanges are described in Chapter 4 while the development of China's market regulatory structure is dealt with in Chapter 5.

The reorganization of SOEs, even if done gradually, is a monumental task involving not simply the creation of the requisite legal, accounting and financial framework, but also somehow instilling in the minds of management an entirely new way of thinking about enterprise operations. Then there is the social issue: until recently enterprises acted on behalf of the state as providers of education, medical insurance and social security services for workers, both active and retired, and their families. Given the continuing reality of over 100 million active employees of SOEs, the inclusion of retirees and dependents makes the number larger than the population of the United States. Understood in this way makes it impossible to assert, as some might on a bad day, that the corporatization process is a sham designed only to help finance bankrupt enterprises. On the other hand, gradualism and a focus on the state owned sector alone have not as yet had anything other than a superficial impact on the way the corporatized enterprises perform. The reasons for this become clear when the restructuring process itself is understood.

State owned enterprises in China are sometimes described as 'big and complete, small and complete (*da er quan, xiao er quan*)'. This refers to the reality that any SOE, no matter what its size (and no matter how size is measured), is a nearly independent society unto itself. Aside from the capital and raw material inputs it may receive from the state and the goods it may sell back, most SOEs are fully integrated entities both vertically and sometimes horizontally as well. On top of this they contain the full scope of social services – schools, hospitals, courts and police, fire departments and, of course, property management, travel and entertainment services. The core of this galaxy of services and related entities is a presumably productive manufacturing entity or service provider. The cash flow from this entity is what supports everything and everyone else. How then, does one go about separating the state from the enterprise to form a profitable and competitive entity which can survive market competition? More to the point, how does one create a company which would be an attractive investment opportunity if shares were offered internationally? And if this is done, what about the remainder of the original enterprise which is not included?

From a technical point of view enterprise restructuring is relatively straightforward, although the work is challenging it is not difficult and relies highly on judgement. The key is the first step: to identify a company in a sector which may have a competitive edge and which investors, therefore, view positively. Although the sector may be attractive, it is nonetheless critical that the final company as restructured be profitable and have strong growth prospects. But, of course, this cannot be known at the outset since there are no proper financial statements and the company as such does not yet exist. This is where judgement is called for, both of the potential company's prospects as well as of investor interests and appetite. After this first step, what might be called the boundaries of the new company are defined, in other words, what assets are in and what are out. Obviously, all the social support and other non-productive assets are excluded. Based on this preliminary definition of the company, accountants are brought in to conduct a full audit and lawyers are brought in to prepare the required documents and formally define the relationship between the new company and what is left outside of it, that is, the former SOE, now called the parent. In other words, what has been done is to carve out the heart of the SOE, form it into a new company, and leave the rest behind in place but without direct access to that cash flow which was its life's blood. A technical triumph, if the international offering of shares is successful, but a looming social disaster for those left behind. This is the true problem in the government's efforts to separate itself from its enterprises (*zhengqi fenkai*). It can be done, but it does not solve the problem.

It is not surprising, therefore, that of the 86 overseas listing candidate enterprises only 47 have managed to complete their full restructuring. This success rate is somewhat smaller when changes in the composition of the listing candidates are considered. Of the 86 candidates only 71 can be considered true SOEs, the remaining 15 are jerry rigged highway, property and agricultural companies added in to the most recent two groups of candidates. In fact, the last group of candidates consisted entirely of highway, port and agricultural assets. Of the 71 SOE candidates only 38 successfully restructured and listed shares and of this number 21 did so prior to 1995 during the initial surge of international interest in Chinese equities.

There are two explanations for these results. First of all, even though the process is technical, its consequences are social. Many SOEs, despite the attraction of new financing, chose not to proceed. Many other SOEs found that they could not proceed since their profitability and prospects were not sufficiently attractive. And still other SOEs decided not to even begin the process due to its expense, the amount of work involved, the social problems eventuating and the ready alternative of the domestic markets, which are significantly easier to access. This, and the reality that China does not have a large number of potentially attractive enterprises, accounts for the growth in so-called infrastructure companies and Red Chip conglomerates which, being entirely artificial, have none of the social problems of a true SOE. The second, and equally critical reason for these results, has been that investors have lost money placed in Chinese shares.

In contrast, the domestic markets have consistently welcomed SOE issuers in the primary market, rationally structured or not. This response has been to a great extent due to government regulated pricing policies which seem to be calibrated to assure both issue success and investor profit in the primary market. And because the SOEs need not drastically restructure their operations, the result is that most domestically listed companies are what might kindly be called conglomerates, although conglomerations is probably a more accurate description. A detailed discussion of the listing and restructuring process is set-out in Chapter 6.

The reason for such different market responses lies ultimately with the investors. International markets and investors are mature and investors as a category represent an extremely diverse group with differing levels of expertise and investment strategies. Moreover, significant amounts of capital have been committed to the markets over time so that such markets can be described as having both breadth and depth. In contrast, in China ten years ago the word 'capital (*ziben*) was still a dirty word and the maybe 100 000 or so equity investors did so for purely speculative reasons. Now, less than a decade later there are 30 million investors, the overwhelming majority of whom are still individuals, and 70 per cent are located in the relatively rich coastal provinces and cities. Even for these provinces account penetration rates, with the exception of Shanghai, remain for the most part in the single digit numbers. Beyond the retail sector work has only just begun to broaden the market beyond the existing

perhaps 70 000 institutional investors which include primarily corporate accounts subject to a variety of shifting restrictions.

China's economy over the past 20 years has given rise to a great
diversity of corporates many of which are active in the stock market.
No systematic publicly available information exists as to the extent
of this investor segment. Whatever might exist represents the proprietary knowledge of China's securities firms. To provide a feel for the
diversity of corporate investors, however, the following types of corporations participated in a recent IPO: SOEs, SOE holding companies, private companies, foreign-invested companies, rural credit
unions and such entities as 'investment' or 'development' companies, which are most likely unregulated banks and money managers.
The corporate investment mentality is not dissimilar to that of individual investors – short term gain, rather than long term investment
results. The 1999 summer rally encouraged many new corporates to
enter the market in the hope of offsetting poor operations, but
results were no doubt mixed due to poor controls and procedures.
In short, in the overall structure of Chinese investors, corporates
are located somewhere above individual accounts, by virtue of
being able to invest more money, but below the mutual funds and
securities houses.

In 1997 the first regulations standardizing the investment fund and
fund management industry came into effect. Prior to this investment
funds were largely found in the local markets created by local governments to provide regional trading centers with their own proprietary
products. Such funds were small, unregulated, invested in projects as
well as securities and controlled by wholly conflicted management
companies. Through 1996 a total of 75 investment funds had been
established. Taken together these funds raised some RMB730 million
(or US$88 million), an extremely small amount which, if averaged out,
comes to only a little more than US$1.2 million per fund. Following
the passage of the 1997 Fund Measures, 15 new funds have been
formed and listed on the two national exchanges, raising some RMB35
billion (US$4.2 billion). According to the new provisions, each fund
must maintain an invested position in equity and debt securities of at
least 80 per cent and can hold no more than ten per cent of the shares
of any one company. During their subscription periods the new funds
have tended to be well oversubscribed despite the fact that the fund
managers themselves have no track record whatsoever. More interestingly, they have traded in the secondary market in the early going at

significant premia over their per unit net asset value showing that investors have yet to fully understand the product.

The success of this new industry has much riding on it as the government seems to believe it provides a less dangerous mode of entry into the markets for others. In late 1999 China's 25 insurance companies, for example, were permitted to invest up to 5 per cent of their assets in stocks, but only through investment in the funds. Over the past few years China has been gradually building up a pension fund industry which is now made up of two types of funds, those managed by local governments and those managed by companies. Like the insurance companies until recently, these pension funds at present can invest only in bank deposits and Chinese government bonds (CGBs). It might be expected that pension funds at some point in the future would also be allowed to invest in equities in a manner similar to insurance companies.

At the current stage of the market, however, the biggest participants by far have been the securities companies and their proprietary trading activity. Much of the 1990s was taken up with the enforcement of a Chinese-style Glass-Steagall Act which separated the banking and securities industries. In China, as in America of the 1930s, the motive was to ring fence savings deposits from securities underwriting and trading. This segregation was confirmed in the 1999 Securities Law. At year end 1998 a survey indicated that there were some 90 securities companies and another 237 securities units operated or controlled by trust and investment companies. All such firms were quite small, only seven had equity capital of RMB1 billion (US$120 million) or more. In fact, the bulk of these security operations were simple brokerages, acting as agents between clients' trading and the securities exchanges (and trading from time to time with their clients' deposits).

The 1999 Securities Law has set in motion an industry consolidation by classing securities firms based on capital as either (1) comprehensive firms; or (2) brokerages. A comprehensive firm is required to have a minimum of RMB500 million in capital, whereas a brokerage needs only RMB50 million. In terms of business scope, as might be expected, the less capitalized brokerage firms can only carry out brokerage business. In contrast, comprehensive firms may broker securities, conduct proprietary trading, act as securities underwriters and seek approval for other securities business from the CSRC. The consequence of such consolidation may be a decline in trading volume. This may be offset, however, by the growing activity of securities investment funds which have tended to adjust their asset structures relatively quickly. A full discussion of investors and other market participants can be found in Chapter 7.

The interaction of share types, regulatory framework, issuers and investors has produced China's unique securities market. Like emerging markets elsewhere, China's equity markets have been characterized by relatively short cycles and, at times, extreme volatility. Unlike other emerging markets, however, the basic fact of China's domestic markets is that they operate in a closed system. The influence of events in the Asian region or elsewhere in the world, including the US, is muted, if not smothered altogether. Over the past three years global and regional markets have experienced such events as the Russian debt default, the meltdown of Long Term Asset Management in the US, the Asian financial crisis and, in China, the spectacular 1999 summer rally. Correlation analysis for this three-year period between China's domestic stock indices and major international and regional indices, as well as Chinese Government Bond price performance versus that of US Treasuries, however, shows very little linkage between domestic and international financial markets. This is primarily the consequence of the Renminbi's non-convertibility on the capital account. It is highly unlikely that this situation will change in the short to medium term, China's accession to the WTO notwithstanding. Impressions of the Mexican financial crisis of the 1980s and the more recent Asian crisis, make the issue of Renminbi convertibility far too politically sensitive an issue to be addressed until a much later date when, it is hoped, a more conducive environment will exist.

Given this isolation, the Chinese market's character to date reflects the influence of two principal factors: (1) investor sentiment about the country's overall economic performance; and (2) government policy. In the twenty years since the start of its liberalization process, China's economy has shot ahead at a growth rate averaging approximately 9 per cent per annum. Given the size of the country, its population and transitional economic structure, it is not surprising that there have been periodic economic dislocations typified by high inflation rates. One such period occurred in the late 1980s when efforts to cool inflation led to a period of economic and political stagnation that extended into the 1990s. Then, catalyzed by Deng's comments in Guangdong, China's economic development once again shot ahead from 1992–94, but this induced extremely high rates of inflation peaking at 21.7 per cent. Strict measures adopted to control inflation proved successful, somewhat unexpectedly, but have overshot their mark and since driven the economy into a period of seemingly unstoppable deflation in 1998 and 1999. This is the big picture.

China's domestic equity markets have shown the strong influence of the two major economic cycles and can be broken down into two complete cycles – two booms with two busts and the apparent start of a third cycle. As an example, the Shanghai A share markets began their first boom in early 1992 on the elimination of daily trading price limits, a scarcity of new issues, then in July a flood of IPOs hit the market leading at once to a technically induced market bust. These were the growing pains of the Shanghai exchange's management, however, and once balance was restored growth soon resumed peaking in mid-1993. This first cycle entered its final stage in early 1994 when it became apparent that the economy had overheated and the government began to strictly implement measures it had begun to put in place in mid-1993. As these measures proved effective, and as the Hong Kong handover of July 1997 grew nearer, the market began to experience an upturn which lasted about one year. Following the Hong Kong handover, however, the markets fell and then lapsed into directionless trading as it became clear that China was drifting into a deflationary period. Despite this, a rally began on 19 May 1999 which had pushed markets up nearly 40 per cent when on 15 June the government joined the party by writing the famous *People's Daily* editorial proclaiming, in preparation for the 50th anniversary of the nation, that the upturn reflected a fundamental improvement in the overall economy. The markets promptly shot straight upward 600 points before falling back once again into directionless trading.

The performance of the shares of the 47 Chinese companies listed on international markets, primarily Hong Kong, has largely mirrored

Chart 1.3: Shanghai A share index (1990–third quarter 1999)

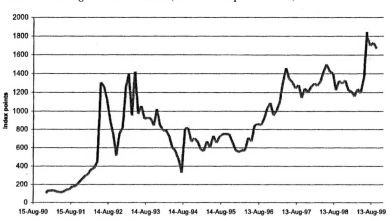

Source: Wind Information System

China's domestic markets. Overseas share performance can be broken down into four identifiable periods: (1) the H share boom era, 1992–94; (2) stagnation, 1995–96; (3) the Red Chip craze and crash, 1997; and (4) the China Telecom era, 1998 on. The single theme that emerges from a review of China's overseas listings has been the growing sophistication of international investors. At the start of the decade, the international investment community had little direct knowledge or understanding of how Chinese companies operated or of the workings of China's economy. After the period of initial enthusiasm and as experience accumulated with the operations of overseas listed companies, this understanding developed and deepened and investor requirements sharpened. At the start of the H share boom, nearly any Chinese company's shares could be sold. By the end of the decade, investors appear willing only to buy shares of China Telecom, a mobile phone communications provider with such profitability and growth prospects, as well as market liquidity, that it can almost by itself satisfy the needs of all investors hoping to add China exposure to their asset mix. At least in terms of profitability and outlook, China Telecom is a far cry from the H share SOEs of the past and suggests that any future China boom will only come in the emerging communications industries, including the Internet. But such transactions in the beginning will be small and, in any event, are only indirectly related to the original aim of the corporatization program, the SOEs.

In terms of financing, over the decade of the 1990s total funds raised through share offerings amounted to US$49 billion, of which the A share markets accounted for 65 per cent, or US$32 billion equivalent (at post-1994 exchange rates). International investors have contributed the remainder with US$13 billion in the H share and other markets and a bit more than US$4 billion in the B share markets. This points out the critical importance, both strategic and tactical, of China's domestic markets to the corporatization effort. While the international markets have been used to absorb bigger companies, the local markets have been directed at keeping smaller and possibly less attractive enterprises afloat, although larger transactions have become increasingly possible in recent years. A review of the data suggests that the maximum amount which can be financed in the two domestic markets each year is around US$9 billion. This has significant implications for the market's overall future development, particularly with regard to the overhang of nontradable state-related shares.

At the same time, it suggests that the international markets will continue to play a critical role especially for the offerings of large SOEs. As the US$4.2 billion 1997 China Telecom IPO demonstrated, the international markets are broad and deep enough to handle almost any size transaction so long as it is seen as an attractive investment opportunity. The government's determination to corporatize and modernize the country's oil and gas industry at almost one go is a clear indication of the significance the international capital markets now have for China. It gives pause to consider the extent to which the Chinese government has exposed itself and its SOE reform program to the whims of international investors.

Liquidity is also an important indicator of a market's strength. Liquidity represents market depth by inferring through trading volume flows capital availability for the purchase or sale of securities. This is important since strong liquidity ensures greater pricing accuracy, enhances the willingness of investors to take larger positions (and assume greater market risk) and, therefore, makes larger transactions possible. Through the third quarter of 1999 the average daily A share turnover on the Shanghai and Shenzhen markets was each around US$600 million versus on average US$800 million on the Hong Kong exchange and only US$38 million for the H share index. Contrast these figures with the average US$29 billion daily turnover of the New York Stock Exchange to highlight the comparative strength of these markets.

Along with liquidity, volatility is another concept used to describe market performance. Market watchers both domestically and internationally often talk about the extreme volatility that characterizes the Chinese equity markets and, indeed, there are many stories of extreme market moves, whether of individual stocks or of the index itself. That this is the case is not surprising given the limited float of most listed companies, the retail character of investors and relatively low trading volumes. However, certain of China's stock indices are comparatively less volatile than other markets in the region including, surprisingly, Hong Kong. Similar conclusions are reached whether comparing 20 day volatility or momentum measures. An analysis of trading performance correlations between different types of Chinese shares rounds out the discussion of volatility and provides a clearer picture of how these markets function. The correlations highlight a fact that is well-known among market professionals: most 'China stocks' are traded based on sentiment and at a country level, as opposed to a more detailed stock by stock, company by company approach. The background and analysis for the commentary on markets is presented in Chapter 8. A brief review of the major challenges confronting China's securities industry can be found in Chapter 9.

In the year 2000 China will join the WTO and over the following five years its domestic securities markets will witness increasing foreign participation just as the international markets will witness the increased participation of the major Chinese securities firms. Domestically, this will come at first through joint venture insurance companies, investment banks similar to China International Capital Corporation, and asset management companies and then followed by full fledged direct participation as the Renminbi becomes fully convertible. Internationally, the major Chinese securities firms can be expected to play an increasingly important role in the Hong Kong and Asian markets. At the same time these years will continue to witness dramatic market changes in China. Such changes will not simply be limited to the types of companies listed and how they are listed and regulated, but also to a much reduced state ownership role and all that that entails. Without question, China's stock markets, with less than ten years of full scale development, are on track to become the largest and most dynamic in Asia.

2
Chinese Equity Securities

The story of equity securities in China involves more than simply Chinese companies issuing shares to investors. Before there could be shares, there had to be companies and these companies had to have equity capital represented in the form of shares. Prior to the reform efforts of the 1980s it is fair to say there were no companies in China, there were state-owned enterprises, or SOEs, and there were factories (*gongchang*). These were the production units of the centrally-planned economy. With a loosely defined collection of assets 'owned by the State on behalf of all of the people', they had no independent legal status and none of what industrial economies consider to be those characteristics associated with property. For example, there was no ability to confer rights associated with 'ownership' on any party. Indeed, the entire thrust of the government's political program up to 1979 had been to eliminate all such aspects of ownership. Thus, all production, revenue and surplus belonged to the state and not the producing enterprise. Investment projects relating to a given SOE were designed and funded by government entities. There was little management independence other than to implement the plan as it was handed down. But this is a well-known story.

It is no surprise that such poorly defined entities were characterized by poor operating results. Following the restoration of social normalcy in 1979, the government's awareness of this problem and its search for a formula which would improve production efficiencies proceeded along two policy paths: the contract responsibility system and the shareholding system. Both reforms were driven by the proposition that production efficiencies would result if enterprise management were given a certain amount of autonomy from state ownership. Both reforms, although they proceeded on separate tracks, in the end

21

dovetailed neatly, achieving the results desired but in a way the government had not foreseen.[1]

By the end of the 1980s enterprises involved in the responsibility system program had become exceptionally autonomous and sought to pursue their own interests through the issue of shares. Enterprises involved in the shareholding experiment had been extremely vigorous and creative in their participation. The shareholding experiment, at this point, had already gone too far for the government to hold back. As of 1988 there were nearly 10 000 so-called shareholding companies whose equity-like securities could be traded over the counter. There were even more enterprises which had retained significant amounts of capital as a result of the contract responsibility system seeking to issue shares.

These companies and enterprises and the securities they had issued, however, had almost no legal basis in law although the Shenzhen government had made some effort toward codification. The securities, at best, were traded over the counter at the business offices of a few semi-regulated securities firms; there were no formal securities exchanges. At worst, securities changed hands at tables set-up in front of the factories which had issued them. The existence of this increasingly active, weakly regulated securities market into which enterprises could virtually offer shares at will, drove the government to establish the Shanghai and Shenzhen securities exchanges in late 1990.

This did not, however, solve the problem of what was being issued and traded on the exchanges. An effort to define the legal status of enterprises and the shares they issued began in the late 1980s but was interrupted by the events of June 1989. So it was not until early 1992 that the State Committee for Restructuring the Economic Systems, or SCRES, produced the Standard Opinion (*Guifan yijian*) which might be better understood as the 'Standardizing Opinion'. This was the first systematic national codification of the legal basis of an enterprise as a corporate form owning and operating productive assets.[2] The issuance of the Standard Opinion, plus a host of supporting regulations,[3] signaled the government's affirmation of the experiment as well as the start of its efforts to channel it along acceptable avenues by establishing a complete legal and regulatory foundation. This effort was to consume most of the 1990s.

The Standard Opinion for the first time in the history of the People's Republic defined the independent legal existence of enterprises, described the characteristics of equity shares in such enterprises and, more importantly, allowed shareholders to benefit from and transfer interests in such enterprises. After two years of further experimentation, the Company Law was passed and became effective in 1994, giving life in law to the concepts of 'companies limited by shares' and 'limited liability companies'.[4] The Company Law confirmed that the corporate form of organization for SOEs would be the key instrument in China's economic development going forward. This, on its face, represented a significant departure for China given the premises on which the People's Republic of China had been founded. But, in fact, the Company Law only recognized the reality of what the contract responsibility system and the experiment with self-financing through share issuance had brought into existence: highly autonomous enterprises and companies.

The Company Law, however, was deficient in many aspects so that in practice it did not and has not superseded the Standard Opinion. For example, the Company Law was almost entirely domestic-oriented with little to say about overseas share offerings by Chinese companies, which in mid-1994 were becoming increasingly common. Nor did it have much to say about the types of shares which had sprung into existence in the 1980s and been codified by the Standard Opinion. Together these two documents plus a third document, the Overseas Listing Rules,[5] provide the principal legal basis for the wide variety of shares to which China's experimentation with the corporate form has given rise.

It is in the existence of this large number of specific share types that the history of China's involvement in state ownership and central planning can be found. The extravagant variety of shares, although always confusing to outsiders, was based on a single, unifying principle: maintenance of unshakable state ownership of Chinese companies regardless of whatever market forces arise. By defining different shares for different investor identities the government made it practically impossible to exchange shares across categories. This, in turn, made it next to impossible to supplant or even dilute state control without first obtaining state approval. On the other hand, if shares are not fungible, market forces will be distorted as they have, in fact, been distorted. But this was beside the point at the outset. For the pro-market reformers, it was enough that shares existed and could be traded on officially approved exchanges. The rest could wait for later.

But progress has been, perhaps, a bit slower than expected. Nearly ten years later the Chinese corporatization effort continues to aim less at creating new types of economic relationships and more at simply giving existing intra-state relationships a new form with the hope of generating greater economic efficiencies. The addition of retail investors to the shareholding mix as minority investors has not altered this reality. It remains to be seen whether this change in form will affect the substance of enterprise operations, or whether China's newly listed companies will continue to be little more than SOEs by another name and with the traditional identifying characteristics. Viewed from the vantage point of the late 1990s, the conclusion must inevitably lean toward the latter reality. But with the tools of the market available, this does not mean that change will not be possible.

After briefly reviewing the history of how shares came into existence in China and the impact of state planning on the definition of shares, this chapter describes the types of Chinese shares as codified by the various laws as the basis for an analysis in the following chapter of the impact this segmentation may have on share valuation and market performance.

2.1   1983–88: the spontaneous development of equity-like securities

The resurrection of shares in China began in the villages of the southern coastal provinces in the early 1980s. Under the encouraging influence of the policies of opening and reform, villages began establishing township and village enterprises (TVEs). Since capital requirements were more than a single family or even a village could meet, experimentation began with a 'co-operative shareholding' structure.[6] Such experiments proved successful in raising capital and soon were quite common, becoming known as the 'Shareholding Co-operative System (*gufen hezuo zhidu*)'.[7] In 1983 a Shenzhen TVE named Baoan County United Investment Company became the first Chinese enterprise to issue shares to the public following the establishment of the PRC in 1949. In July 1984, Beijing Tianqiao Department Store, was the first SOE restructured as a company limited by shares. And in November of the same year a Shanghai SOE, Shanghai Feile Acoustics Company, issued shares to the public. All of these early transactions were unregulated private placements and represented the tip of a development which would not gather momentum until 1987 with the public offering of Shenzhen Development Bank (see below).

The 1986 Shenzhen Provisions

Experimentation with shareholding ownership structures was given further impetus in October 1984 following the Communist Party's momentous passage of 'The decision on the reform of the economic system', which promoted the broad development of co-operative and individual enterprises. Encouraged by this new policy and seeking to manage the widespread activities in its jurisdiction, the Shenzhen government in 1986 was the first to standardize procedures relating to the restructuring of enterprises into shareholding companies.[8] These regulations, more than any of those which came out in the early 1990s, truly empower the SOEs to take charge of their own fate with minimal State intervention. As such, they suggest a possible outcome different than the one facing SOEs and the state at the end of the century.

The Shenzhen provisions were directed primarily at the restructuring of Shenzhen's own SOEs, but the government welcomed all to use them as a guide: 'other SOEs, co-operative enterprises implementing restructuring, and newly established internally capitalized companies limited by shares can also proceed based on these regulations.' This was a very refreshing approach as it was non-compulsory. The Shenzhen provisions defined the restructuring of an SOE into a shareholding company as follows: '... transforming the net asset value of an SOE into shares representing the state's equity ownership, then transferring a portion of the state's ownership to other enterprises and individuals or taking in new shares from the state, other enterprises or individuals, then transforming the original enterprise into a company limited by shares in which the state, other enterprises and individuals participate in the shareholding'.

This definition is notable for permitting two ways of attracting capital through the sale of shares. Like overseas companies, the owners of the 'original enterprise' could choose to either sell down their existing stake, that is, sell primary shares, or sell new, or secondary, shares in the company, thereby diluting the original ownership. The economic result in both cases is the same: the original ownership interest is diluted. Once the central government took control of the process in 1992, however, the direct sale of state ownership interests was prohibited for ideological reasons: the state did not want to give the impression that it was privatizing SOEs. Since it had accommodated itself to the notion of attracting capital via the equity JV path, the state now saw little difference in selling new shares and, thereby, creating a minority stake in what continued to be a state-controlled company, regardless of the name. The codification in the Standard Opinion of primary shares as nontradable state or legal person shares has had a lasting impact on the market's development, as discussed in Chapter 3.

Also of interest, the Shenzhen provisions made it possible for foreign investors to acquire up to 25 per cent of an SOE, but anything larger triggered the JV laws of the central government. Thus, the state, other enterprises and legal persons, foreigners and individuals could all become shareholders. The company, with approval, was also allowed to raise money through the sale of shares overseas. Such measures were the forerunners to the B shares provisions. Investors, including banks, owed money by the potential shareholding company could carry out debt for equity swaps. Limits to how much the state, other enterprises, foreigners and individuals could own of a given company's equity were to be set out in the company's articles of incorporation and not by the state. Shares were permitted to be sold, given as gifts, inherited and used as collateral for bank loans: they were, for all purposes, the private property of the owner, or the Shenzhen Finance Bureau as the state's designated trustee.

In terms of corporate governance, the shareholders' general meeting was the locus of highest authority of a company under the provisions and was required to be held once a year. The shareholders meeting was empowered to elect members of the Board of Directors and the Board was wholly responsible to the shareholders meeting. There is no mention of the majority owner controlling the process.

The corporatization process laid out in the provisions was driven by the Shenzhen government which selected the SOEs to be involved. Following selection a work group led by the Finance Bureau and including the PBOC branch and enterprise management was formed. Much like the work done in the 1990s this group was responsible together with a preparatory group from the enterprise itself for the 'packaging' of the SOE: '... non-productive assets (non-operating assets) and unused assets in general are not to be turned into shares, they can, through certain procedures, be transferred to the administration of other SOEs or institutions.' Such packaging, designed to achieve enterprise profitability by carving out the best part of an SOE, came to have a bad name in the mid-1990s when it was seen by investors to be unsustainable.

In terms of actual practice, five different sorts of companies evolved under the Shenzhen regulations.[9] The first included SOEs without significant state investment which divided their net assets into both state and enterprise shareholdings and, at the same time, solicited investment by other enterprises as well as individuals; second, SOEs with significant state investment which became companies with a single state shareholder and then solicited investment by other state enterprises; third, existing Sino-Foreign Joint Ventures which restructured as shareholding companies; fourth, entirely privately-owned companies; and fifth, limited liability companies with multiple shareholders including state, collective and private sector investors.

In short, the liberal implementation of the 1986 Shenzhen Provisions clearly show the influence of Hong Kong and Western capitalism as well as the *zeitgeist* of the period. In 1987 the Party at its 13th Congress reaffirmed such experimentation with the shareholding structure stating, 'The shareholding system form that has appeared during the reforms, including state majority ownership with participation in shareholding by ministries and local enterprises as well as investment by individuals, is one kind of organizational form of enterprise property and can be continued.' By the end of 1987 there were reported to be 6000 shareholding enterprises across China and a further 3800 were added in 1988.[10] Although no statistics on the number of such enterprises in Shenzhen at this time are available, by the end of 1986 Shanghai alone had 1500 shareholding companies which had issued either debt or equity-like securities. Shenyang, remarkably, was the capital of equity issuance with 216 SOE-based shareholding companies having issued equities-like securities to the public. And at the end of 1989 Shenzhen is recorded as having over 200.[11]

On the eve of the Deng Xiaoping's 1992 Southern Tour, which marked the beginning of China's equity market explosion, Liu Hongru, as authoritative a figure as any, put the number of pilot SOE-derived shareholding companies at 3220, a figure which excluded rural TVE figures.[12] Of these, 380 companies represented cases in which other SOEs had invested, 2781 represented cases in which employees had invested in the shares of their own company and 89 companies had issued shares to the public.[13] The consolidated shareholding structure of these 89 companies, as presented by Liu, is shown in Table 2.1 based on the share types codified in the Standard Opinion and compared to a sample of 20 Shenzhen companies reported by SCRES as of 1989. These

Table 2.1: Shareholding structure, national vs Shenzhen samples (31 Dec. 1991)

Type of share	National sample	State %	Shenzhen sample	State %
State Share	47	76	23	36
Legal Person Share	29		13	
Individual Share	14		27	
Foreign Share	9		37	

Source: Renmin Ribao, 23 June 1992, p. 5; and Gao Shangquan and Chi Fulin, p. 88

limited data suggest that this 'experiment', had it not been interrupted by the events of 1989, might have had untold consequences for Chinese companies and the Chinese economy, had the path China later on pursued closely followed the Shenzhen practice.

The 'coupon clipping' investor mentality

The late 1980s was obviously a period of spontaneous fundraising through the sale of a wide variety of nonstandardized securities. 'Shares', moreover, bore a strong resemblance to debt securities since they were issued at par value and paid dividends at a rate fixed in excess of the bank deposit rate. There was no understanding among investors that shares could appreciate (or depreciate) in value in line with the given issuer's economic performance or even simply as the result of supply and demand. Investors at this stage were simply passive 'coupon clippers'. This was, in part, due to the limited number of formal locations where shares could be bought or sold following their initial issue. The first officially approved trading entity was established in Shanghai in 1986 with the opening of a business office dedicated to OTC trading by the Industrial and Commercial Bank of China.[14] It is unlikely, however, that this was the first formal OTC trading entity in China if Shenzhen is taken into consideration. Even at the end of the 1990s the competition between Shanghai and Shenzhen remains intense and extends even, and perhaps most especially, to the early history of China's markets.

By the end of the 1980s, this unregulated 'experimental' activity involving what was, in effect, the sale of state assets had gained sufficient critical mass and momentum to pose a potential threat to the state or at least to those representatives of the state who opposed anything smacking of capitalism. When an SOE restructured as a shareholding company and offered shares, there were as yet no restrictions on who could buy them. For example, the previously mentioned Beijing Tianqiao Department Store post-offering shareholding structure was as shown in Table 2.2.

This department store, originally 100 per cent owned by the Municipal Government of Beijing, had sold shares amounting to a 49.1 per cent ownership interest to a group of banks, which were owned by the central government, enterprises, which may have been owned by governmental agencies outside Beijing, and individual employees. There was no restriction on how these shares could be transferred or at what price. And unlike Shenzhen, Beijing appears not to have enacted any formal regulations providing for shareholders

Table 2.2: Beijing Tianqiao Department Store equity structure

Shareholder	Percentage held
Beijing Tianqiao Department Store	50.9
Banks	25.9
Enterprises	19.7
Employees	3.5
	100.0

Source: Li Changjiang, p. 54

meetings and boards of directors. It would be surprising if the city had, given its proximity to the central government and the contentiousness of the shareholding experiment. If this could happen in Beijing, then clearly things had progressed almost to the verge of spontaneous privatization among Chinese enterprises elsewhere.

2.2 1989–90: 'share fever' – stocks can appreciate in value!

This transformation in ownership structure and the potential dilution of state control, however, did not in themselves trigger a backlash. Rather the high rates of inflation and subsequent social unrest that led to June 4 triggered a conservative reaction which put a name to the entire political line that made the 1980s possible: shares were a capitalist manifestation. Yet it was a congenital fear of social unrest which provided the drive towards greater control of the burgeoning securities markets. And in this regard, Shenzhen was without question the key catalyst, just as it would be again three years later in 1992. The match that lit the fire, however, came from the Shenzhen Development Bank.[15]

In March 1989 the bank announced its dividend based on 1988 results. This announcement marked a major turning point in China's equity markets. The bank was exceedingly generous to its investors awarding them with a cash dividend of RMB7 per share, a two for one stock dividend, and a one for one stock split. In the blink of an eye, investors who had bought the bank's shares in 1988 for about RMB20 per share now enjoyed a profit several times their original investment. Investors did not need a market guru to tell them that shares were worth (potentially) more than their face value suggested. The bank's shares soared in OTC trading from a year end price of RMB40 to RMB120 just before June 4 and ended the year at RMB90, the June interruption notwithstanding.

Through the summer of 1990 prices for the five publicly traded Shenzhen companies snowballed creating 'share fever' with funds pouring in from all across China. In addition to raising investors' understanding of the long term value of investing in shares, this experience had a second, and equally strong, effect of orienting investors toward a quick short term capital gain: the market expanded and became speculative in nature. Just how hot shares had become can be seen in the significantly increased trading volumes of the five shares as a per cent of total trading volume in Shenzhen's OTC market as shown in Table 2.4. At times, share trading seems to have virtually eclipsed bond trading in Shenzhen. At the time government bonds were usually more actively traded.

This frenetic activity, and the birth of an active black market, did not pass unnoticed by the Shenzhen government which imposed a variety of measures beginning in May 1990 to bring the market under control.[16] These measures included ceilings on daily share price movement. And as shares became highly priced in Shenzhen money from the South began to buy up the relatively cheap Shanghai shares as well. Although the Shanghai market was still quiet, events in Shenzhen caused PBOC Shanghai branch to halt approvals for the establishment of new OTC trading offices by banks at this time.[17] In the short term, shares continued to trade up against their price ceilings each day and the black market flourished. Even worse, many companies took advantage of the craze to illegally issue shares. The speculative frenzy subse-

Table 2.3: Market price of the five publicly traded Shenzhen shares (in RMB)

	SZ Dev Bank	Vanke	Jintian	Anda	Yuanye
Face value	1	1	10	1	10
May 1990	11.99	2.00	28.58	2.60	17.26
June 1990	18.18	5.80	50.91	3.59	30.63
per cent change	52	190	78	38	78

Source: Cao Er-jie, p. 141

Table 2.4: Five traded Shenzhen shares OTC market peak trading volumes (%)

	SZ Dev Bank	Vanke	Jintian	Anda	Yuanye
4th quarter 1989	2.4	0.8	4.5	Not issued	Not Issued
1st quarter 1990	6.1	12.3	7.9	Not issued	Not Issued
2nd quarter 1990	13.7	18.0	25.9	40.9	20.6

Source: Cao Er-jie, p. 142

quently died down as a result of strong government intervention beginning in November 1990, which later led to a market crash in Shenzhen. But the experience had taught investors, actual and potential alike, that shares had value over and above the dividends paid. The equity investor mentality was born.

2.3 The state reins the market in

'Share fever', as the period was characterized, produced a strong reaction in the central government. From early 1989 the State Committee for Reform of the Economic Systems, the putative government department in charge, initiated the development of a variety of measures which would ultimately channel the experiment towards ends acceptable to the State.[18] As SCRES noted in its 1990 English language yearbook, 'The stock system involves changes in the system of property rights and, if there is not [sic] a unified method and if the rules are not clear, then if the work is mishandled, it will be difficult to correct.' Consequently, over a year's period beginning in the second half of 1988 SCRES drafted a number of measures based on a survey of practices in Shenzhen, Shanghai, Beijing and Shenyang as well as by reference to foreign laws and regulations. Such draft measures included 'Provisional measures on the experiment with the shareholding system by enterprises', 'Regulations on shareholding companies', and 'Regulations on limited liability companies'. At the same time the SAMB and the PBOC prepared drafts including 'Provisional measures for the appraisal of assets' and 'Provisional measures for the administration of the issuance and trading of shares'. These drafts were then submitted to the State Council for review and approval. Unfortunately, the events of June 4 intervened and these measures, which would lead to national standards for corporatization and share issuance, were not taken up again until after Deng's trip. Thus, it appears that the measures eventually implemented in May 1992, such as the 'Standard Opinion' discussed below, had been fully prepared three years earlier.

This failure of the government to act, however, did not stop the evolution of the 'experiment'. From late 1990 the state was able to agree internally to place a loose framework on the process. The principle result of this effort came in May 1990 when the State Council approved a SCRES report which imposed restrictive limits on the experiment. This included such measures as proposing: (1) the continuation of experiments wherein only other state enterprises participated in the share capital of restructured companies; (2) restrictions on the further spread of the sale of shares to employees; and (3) the restriction on the development of OTC markets in cities other than Shanghai and Shenzhen.[19] Later the same year formal securities exchanges were established in Shanghai and Shenzhen, but the intent was not to expand the experiment, rather to rope it in by halting OTC trading and concentrating it in one of the two exchanges.

2.4   Shares of what?

There is no question that by the end of the 1980s some sort of national effort aimed at standardizing the corporatization process was needed if 'experimentation' was to develop in a healthy manner. For one thing, what were these newly restructured companies limited by shares offering to investors in the form of a piece of paper called a 'share'? Putting aside the issue of a legal foundation, a company limited by shares quite obviously presupposes an operating objective quite different than an SOE: the maximization of shareholder value rather than maximizing output units of whatever product.

Underpinning this objective must be a fundamental reworking of a company's operations and, most importantly, its financial reporting and accounting practices.[20] It was not until mid-1993 that the Ministry of Finance enacted an accounting revolution for SOEs by requiring the adoption of general accounting principles based on International Accounting Principles ('IAS'). Until that date SOEs did not even have an equity capital account available on their balance sheets (although SOEs already restructured as shareholding companies were meant to adopt a Western balance sheet and income statement as of mid-1992). Prior to 1993 Chinese SOEs had functioned as production units in a relatively centralized planned economy and accounting practices were oriented to suit the needs of compiling the national plan. In fact, accounting practices developed by the MOF differed between industries. So what was being sold to investors? The answer to this question and to the emergence of investor-specific share types can be found in how the financial side of an enterprise's operations was portrayed via Chinese accounting practices.

Chinese accounting practices, like those of the Soviet Union from which they were inherited, were rule based, as opposed to principle based, and adopted the concept of 'fund' and fund source and fund use.[21] By rule based is meant an entire code of extremely specific accounting treatments existed to meet every situation. Rather than proceeding from principles, accountants had only to determine in which 'box' a specific item should be placed. Fund accounting is an example of this approach. In fund accounting, fund use means the use of funds to acquire property or supplies and fund source is the specifically identified channel for obtaining funds. There were three categories of funds – fixed, current and special. These three funds were actually separate balance sheets representing different aspects of one enterprise's operations. There was no integrated balance sheet as Western accounting understands it. Fixed funds were those used for what the West would understand as investment in fixed assets. Current funds can be understood as working capital while special funds refer to monies set aside for purposes such as major renovations of fixed assets and employee welfare. These special funds were sourced from an enterprise's cost of production while others, such as the employees' incentive fund and product development fund, were sourced from an enterprise's profit.

Enterprises were required to comply with the principle of a specific fund for a specific purpose and there could be no flexibility (in theory at least) in transferring funds from one specific use to another use. At specific periods the enterprise had to provide its supervising ministry or bureau with a copy of its fund balance sheet which was based on the principal of 'fund use = fund source' as shown in Table 2.5. Given the

Table 2.5: Summary SOE 'balance sheet' using fund accounting

Fund application		Fund source
Fixed assets		**Fixed fund source**
Original cost	=	State fixed fund – state budget grant
Less Depreciation		Enterprise fixed fund – enterprise funds
Net Book Value		Fixed fund loan – state bank loan
Sub-total		*Sub-total*
Current assets		**Current fund source**
Inventory	=	State current fund – state budget grant
Accounts receivable		Enterprise current fund – enterprise funds
Cash		Current fund loans – PBOC loan
Sub-total		*Sub-total*
Special Assets		**Special Fund Source**
Bank deposit	=	State special fund – state budget grant
Special fund assets		Enterprise special fund – enterprise funds
		Special fund loans – state bank loan
Sub-total		*Sub-total*
Total fund use		**Total fund source**

Based on Tong, Chow and Cooper, *Accounting and Finance in China*, pp. 25 and 110

absence of any relevant regulations on the topic, how did enterprises which transformed themselves into shareholding companies show this in their accounting? Even more important, if the company sold shares to outsiders, whether state entities, other enterprises or individuals, how was this evidenced and what implications were there of the treatment used.

One common method simply had the company allocate share capital according to its source to each of the fixed and current fund accounts, as shown in Table 2.6. But it should not be surprising that there was apparently no single dominant accounting treatment which emerged from the many proto-shareholding companies, although some local governments were prescient enough to have shareholding enterprises adopt Western-style balance sheets. The results of the effort to reconcile fund accounting, in which enterprises had no equity capital, with shareholding companies with equity capital accounts sheds significant light on the laws and regulations adopted in the early 1990s during the heyday of the effort to 'standardize (*guifan*)' the securities industry.

As is further discussed in Section 2.5, the transformation of an enterprise into a shareholding company involved one or more pro-

Table 2.6: Representation of early shareholding company 'balance sheet'

Original fund source	Equity Contribution	Post-equity contributions
Fixed fund source		**Fixed fund source**
State fixed fund		'State share' fixed fund
Enterprise fixed fund		'Enterprise share' fixed fund
Fixed fund loan		Enterprise fixed fund
		'Individual share' fixed fund
Sub-total		*Sub-total*
Current fund source		**Current fund**
State current fund		'State share' current fund
Enterprise current fund		'Foreign share' current fund
Current fund loans		'Individual Share' current fund
Sub-total		*Sub-total*
Special fund source		**Special fund source**
State special fund		State special fund
Enterprise special fund		Enterprise special fund
Special fund loans		Special fund loans
Total fund source		**Total funds plus equity shares**

Based on Tong, Chow and Cooper, pp. 25 and 110

moters contributing physical assets to the new company and, in return, receiving shares. Thus, if a state agency, for example, the Bureau of Heavy Industry, contributed certain equipment which it owned to the company, it would received shares representing that equipment's value. Under fund accounting, such shares would be treated as 'state share fixed funds'. Again, if individuals used cash to buy shares in the company, their shares would have been carried as 'individual share current fund'. So, depending on what type of asset was contributed, the related shares would be carried in the old fund source location on the fund balance sheets.

This treatment is, from a Western accounting viewpoint, entirely confusing and off the mark. For example, under the Western system, the purchase or disposal of a fixed asset or the write off of inventory does not directly impact the equity accounts. In contrast, the fund accounting methodology would result in an addition or subtraction from, for example, the state share fixed funds. This approach simply doesn't work: equity shares do not represent a defined chunk of a company, but a share of a company's total assets after deducting various obligations to arrive at equity. Under fund accounting, presumably, if the specific assets related to the shares were used up or destroyed, the investment would be lost entirely, even if the company as a whole continued in existence! In short, fund accounting leads to a fragmented view of a company, whereas the Western approach views the company as an integrated whole.

This convoluted discussion of fund accounting goes a long way toward explaining Article Four of China's first Company Law, which came into effect in July 1994 on the eve of the first New York Stock Exchange listing of a Chinese company. This article stated: 'The ownership rights to the state-owned assets of a company belongs to the State'.[22] This incredible pronouncement can be understood quite easily by reference to fund accounting. So too can the ossified categorization of different share types as contained in the Standard Opinion. Given this mindset, state shares and third party enterprise invested shares were obviously those related to a fixed fund source and fixed assets and, therefore, could not be sold without threatening state ownership of its original investment, while individual or foreign shares, since they were most likely purchased in exchange for cash, should be a current fund source which could be exchanged for other, equally fungible cash. Clearly, despite the ambitious efforts of enterprise management, Chinese companies were not going to escape the bounds of a planned economy just by changing their names.

2.5 The 'standardized' creation of a shareholding company

The Standard Opinion and supporting legislation, drafted in 1989 and implemented in 1992, was aimed at 'standardizing' the helter-skelter approaches of the 1980s to creating shareholding companies. Under the Opinion, a shareholding company is established when a promoter exchanges his ownership of certain assets for shares of a new company. The Opinion, wholly unlike the 1986 Shenzhen provisions, at the outset in Article 10 limited corporatization to the state sector exclusively. Promoters were required to be domestic Chinese legal persons in the state sector; private sector entities of any kind were excluded.[23] In general, however, many of the roots of the Standard Opinion can be found in the 1986 Shenzhen provisions discussed previously. In fact, even after enactment of the Standard Opinion, Shenzhen was allowed to continue to use its own provisions to carry out corporatization of its SOEs to the extent they did not conflict with national regulations.

To preserve the state's investment, the critical part of enterprise restructuring lies in the determination of where the state ends and the corporation begins.[24] The process, overseen by the State Asset Management Bureau, involves the engagement of an approved asset appraiser as well as a certified public accountant as auditor. These two professionals working with enterprise management are held responsible by the state for defining the boundary between the original collection of assets, which is to say the state, and the new company which is to be incorporated. This 'boundary setting' involves not a few disputes and it is always amazing how in an economy characterized by 'ownership by the whole people' there can be so many claimants to any given article of value. On completion of the appraisal and audit, the net asset value (NAV) of the new company is set as its registered capital, transformed into shares with a par value of RMB1 and the company is incorporated following a vote by a founding meeting of shareholders/promoters and approval by relevant company registration agencies.[25]

The Chinese tend to experiment, back peddle, try again, then back peddle again. This has been particularly true in areas as ideologically sensitive as corporatization. The result, as usual, was a melange of laws and 'provisional' regulations reactive to specific problems encountered, but not systematically thought out. Indeed, it was likely to be inconvenient to systematically think out the ramifications of the corporatization process in China, particularly at the early stage. Hence, the Company Law cannot wholly replace the Standard Opinion since it fails to address many aspects of the reality to which the Opinion gave rise. Similarly, since the Company Law fails to deal with listings of Chinese companies overseas, the Overseas Listing Rules were quickly elaborated and ratified to fill the gap. It is assumed in this discussion of share types that such inconsistencies were not aimed at undermining the legal status of what has been glossed over or ignored. From a Western viewpoint, however, this may be seen as precisely the effect. Whatever the case, any understanding of the current reality of China's equity markets requires a general understanding of the legal basis supporting the variety of Chinese shares starting first with the Standard Opinion.

2.5.1 The Standard Opinion

Under the Standard Opinion, SOEs can be restructured into companies limited by shares in two principal ways: (1) the promoter method; and (2) the fundraising method.

The promoter method

This approach requires the package of assets to restructure itself into a company limited by shares. Whether there might be any packaging involved at this stage, as clearly addressed in the 1986 Shenzhen provisions, is not mentioned. Perhaps not, since the transfer of non-productive assets to other entities can be extremely contentious. Shares must then be placed in their entirety with the single promoter of the company. The promoter will normally be the original state agency which invested in and, therefore, 'owned' the assets being restructured, for example a local government or ministry. This path was used principally by the larger SOEs in preparation for public listings at a later date.[26]

The fundraising method

This approach takes two different forms: (1) the directed offering (*dingxiang muji*) method; and (2) the public offering (*shehui qunzhong muji* or *shehui muji*) method. In a directed offering the shares of the restructured company are acquired by the promoter as well as other legal persons in a manner not unlike a private placement. If additional approval is obtained, shares can be sold to employees of the given company as well.[27] In contrast, in a public offering shares can be sold to the public in addition to being acquired by the promoter. Companies established using the directed method can, on approval, offer shares to the public after one year when making a secondary offering of shares to further increase capital.

Approval procedures

Once the promoters have decided to establish a company, the supervisory authority for the company's given industry, either a ministry for a centrally owned enterprise or a provincial industrial bureau for a locally owned one, acts as sponsor and oversees the entire application process.[28] The promoters must prepare a package of documents in support of their request including promoters' agreement, application, feasibility study, articles of incorporation, asset appraisal report, verification report (by which a lawyer attests that all facts are validly documented), prospectus and the approval of the supervising ministry or bureau. This package is then reviewed and approved by a variety of government agencies with the process co-ordinated by SCRES or its local government counterpart. On approval the promoters have 30 days to complete preparatory registration procedures with the appropriate level Bureau of Industry and Commerce. But this hardly marks the end of the process.

Next the promoters must make their appropriate capital contribution. Once this has been fully paid in to a pre-approved bank account or the ownership of specific assets has been transferred, they must call a shareholders meeting to establish the new company within 40 days. The meeting must be attended by share subscribers holding over two-thirds of the total shares. The purpose of the meeting is: (1) to review and comment on the promoters' plan to establish the company; (2) to approve the draft articles of incorporation; (3) to elect the companies directors; and (4) to elect the company's supervisors. Within 30 days of this meeting the Board to Directors must meet to approve the application to register the new company at the Bureau of Industry and Commerce. On completion of registration, the company commences its existence as a legal entity.

There is obviously a significant degree of risk in this process for potential shareholders. Public investors are particularly at risk since their capital is being contributed to an entity which is not yet in legal existence and will not be for perhaps two–three months after they have put up their capital. The promoters are, as a result, made jointly liable for all costs associated with the effort, as well as the return of any public funds, with interest, in the event the new company is not established as expected. This requirement is likely to have been poor solace to those investors stuck with an investment in a potential deal which never went through.[29]

Basic shares types

The Standard Opinion permits a company to issue both common and preferred shares. At the same time, however, it also clearly defines a number of different types of shares reflecting the ownership characteristic of the assets contributed by the promoter or investor to the new company. This definition did not just formalize the status quo of how shareholding companies were created during the 1980s, it froze it in place with the consequences discussed in Chapter 3.

State shares are the consequence of a government agency contributing its lawfully held assets to the formation of a company limited by shares and receiving shares in return. Legal person shares represent the contribution by government-invested SOEs of their legally owned assets to the formation of a company limited by shares and receiving shares in return.[30] To further complicate matters Legal Person shares are often called state-owned Legal Person shares since '... the entities holding this type of share are state-owned in nature ...'[31] This is apparently an effort to differentiate among Legal Person shares since non-state owned companies are also legal persons under Chinese law. But the approach again indicates the reality that the entire exercise was exclusive of the non-state sector at least at the start.[32]

These three share types are all considered 'Public (that is, state) Shares(*gongyou gu*)' given the underlying ownership characteristic of the assets contributed, that is, ownership by the state on behalf of the people. By logical extension, this terminology means that shares held by the investing public, that is the 'people', are non-Public shares (*feigongyou gu*). It seems rather odd that the people's ownership of non-Public shares is considered by the state to be in some way at odds with the same people's interests as represented by the state.[33]

These are the basic share types, but reality over the eight years since the enactment of the Standard Opinion has resulted in some highly creative, if not wholly confused, elaborations on this theme as shown in Table 2.8. These multitudinous share types are the result of hair-splitting fights over who owns the assets contributed to a given listed company which has been taken to its wildly logical conclusion by the creation in 1998 of 'Individual shares of companies listed in the local OTC markets which have been acquired by a listed company but not yet listed.'

The multiplication of share types led to a variety of technical problems, for example, disclosure in annual reports, classification in the electronic data systems of the two exchanges and so on. While the CSRC in early 1997 attempted to standardize the categories of shares,[34] there has been no questioning of the basic validity of the approach even by reference to the set of companies formed in the 1980s which floated all of their shares, which are discussed in Chapter 3.[35] The simple fact is that China must address the proliferation of share types,

Table 2.7: Types of shares of non-listed shareholding companies

Type of share	Legally permitted holder of share	Assets contributable
State share	State Council authorized representatives of the state's investment in the company, typically state agencies or organizations at either the central or local levels	Buildings, equipment, patents, technology, land use rights, cash
Legal person share	Enterprises, institutions or authorized social groups with legal person status	Buildings, equipment, patents, technology, land use rights, cash
Individual share	Either public retail investors or employees of a company who have invested their own wealth in the company	Renminbi cash
Foreign share	Foreign investors using foreign currency to acquire RMB shares	Foreign currency

particularly since shares in law enjoy the same rights except for free transfer of ownership.

Transfer of ownership

On paper state shares and legal person shares are transferable, but the purpose and scope of transfer is narrowly defined and the procedures drawn to make any such transfer of ownership difficult.[36] State shares for all intents and purposes are not transferable, while to date legal person shares have been transferable only among legal persons and in some cases through STAQ, the automated OTC trading system which has been moribund since 1994. It is clear that the intent of the State at the time the Standard Opinion was formulated (1989–90) and enacted (1992) was to prevent its loss of control over state-owned enterprises as well as the assets contributed to them.[37] An example from 1999 provides some insight into the kinds of situations government leaders must have thought about when these share types were formulated.

In the autumn of 1997 the Chengdu Lianyi Group sought new funds by selling a portion of its shares equal to 40 per cent to another legal person, the Guangdong Feilong Group for RMB68 million consideration.[38] The two companies signed a 'Legal Person Share Transfer Agreement' which specified the terms of Feilong's investment including the fact that the investment would be done on an instalment basis. On formal signing, the shares were transferred and Feilong became Lianyi's largest shareholder. Unfortunately, relations between the two companies quickly degenerated, as Feilong was unable to make the

Table 2.8: The elaboration on Chinese share types

Year	Types of share	Comment
1991	State shares, 'unit (*danwei*)' shares	Unit shares appear for first and last time
1992	State shares, Legal Person shares	Promoter shares, foreign capital promoter shares, overseas legal person shares, legal person shares and individual shares become commonly used
1993	State shares, Legal Person shares, Internal Staff shares, and Preferred shares	Internal staff shares and Preferred shares come into usage
1994	State shares, Chinese Promoter shares, Foreign Promoter shares, Social Legal Person shares, Leftover Rights Offering shares, and Internal Staff shares	Leftover Rights Offering shares (*zhuanpeiyiliu gufen*) for disclosure purposes are entered as Individual shares
		'High Official' shares appear in SZSE listed companies
1995	State shares, Domestic Promoter shares, Foreign Capital Promoter shares, Social Legal Person shares, Leftover Rights Offering shares and Internal Staff shares	Types of shares gradually become a bit more defined and taken as a whole are considered as either nontradable or tradable, each major category having a number of sub-types
1996	Promoter Shares: – State-owned shares – Domestic legal person – Foreign legal persons – Other Social Legal person shares Internal staff shares Preferred and Other shares	The CSRC on 1 January 1997 makes a clarification of share types for first use in 1996 financial statements
1997	Same as 1996	State-owned Legal Person shares comes into usage
1998	Same as 1996	Fund Offering shares, Strategic Investor shares, General Legal Person shares and Individual shares of companies listed in the local OTC markets which have been acquired by a listed company but not yet listed themselves

Source: *China Securities Daily*, 7 December 1999, p. 4

Table 2.9: CSRC 1997 categorization of principal share types

Principal category of shares	Share sub-types
I. Shares as yet untraded	
i. Promoter shares, including:	State owned shares
	Domestic legal person shares
	Foreign capital legal person shares
	Other
ii. Social Legal Person shares	
iii. Internal Staff shares	
iv. Preferred shares and Other	
II. Shares already traded	
i. Domestically listed RMB common shares	
ii. Domestically listed foreign capital shares	
iii. Overseas listed foreign capital shares	
iv. Other	

Source: CSRC, 22 January 1997, p. 166

Table 2.10: Rights of ownership transfer by types of shares

Type of share	Legally permitted holder of share
State share	Can be transferred subject to other state provisions
Legal Person share	Cannot be transferred for 1 year following establishment of company
	Cannot be transferred to employees of company in any manner
	Can only be transferred to other legal persons
Individual share	Cannot be transferred for three years following establishment of company
	Can only be transferred among other employees of same company; the transfer or sale of these shares outside of the company is prohibited
Foreign share	Can be transferred subject to other state provisions

instalment payments for the shares of Lianyi which it had received. Consequently, a supplement to the original share transfer agreement was signed in late 1998 which stated that the shares continued to belong to Lianyi Group and prohibited Feilong from disposing or otherwise using Lianyi's shares in any fashion until proper payment was made. Feilong informed Lianyi that it had more than sufficient funds and produced bank deposit books showing this. But these later turned out to be counterfeit. Lianyi at the time was satisfied, until in August 1999 it received a notice from a bank in Guangdong that the RMB30 million loan it had borrowed had come due and must be repaid. Lianyi had made no such loan. An investigation began which showed that Feilong had used the Lianyi legal person shares as collateral to procure the RMB30 million loan. All attempts to locate the Chairman of Feilong failed and the Lianyi chairman was sacked shortly after the case was made public.

Regardless of the practical realities of business in China, the stringent limitations on transfer, in part, explain how situations such as the Lianyi case arise. Moreover, these regulations severely curtail the right of ownership, which shares notionally provide to their owner, and have an impact on tradable share and overall market valuations as discussed in Chapter 3.

2.5.2 The Company Law

In what appears to be wilful disregard of reality, the Company Law makes no mention of the four share types defined by the Standard Opinion, nor of the concept of ordinary or preferred shares.[39] By July 1994 when the Law was signed into effect, thousands of companies limited by shares had been established across China of which some 290 had actually listed their 'non-Public' shares on the two domestic exchanges. The Law refers to this situation by requiring companies 'not completely satisfying' the requirements of the law to do so 'within a specified time limit'.[40] A national effort to conform Standard Opinion companies with the requirements of the Company Law was initiated in July 1995 by the State Council.[41] However by the end of the year little apparently had been accomplished. The State Council Office for Economics and Trade issued a further notice in late 1995 setting the end of 1996 as the cutoff date.[42]

The work involved in bringing the older companies into conformity with the Company Law did not address the issue of share types. Rather, it was designed to obtain complete corporate documentation of existing limited liability and companies limited by shares with the threat of revoking their business licenses. The reapplication work called for full disclosure of a company's shareholders or promoters, its registered capital, its articles of incorporation, its management structure, its financial accounting system, a new asset appraisal and a verification of the documents which entitled the company to ownership of its assets. This was a simple clean up of spotty government records and by choosing to ignore the larger reality of the various share types and corporate forms created under the Standard Opinion, the government allowed the Company Law to, in effect, call their legal basis into question. But market practice ignores this and moves on. The Standard Opinion remains as the foundation document of the securities industry.

In addition, the failure to distinguish between common and preferred shares or provide for other share types or classes, as the Standard Opinion does in part, virtually precludes the development of equity securities bearing different investment characteristics, for example different voting rights. Since all shares enjoy the same rights and the same benefits under the Law,[43] without further reworking it will be difficult to establish a basis on which minority shareholders or investors giving different value can be protected.[44]

Financial sophistication, or even protection of the minority interests of domestic shareholders, was not, however, the principal priority of the government. This is made very clear by the previously mentioned statement that 'The ownership rights to the state owned assets of a company belong to the State.'[45] Such a statement is only slightly less mindboggling when reference is made to China's 30 years of fund accounting. Notwithstanding this, the Law's purpose is to provide the legal basis for shareholding companies, the shares of which represent an interest in a company as a whole and not simply a certain asset category. By piercing the veil of a shareholding company's equity structure, the Law makes it black and white that contributed assets continue to belong without question to the state. Thus, if the state contributed factory buildings and equipment, these continue to belong to the state regardless of their inclusion in a shareholding company. But this statement should perhaps be taken with a pinch of salt, since it seems to be simply a sop thrown at the political sensitivities of certain factions of the government at the time, so that the process could go forward. If, in 1990, it was just barely conceivable that this process could be halted, by 1994 it was entirely inconceivable.

The Law also narrows the options for establishing a shareholding company to two methods: (1) the offer method; and (2) the promotion method.[46]

The offer method

Creation of a company via the offer method requires the promoters to subscribe to not less than 35 per cent of the shares to be issued by the company with the remaining up to 65 per cent to be issued in a public offering, *all prior to formal legal establishment* of the company. This is similar to the public offering method defined by the Standard Opinion.

In reality, promoters, which overwhelmingly have been SOEs to date, have traditionally subscribed to approximately 75 per cent of the original share capital, with the remaining 25 per cent offered to the public. This has been the case to absolutely ensure the unchallenged ownership and control of listed companies by the State.

The Law eliminated the directed offering option contained in the Standard Opinion, which allowed for the private placement of equity to other legal persons and, with approval, company employees prior to the legal establishment of the company. This merely formalized the SCRES decision of 1993. Nonetheless, the problem of how to address the ticklish reality of individual, employee shares remained. Also, the problem of a public offering of a company not yet in legal existence remained. As noted before, such a procedure represents significant investor risk, particularly to minority shareholders and for obvious reasons is not currently international practice in the world's major jurisdictions, nor has the practice been attempted for overseas listings.

The promotion method

This method requires the promoters to purchase all shares in the company to be established with subsequent capital raising via share issuance restricted for one year. The new shareholding company is legally established only after all promoters have fully made their capital contribution. Companies are required to have at least five promoters, by number, not economic interest, and more than half must reside in China. The principal promoter has generally satisfied this requirement by giving extremely small, minority roles to entities owned by either the local government or other legal persons within its own group. In contrast, the Standard Opinion allowed 'large scale' SOEs to transform themselves into shareholding companies using themselves as the single promoter.

Relative to the provisions of the Standard Opinion, the combination of these requirements makes it difficult for enterprises to carry out the establishment of a shareholding company with the aim of completing an increase in capital via an initial public offering. This problem was at once resolved for those SOEs approved to undertake overseas public offerings by a special regulation passed by the State Council exactly one month after the Company Law went into effect.[47] Overseas listing candidate enterprises must adopt the promotion method of establishment and may have fewer than five promoters. Moreover, on establishment the company may at once issue new shares, in this case, to overseas investors.

Transfer of ownership

The Law states that all shares possess the same characteristics of issue price, ownership rights and benefits (*tongjia, tongquan, tongli*). Similar to state-held shares under the Standard Opinion, shares held by 'state authorized investment organizations' can be legally 'transferred' and such entities can purchase shares from other shareholders. However, the Law restricts shares held by the state from being transferred within three years of a given company's formation. The Law did not specify how the ownership of such shares should be transferred, noting, like the Standard Opinion, that the issue will be separately dealt with in other laws or regulations.[48] More than five years later there has yet to be clarification and none is expected in the medium term future. Shares defined as those not held by state organizations can be freely traded, but only after listing and then only on legally constituted stock exchanges. Presumably this refers to legal person shares which, in theory, could be traded on the STAQ exchange. In short, state-held shares, and in practice, legal person shares, do not possess the same characteristics and rights as those held by non-state investors. This problem has long been recognized and, in late 1999, public discussion began as to means of dealing with the issue. This is discussed in detail in Chapter 3.

2.6 Listed company shares

The Standard Opinion was written in early 1992 when the only Foreign or 'Special shares' available to foreign investors were B shares (or, presumably shares in a Sino-Foreign Joint Venture which had transformed itself into a company limited by shares). These B shares were offered and listed on the two domestic stock exchanges and are available only to foreign investors (or, rather, investors who hold foreign passports). The State Council issued further special regulations applicable only to B shares in 1995.[49] But all of this, as well as almost annual efforts by the Chinese government to 'do' something (anything) to revive interest in the B share markets, was to no avail, pushed aside by what the international market saw initially as the 'real thing', H shares and Red Chips.

This 'real' effort to attract foreign equity capital began in October 1992 when the government announced the selection of nine companies designated as listing candidates on the Stock Exchange of Hong Kong. On hearing this, investors said goodbye to domestically listed B shares and hello to Hong Kong. These companies' shares quickly came to be called H shares after Hong Kong. There followed, not long after in early 1994, a group of five companies designated to list on the New York Stock Exchange and these, of course, came to be called N shares. In late 1996 another two companies were designated to list on the Tokyo Stock Exchange, becoming potential T shares and so on.

As noted previously, the Company Law makes no provision at all for companies intending to offer shares or list on overseas stock exchanges. Therefore, shortly after it went into effect in July 1994, the Overseas Listing Rules, sometimes called the 'Small Company Law', were passed by the State Council. The Rules defined shares listed overseas as 'foreign (capital) shares', whereas the shares of the same company listed domestically were called 'domestic (capital) shares'.[50] Despite this alphabet soup of different names of convenience (or satire), all such Foreign or 'Special shares' generally enjoy the same rights and obligations as those enjoyed by holders of domestically listed shares of a Chinese company with the exception that, for example, H shares are priced and traded in Hong Kong dollars and dividends are paid in Hong Kong dollars.[51]

It has been Chinese practice to conclude Memorandums of Understanding with each separate regulator of the international stock exchange on which Special shares may be listed.[52] These agreements are aimed at co-ordinating and settling any differences between the specific listing and regulatory requirements of the particular overseas exchange and Chinese regulations and practices governing listed Chinese companies.[53] In certain instances, the arrangements reached provide holders of Special shares or 'Foreign shares' greater rights and protection than holders of Domestic shares. For example, in the case of an SEHK listed Chinese company, foreign shareholders are permitted to vote on certain matters of material import to the company's operations while the majority mainland shareholders are excluded. This is certainly not the case in the Chinese legal and regulatory context. Should an individual overseas shareholder, however, wish to voice disagreement or claim damages from a listed company, this dispute would be settled under Chinese law. Hence, any extra rights foreign shareholders might have exist more on paper than in actual practice, so for all practical purposes their rights are equivalent to domestic Chinese non-state shareholders.

Providing some insight into what this might mean is the recent case in China of an individual shareholder who sued an A share company in court for false disclosure. There appears to have been merit to the case since the company's chairman and chief financial officer were

Table 2.11: Types of shares of listed companies

Type of share	Legally permitted holder of share	Legal basis
Foreign or 'Special shares' also called 'B shares'	Foreign investors who directly purchase RMB denominated shares using foreign currency	Standard Opinion Art. 24.4 and Art. 29; and 1995 Provisions
RMB denominated share also called 'A share'	Domestic investors only are allowed to purchase, hold and trade	Standard Opinion Art. 29
H shares or 'Special shares' similar to B shares	Foreign investors who directly purchase RMB denominated shares using foreign currency	Standard Opinion Art. 29; Company Law, Arts 85 and 155 and Overseas Listing Rules, Art. 3
N shares or 'Special shares' similar to H shares	Foreign investors who directly purchase RMB denominated shares using foreign currency	Standard Opinion Art. 29; Company Law, Arts 85 and 155 and Overseas Listing Rules, Art. 3

both sentenced to jail and the firm's auditors barred from practice. The court, however, told the plaintiff that it declined to hear his suit since it was the CSRC's responsibility to address illegal acts by listed companies. The court's ruling reflects the fact that the 1999 Securities Law does not explicitly grant individual shareholders the right to take action against issuers. Moreover, the law suggests that any compensation for damages is owed the state not the individual investor.[54] The case once again underlines the nature of China's experimentation with equity securities and stock markets.

2.7   The 1999 Securities Law

The promulgation of the new Securities Law in 1999 was much anticipated in the hope that it would provide a solid foundation for the existing hodge podge of laws and regulations. Indeed, the 1999 Securities Law in Article 1 states as a general principle the objective of standardizing the issue and trading of securities.[55] Unfortunately, however, the scope of the new law governs only the issue and trading within China of shares, corporate bonds and such other securities as are approved by the State Council. Government bonds are subject to separate laws and regulations. Insofar as equity securities go, the law seems to apply to both A and B shares, however, Article 213 notes that B shares are subject to other measures separately enacted by the State Council. This suggests that B shares continue to be subject to the 1995 Provisions. The Securities Law, like the Company Law before it, makes absolutely no reference to State shares and Legal Person shares. As a result, there is no clear legal treatment of how, or whether, such shares can be listed or traded. As Table 2.12 illustrates, this is not an insignificant omission since at present State and Legal Person shares constitute nearly 70 per cent of the Shanghai Stock Exchange's market capitalization. The proportion is similar for the SZSE.

Article 29 is the only part of the Securities Law which directly applies to overseas listed shares. The article imposes the condition that such companies as desire to list and trade their shares overseas must first obtain the approval of the CSRC. In this case, the catchall general principle stated in Article 2 most certainly applies: 'For matters not provided for in this Law, the provisions of the Company Law and other relevant laws and administrative regulations shall apply.' This at least gives the market comfort that previous laws have not been superseded but, given the confusing state of all such laws and regulations, it does little to develop the market in a positive manner.

Table 2.12: Shanghai market capitalization structure (30 Sept. 1999)

	(MM) RMB	A shares US$	%	B shares US$	%
State shares	426 311	51 487	27.3	2 836	38.2
Domestic Legal Person shares	509 207	61 498	32.6	1 416	19.1
Overseas Legal Person shares	19 762	2 387	1.3	132	1.8
Social Legal Person shares	104 943	12 674	6.7	284	3.8
Internal shares	19 927	2 407	1.3	103	1.4
Other	37 337	4 509	2.4	74	1.0
Total non-tradable	1 117 487	134 962	71.6	4 845	65.3
A Shares	444 523	53 686	28.5		0.0
B Shares	0		0.0	2 574	34.7
Total market capitalization	1 562 010	188 648	100.0	7 418	100.0

Source: Wind Information System

In summary, the Securities Law does not relieve the uncertainty associated with the legal foundation of China's equity shares. State shares, a variety of Legal Person shares, foreign shares as well as 'other' shares have not been formally recognized by the two principal laws governing the establishment of shareholding companies and the resulting equity securities evidencing ownership in such companies. Instead, the approach has been to patch-up inadequacies which further adds to confusion. The principal arbiter of such confusion, in the first instance, has been the CSRC, and then ultimately the State Council. This approach to matters can be expected to continue.

3
The Impact of Share and Ownership Structure

The enactment of national securities regulations and a company law together with the creation of a national industry regulator were without question necessary to promote the continued development of China's equity capital markets. By the late 1990s, however, the costs of the political compromises and the historical burden of central planning had become clear. By avoiding at the birth of the equity markets the politically sensitive issue of whether the ownership of state and legal person shares could be transferred and, if so, to whom, the government in the end has created a huge market overhang.

The question pending in late 1999 was what to do about this problem. Approximately 70 per cent of domestic market capitalization is currently frozen in place in the form of state and legal person shares, themselves a leftover of the planning process. In normal market circumstances elsewhere such an overhang would have a significant impact, not simply on the market's valuation, but also on that of individual listed shares. This should also hold true for Chinese markets.

In China this impact has been obscured since the sale of state or legal person shares has until very recently been a moot point in public discussions and the markets have fulfilled their SOE financing function in an acceptable fashion. With China's presumed addition to the WTO in the year 2000, however, the government is confronted with a planning problem: how and when to make domestic markets accessible to international capital. This raises the issue of the non-convertibility of the Renminbi on the capital account. And, even more pressing at the moment, how can companies already listed raise more money after they have already sold down to the limits imposed by the requirement of absolute majority state ownership.

This chapter proceeds to look at the market overhang problem in three ways. First of all, the problem need not have been created, as early experience in Shenzhen suggests. There are, as of the end of 1999, 89 companies, or roughly 10 per cent of all domestically listed companies, which have free floats of greater than 50 per cent and eight with 100 per cent. Most of these companies listed shares in the very early days of the two markets prior to the enactment of the Standard Opinion. Two of these companies, however, diluted the state's portion below 50 per cent in 1999. A look at these 89 shares sheds light on the market overhang problem and how the government is currently planning to address the problem going forward. Second, a further issue is that the market overhang has been understood by some market observers to suggest the penalization of the owners of state shares while retail owners of A shares rake up huge capital gains. Such an understanding of how China's equity markets function is not correct. Finally, the segmentation of the share markets for the handful of Chinese companies which have listed shares both domestically and internationally is highly suggestive as to the true valuation of China's domestic equity markets and provides another angle to view China's market capitalization and the issue of Renminbi convertibility.

3.1   Companies with state ownership of less than 50 per cent

There are 89 domestically listed companies whose combined A, B and H share free float is in excess of 50 per cent of their total equity capital. This suggests that these companies may not be controlled by the state. The companies account for nearly 10 per cent of the total number of domestically listed companies and for US$33 billion, or roughly 8 per cent of the total market capitalization of the two exchanges as of late 1999. Among them, the shares of five companies are entirely listed and trading on the market, for example, Shanghai Feile Acoustics, the first SOE to publicly offer shares. Is this situation simply an anomaly, were these companies really privatized and what, if anything, is their significance?

A review of their offering histories shows that most of these companies carried out private placements of shares prior to 1994 when the Company Law replaced the Standard Opinion. This supports the case that they are an historical anomaly together with all the other state-controlled companies which carried out subscriptions at that time. During the 1980s 21 of the 89 companies offered shares for subscription and a further 46 did so prior to the implementation of the Company Law. These companies later on listed their shares on the newly established exchanges through a legal process known commonly

Table 3.1: Shanghai Feile Sound Company equity structure (30 Nov. 1999)

Share type	Number of shares	%
State share	0	
Legal Person share	0	
A share	14 638 400	100

Source: Wind Information System

as listing by way of introduction, that is, no new shares were offered or funds raised. These companies are truly remnants of the previous era of experimentation, particularly the cases of the 1980s. Once Deng's imprimatur was added to the securities markets in early 1992 the number of placements surged. This led to a rapid build-up in the queue to list through 1993. Thereafter, the prohibition of placements enacted in 1994 gradually eliminated the problem as subscriptions and listing were made more or less simultaneous.[1]

Table 3.2 illustrates these events. It provides data on the timing of subscription versus formal listing for all listed companies as of 1999 September 30. Of the total number of 903 companies, 88 (not to be confused with the 89 companies with a float greater than 50 per cent) had carried out share subscriptions prior to the formal establishment of the two exchanges in late 1990 (with eight of these listed on the Shanghai exchange in December 1990). This figure of 88 includes 23 of the group of '89 companies' with a free float greater than 50 per cent, of which a further 44 completed placements before 1994 when the Company Law took effect. As noted previously, all companies formed prior to the Company Law were required to conform with the law by the end of 1996. By this time, some 80 of the 89 companies with minority state ownership had completed formal listings of their shares.

The listing of the shares of the seemingly 'privatized' shareholding companies of the 1980s marked the end of one potential outcome for the shareholding experiment: apparent privatization,[2] or at least the elimination of the proliferation of various share types which over time led to the severe illiquid overhang in China's stock markets. This latter point is illustrated well by comparing Tables 3.3 and 3.4 which show the share composition of the Shanghai market in 1991 and 1999.[3] A closer examination of the A share ownership of the 'privatized' companies, however, shows what one might expect: a preponderance of state and legal persons. This explains why these shares perform in every way like the shares of their SOE brothers and sisters which were

Table 3.2: Subscription vs listing for the 89 companies vs. all others

Year	The 89 companies			Other companies		
	Placement	Listing	As yet unlisted	Placement	Listing	As yet unlisted
1984	3	0	3	0	0	0
1985	2	0	5	0	0	0
1986	4	0	9	0	0	0
1987	6	0	15	6	0	6
1988	4	0	19	31	0	37
1989	2	0	21	26	0	62
1990	2	6	17	11	2	71
1991	5	4	18	11	0	82
1992	16	8	26	74	32	124
1993	23	32	17	101	90	135
1994	5	16	6	33	94	74
1995	1	3	4	12	21	65
1996	8	11	1	164	192	37
1997	5	6	0	183	200	20
1998	1	1	0	102	105	17
1999	2	2	0	60	77	0
Total	89	89	0	814	814	0

Source: Wind Information System

restructured under the Standard Opinion. But the experience is significant nonetheless. Had the government adopted a slightly more sophisticated approach at the outset of the process, state control could have been maintained even with shares which were tradable. This would not have been privatization and the 'pilot enterprises' existed to support such a policy direction. This is their immediate significance. But given the times, the political sensitivity of the share reform effort, as well as China's heritage of central planning, such an outcome is actually beyond reasonable expectations.

The chosen path is well known now and has found the public offering process dominated by state and legal person promoters who receive non-tradable state and legal person shares so that the market capitalization of both exchanges has evolved to reflect the growing weight of illiquid shares. The consequence for today's policymakers is shown in the case of the Shanghai exchange in Table 3.4.[4]

The two minority state-controlled companies which listed shares in 1999, Guangdong Kelon and Beijing Zhongguancun Science-Tech ('Beijing ZGC'), may represent the future, and not the effort to deal

Table 3.3: 1991 Shanghai market capitalization structure

	SSE market capitalization A share companies			
	No. of shares	RMB (MM)	US$ (MM)	%
State shares	1 778 841	977	118	33.2
Domestic Legal Person shares	211 190	115	14	3.9
Individual shares	692 359	380	46	12.9
Total nontradable	2 682 390	1 472	178	50.0
A shares	2 682 390	1 472	178	50.0
Total market capitalization	5 364 780	160 228	356	100.0

Source: Annual Trading Statistics 1990–91; for comparability, US$1 = RMB8.28

with the consequences of early practice. Guangdong Kelon, a successful producer of consumer durables, is one of China's earliest H share companies dating from July 1996. Kelon had not been allowed to issue A shares at the time of its H share offering. Beijing ZGC takes its name from that of the locality in Beijing's university district which has become synonymous with computers, software development and similar hi-tech enterprises. In both instances, the state retained a majority share after their initial public offering, and in both cases subsequent offerings diluted the state's holdings to less than 50 per cent. These two cases throw light on the problem of how the government appears to have decided to solve the issue of non-tradable shares.

The promoters of Beijing ZGC did not include state agencies: only legal persons contributed to its formation as a shareholding company. The company's capital consisted of 300 million legal person shares. On 12 July 1999, the company, following a private placement of shares to the initial promoters, completed its listing of 187 million A shares at a price of RMB5.78.[5] The shares performed well, rising to RMB30 in a matter of days. Three weeks later in August 1999 the company announced a one for one rights offer for A share holders priced at the original IPO level of RMB5.78. Given the secondary market price at the time of RMB30, the rights issue was a guaranteed money winner for any current A share investor. Why was the rights subscription price set so low? After all, the stock was trading at RMB30 per share and the rights price was only 20 per cent of this. The explanation revolves largely around past market practice, investor expectations and poor understanding of cost of capital issues. But proper pricing for the rights offering is not the point here. The question is: at what price did the shares open for trading again? As professionals in other markets will

Table 3.4: Shanghai market capitalization structure (30 September 1999)

| | SSE market capitalization | | | | |
| | A shares | | | B shares | |
	RMB (MM)	US$	%	US$	%
State shares	426 311	51 487	27.3	2 836	38.2
Domestic Legal Person shares	509 207	61 498	32.6	1 416	19.1
Overseas Legal Person shares	19 762	2 387	1.3	132	1.8
Social Legal Person shares	104 943	12 674	6.7	284	3.8
Internal shares	19 927	2 407	1.3	103	1.4
Other	37 337	4 509	2.4	74	1.0
Total non-tradable	1 117 487	134 962	71.6	4 845	65.3
A shares	444 523	53 686	28.5		0.0
B shares	0		0.0	2 574	34.7
Total market capitalization	1 562 010	188 648	100.0	7 418	100.0

Source: Wind Information System

Table 3.5: Post-offering share structure, Beijing ZGC and Guangdong Kelon

Share type	Beijing Zhongguancun	%	Guangdong Kelon	%
Promoter Legal Person shares	300 000 000	44.5	337 920 000	34.1
Internal Staff shares			84 500 000	8.5
A shares	374 847 000	55.5	110 000 000	11.1
H shares			459 590 000	46.3
Total shares	674 847 000	100.0	992 010 000	100.0

Source: Wind Information System

attest, the market is the final determinant of pricing and what the market decided here is quite illuminating.

The closing price of the share prior to going ex-rights was RMB33.80. The next morning the Shenzhen exchange announced the new price reflecting the dilution caused by the rights issue. The exchange's calculation showed a weighted average price of RMB26.02 per share and was carried in the *China Securities Daily*, the newspaper of record for the securities industry. The calculation, shown below, can be summarized as adding the total market capitalization of the company (A shares and legal person shares) to the funds raised through the rights offering and dividing by the new total number of shares. This results in the exchange's per share value of RMB26.025.

Total: number of pre-rights offering shares: $(187 + 300) \times RMB33.80$
(A shares + LP shares) times market price

Plus: shares in rights offering times offering price $\qquad 187 \times RMB5.78$

Divided: by total post-rights offering number of shares $\qquad (187 + 300 + 187)$

Unfortunately, the market that morning for the Zhongguancun shares opened at RMB23.42, down by the 10 per cent mandated daily trading limit, and the next day the shares traded down again by the 10 per cent limit to RMB21.08. It was not until the third day that the shares began to trade normally, closing at RMB19.01, down almost 44 per cent from the pre-rights share price.

After some thought as to why the fall to the RMB19 level occured, it becomes clear that the market had decided that the post-rights price should reflect *only* the tradable A shares in the company's capital base and not the non-tradable legal person shares. Though surprising, this finding is completely in line with how the state thinks, or had thought, about its own share contribution. This interpretation is supported by a recalculation of the price based on this understanding with the result, as shown below, of a price per share of RMB19.79. Thus, it seems clear that Chinese retail investors do not attribute any value at all to non-tradable shares.

Total: number of pre-rights offering A shares:

A shares times market price	187 × RMB33.80
Plus: shares in rights offering times offering price	187 × RMB5.78
Divided: by total post-rights offering number of shares	(187 + 187)

The 'correct' answer to the Zhongguancun pricing problem is unclear. If, however, one believes that the market is always right and that the market will ultimately determine the true value of a company, then the impact of loosening restrictions on the sale of state and legal person shares could be devastating, not only to the valuation of the company in question, but to market capitalization as well.

How the market reacts in large part reflects investor expectations, so it is important to consider the element of investor psychology including that of the state itself. It is likely that a part of the reason for the lower than expected trading price for the Zhongguancun shares is that it accurately reflects how investors understand what they are investing in. This goes back to the perspective of the state as embodied in Article 4 of the Company Law quoted in Chapter 2, which can be summarized as the 'State assets contributed belong to the State'. If the state simply contributes its own assets and receives shares in return which do not trade, it will not care less how shares representing other assets trade except as a policy issue relating to social unrest. Moreover, it will not care how many shares are issued and at what price. Those shares are some other investors' property and concern. In other words, the state's consideration of a company's cost of capital extends only to the cost of its original investment of equipment, land or buildings. Similarly, A share investors who contribute cash seem to give no credit to any valuation which attempts to include the contributed state assets – they might be taken back! The retail investors, like the state, thus behave in an equally compartmentalized way and are concerned only about their original cash investment since they might want to take their cash back, just as (in theory) the state can recoup its assets. This explanation is outlandish, but do not underestimate the possibility that such thinking may be true, at least in part.

The importance of accurately valuing companies should be, but has only superficially been, a critical part of China's SOE reform program.

This does not mean that the tools for technical valuation have not been popularized, rather that such tools do not produce practical results in the Chinese context. The market's current inability to value listed company shares properly appears to be a consequence of the state's perpetuation of illiquid classes of shares and a consequent fragmented view of a company. In turn, this goes back to state planning and fund accounting which, in fact, did treat an enterprise not as an integrated whole, but as three distinct parts which may, or may not, have represented a company from a financial viewpoint.

There does not appear to be any easy way out of the current situation. At a recent China business conference a senior government figure suggested that the value of state and legal person shares is approximately 20–25 per cent of the market price of A shares trading on the secondary market.[6] It is universally true that large shareholders are seldom able to realize, all at once or even gradually, the theoretical value of their holdings as set by the current market price. Any attempt to sell a portion of their holding will move the market price down. Nonetheless, the Chinese official's comment tacitly accepts the market's exclusion of non-tradable shares as part of the overall market capitalization. An approximation of this 20–25 per cent valuation can be arrived at by assuming that only the market capitalization of tradable shares is real as shown in the example below:

- Shanghai Official A share Market Capitalization = US$200 billion
- If 100 shares total, then the price per share = US$2.00 per share
- A share free float alone of 30 per cent or 30 shares = US$60 billion
- Assume not 30 shares but 100 shares then = US$0.60 per share

In other words, the fully diluted market capitalization, if all non-tradable shares were listed, would be roughly 30 per cent (0.60 divided by 2.00) of the current official market capitalization. Put another way, the value of the non-tradable shares is roughly 30 per cent of the current market price, approximating the official's estimate. This calculation, however, assumes: (1) that the pool of capital devoted to the market is limited to the value currently invested; and (2) that none of this money leaves the market during the listing of the previously non-tradable shares. While neither of these assumptions need be true, the example does indicate the huge impact of any major state divestment within a short time period.

Regardless of the implications of this approach, this appears to be the direction of state policy, as was publicly suggested recently by the

Chairman of the CSRC.[7] Shortly after his comments, on 29 November 1999, the CSRC announced the final selection of ten listed companies which will auction off (*paimai*) an as yet unspecified amount of state shares to current holders of A shares based on a pricing range set in excess of each company's NAV, but less than a P/E ratio of ten times earnings.[8] Given that the average P/E ratio for the domestic markets is approximately 50 times, the CSRC's suggested pricing range reflects the thought that non-tradable shares are worth only 20 per cent of tradable shares. As a CSRC official put it when announcing the plan, 'The sale of state shares fully considers the actual situation of China's equity markets, the pricing is relatively reasonable and leaves a fairly large opportunity for profit. The reason why we are giving preference to original shareholders is because we want to fully care for the interests of current [A share] investors.'[9]

It is interesting that in the days following the announcement, the shares of the two companies meant to complete their offerings before year end 1999 traded up an average of 24 and 12 per cent on the secondary market as shown in Table 3.6. This surprising outcome reflects the investor belief that acquiring the shares now will enable them to acquire an equal number of cheap shares later so that, overall, they will book a nice gain (but will they be able to realize it later!). The only answer to this can be that it all depends how high the initial buy-in cost is. And while this approach may succeed in reducing the proportion of state shares, the case of Beijing Zhongguancun strongly suggests such success will come at the cost of a significant decrease in secondary

Table 3.6: CSRC designated ten companies auctioning state shares

Code	Name	Mkt Cap (RMB BN)	% State	26/11/99 (RMB)	3/12/99 (RMB)	Rise %
0667	Huayi Investment	2.23	74.1	8.51	8.58	0.8
0692	Huitian Power	3.06	75.0	13.04	13.23	1.5
0589	Qianluntai A	1.87	63.3	7.13	8.87	24.4
0426	Fulong Power	1.72	72.4	8.61	8.93	3.7
0401	Beidong Cement	5.29	80.5	6.3	6.29	–0.2
600663	Lujiazui	18.73	91.4	14.01	14.01	0.0
600877	Jialing	3.47	74.8	7.29	8.19	12.3
600129	Taiji Group	4.02	74.4	15	15.84	5.6
600717	Tianjin Port	3.40	72.9	9.73	9.82	0.9
600828	Chengshang Group	1.81	74.9	9.5	10.29	8.3

Source: Wind Information System; state share as of 30 September 1999; bold represents companies to offer before year end 1999

market values and the overall market capitalization of the companies involved.[10]

Returning to the Zhongguancun issue, there is an additional reason which might explain its low rights price and the subsequent post-offering price collapse. This is simply that even at a lower share price not enough demand was generated from other, new investors to provide price support in the secondary market. If the State truly believed that one of the companies whose shares were being offered to investors was at an unacceptably low price, there is nothing preventing it from using international techniques to generate greater demand and higher prices. By treating each company's shares as a commodity, prices will naturally be lower and the entire market is unlikely to develop much beyond-its current level.

Nonetheless, the conclusion must still be made that the Chinese domestic equity market is still not broad enough or deep enough to absorb the huge state sector. This explains the continued reliance on overseas offerings for major transactions. The way out will require time and the development of an investor base beyond the retail sector. (The development of companies which truly act as companies is the other critical part of this equation.) As discussed later on, securities investment funds, insurance companies, pension funds and similar professional investors are only very recent market participants. Without professional investors it is very difficult to imagine how China's equity markets can move beyond their current achievements.

3.2 Impact of share structure on the value of state and legal person shares

Interestingly, some analysts have argued that China's rigidly defined mix of shares has been prejudicial to the economic and ownership interests of the state. While surprising and incorrect, this view as expounded below is useful in highlighting the entire issue of who benefits from China's current state dominated equity markets.

> … where the assets of a state-controlled firm appreciate, the non-tradable, majority state shares are effectively transferring part of their appreciated value to the tradable, minority public individual shares, by virtue of the market forces of demand over supply, thus resulting in a reduced value of the illiquid state ownership interests and a windfall to the selling individual shareholders. … no law has been adopted to address the latent transfer of value from state

ownership interests to the few individual shareholders caused by the government's self-imposed illiquidity.'[11]

Although it is unclear, this analysis seems to suggest that there is a value to a listed company's assets independent of the value assigned to them by the market. Of course, this is exactly the state's view as expounded in the Standard Opinion and Company Law. But the analysis quoted above seems to assert that the book value of a company's assets is what moves stock prices. Based on this view, the argument develops the concept of a 'latent transfer of value' from the non-tradable shares of the state to owners of tradable shares.[12] This view is entirely incorrect. If there has been any such kind of 'latent' transfer on China's stock markets, it has been the continuing open transfer of wealth from individual investors to Chinese companies and their state shareholders as a result of the public offering and trading process. Indeed, recapitalizing highly leveraged Chinese SOEs so as to maintain employment has been the entire reason for being of China's stock markets from the start.

The book value point of view is, however, shared by the state which requires by regulation a company seeking an IPO to price its equity at a value in excess of the officially appraised net asset value per share. As anyone involved in China's IPO process is aware, whether for a domestic or international issue, the share price must exceed the NAV per share even if only by a penny. How to arrive at this result is usually an object of intense discussion during the preparation stage of an offering. Whether the answer is correct or not is first of all up to the State Asset Management Bureau, but the real test lies with the market.[13]

The asset appraisal of any SOE attaches an inflated value to the assets due to the use of the replacement value of the given assets. The replacement value is based on the question, 'What would be the cost of acquiring similar assets in today's market?' For example, a given machine may have been in operation daily for five years with the company's financial records reflecting its depreciated value. On application of the replacement value, however, the machinery is revalued upward with the resulting premium shown in the company's equity capital accounts under PRC generally accepted accounting principles (PRC GAAP). Downward revisions in value, while theoretically possible, are in practice not permitted in accordance with the spirit of SAMB regulations. It is the State Asset Management Bureau's mission to ensure that state assets increase in value year by year. Consequently, at the company's IPO the state sells a minority stake in the company at an inflated asset price and based on an administratively predetermined multiple of earnings. There can be no doubt that this leads to a net transfer of value from the share investor to the state at the outset. The entire approach, by focusing on the book value of a company's assets, wholly ignores the real question of whether such assets, whether fully depreciated or completely new, actually create value, that is, profit through their operation and management.

Once the listing has been completed the company's shares trade freely in the secondary market between individual investors and other market participants. On the market shares not only appreciate in value, they depreciate as well, as everyone investing in the A share (or any other) market is more than well aware. As the discussion in Chapter 8 demonstrates, secondary trading levels of all Chinese shares is a consequence of market sentiment, overall trends in the economy, and government actions or pronouncements as well as supply and demand. Chinese shares, and particularly A shares, do not move based on appreciation in asset value, if by this is meant profitability. The market at its current stage of development in China does not price shares based on any kind of fundamental analysis of company performance.

The latent value argument can be looked at from a further angle. The secondary market value of a company's shares is used to calculate not only the single company's market value but also the entire market capitalization of the given exchange as shown in Tables 3.4 and 3.7. Thus, if a company has 100 shares of which 30 are listed and trade at RMB20 per share, all of the company's shares, including the state shares, are attributed this value and its market capitalization is, therefore, RMB200. The exchange's market capitalization represents the aggregate valuation of all shares of all listed companies at their price at a given moment in time. But as has been shown, Chinese market participants currently reject this approach to the extent of denying that any value attaches at all to non-tradable shares. So even though its shares are nominally valued at the market price, the state is unlikely to be able at this time to realize their value at any price approaching this level. This situation, however, is a consequence of the state's desire at the inception of the equity experiment to own and control the listed companies. If the state should desire to realize value for its controlling stake, it can choose to write rules which would permit the use of shares in a number of financing transactions. For example, the state could use its shares as collateral either for bank loans or repo transactions. Or it could use its shares to acquire other assets in M&A transactions. Or it can, as it intends to do, sell off some of its holdings. In each of these cases the

Table 3.7: Shenzhen market capitalization structure (30 September 1999)

| | Shenzhen Stock Exchange market capitalization | | | | |
| | A share companies | | | B share companies | |
	RMB (MM)	US$	%	US$	%
State shares	306 596	37 028	23.6	1 765	29.8
Domestic Legal Person shares	428 553	51 758	33.0	1 371	23.2
Overseas Legal Person shares[1]	20 599	2 488	1.6	449	7.6
Social Legal Person shares	84 260	10 176	6.5	251	4.2
Internal shares	38 263	4 621	2.9	69	1.2
Other[2]	8 807	1 064	0.7	23	0.4
Total non-tradable	887 078	107 135	68.3	3 927	66.4
A shares	412 213	49 784	31.7		
B shares				1 993	33.6
Total market capitalization	1 299 290	156 919	100.0	5 920	100.0

Notes: 1. Legal Person Shares are created when a company uses state assets which it is authorized to dispose of to invest in a company limited by shares. Presumably Overseas Legal Person Shares represent the investment by properly authorized overseas Chinese state enterprises. Social Legal Person Shares represent investment by third party legal persons in the public offering of a company.

2. Aside from preferred shares, what 'Other' shares may include is anyone's guess. One likelihood is that a portion of these are shares to which the State or Legal Persons failed to subscribe during Rights Issues. In such a case, such shares may have been sold to the public.

Source: Wind Information System

reference value for the shares should be the secondary market price, not some notional asset value subject to the whims of asset appraisers, accountants and the SAMB as is the current practice.

This notion that there has been a hidden transfer of value from the state to the individual investors (at least in up markets) confounds the entire nature of the share reform. Without the existence of the markets, the state's assets would have remained significantly undervalued to the extent that many of the currently listed companies would most certainly have long since gone bankrupt. This, in reality, is the case of the 64 so-called 'Special Treatment' companies already listed which have not shown a profit, even by lax Chinese standards, for two years in a row.[14] What is required is the further development of the market and not another law or regulation which, in any event, would lead to even further market distortion. Indeed, such an approach would without question lead to the collapse of China's equity markets just as it would if this notion were brought up in any other country with an equity market.

3.3   Impact of segmented share structure on market valuation

The existence of segmented, or different share classes, has been a fairly common phenomenon throughout developing Asian markets and generally reflects policy decisions to limit foreign participation in domestic equity markets. The same is true for China but with the twist that the policy decision has been to limit all non-state equity ownership, domestic or foreign. The situation is further complicated by the non-convertible Renminbi. For example, China Eastern Airlines has successfully listed shares in New York, Hong Kong and Shanghai. Whether the shares are listed on the SEHK or on the NYSE or on the Shanghai Stock Exchange, each share represents the same entitlements and same return characteristics. This is fully demonstrated in the international markets by the fact that the New York/Hong Kong shares trade at the same price after adjustment for currency differences.

In contrast, China Eastern's Shanghai A shares trade at a price in general about five times that of the international markets.[15] There are 13 Chinese companies like China Eastern which have shares listed domestically and internationally and an analysis of the trading patterns and valuations show the same results for each of them as shown in Table 3.8. The price ratio between A and H shares for each of the 13 companies' shares as of September 30 1999 and after translating the

Chart 3.1: China Eastern Airlines N, H and A share performance

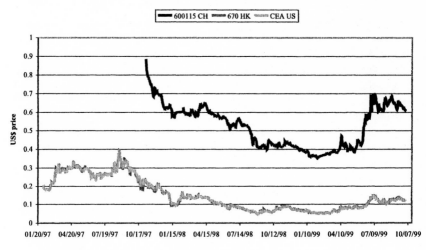

Source: Bloomberg and Wind Information System

value of each share into RMB is shown in Chart 3.2. The ratio ranges from a low of about two times for Yizheng Chemical Fiber to over 14 times for Kunming Machinery.

In addition to the impact of a non-convertible currency and, therefore, a virtually closed domestic market, this wide valuation gap for shares of the same company reflects a further difference between China's domestic markets and international markets: the new Securities Law prohibits short selling of any securities. The inability of an investor to take advantage of this valuation differential, for example, by buying the cheap Hong Kong shares while selling the expensive A shares short (or, if the situation is reversed, vice versa) prevents the arbitrage transactions which take place between the New York and Hong Kong markets and keep the shares of a given company in line in both markets. The same holds true, not surprisingly, for the 40 B share companies which also have listed A shares. Here the ratio of the price of an single A share to that of a single B share ranges from nearly four times to almost 11 times.

This discrepancy in the valuation of the same shares listed in different markets can be looked at from a second angle, but the story is the same. The Price/Earnings ratio[16] is the more typical method used to compare share valuations across different markets. Table 3.9 shows year-end average market P/E ratios for Chinese shares over a nine year

Table 3.8: Chinese companies with domestic SSE and international listings

	Overseas share data				A share data		
	Listing date	Location	Shares (MM)	PE	Listing date	Shares (MM)	PE
Tsingtao Beer	7/15/93	HK	317.6	17.89	8/27/93	100	0.00
Shanghai Petro.	7/26/93	HK/NY	1 680	0.00	11/8/93	550	0.00
Guangdong Shipping	8/6/93	HK	145	9.50	10/28/93	126.48	0.00
Beiren Printing	8/6/93	HK	100	11.50	5/6/94	50	18.93
Maanshan Iron	11/3/93	HK	1 733	13.00	1/6/94	687.81	12.06
Kunming Machinery	12/7/93	HK	65	10.62	1/3/94	60	0.00
Yizheng Chemical	3/29/94	HK	300	13.83	4/11/95	200	9.93
Bohai Chemical	5/12/94	HK	340	12.60	6/30/95	68.98	0.00
Dongfang Electric	6/6/94	HK	170	11.94	10/10/95	60	0.00
Luoyang Glass	7/8/94	HK	250	10.50	10/31/95	50	0.00
Panda	5/2/96	HK	242	0.00	11/18/96	23	13.60
China Eastern	2/5/97	HK/NY	1 400	0.00	11/5/97	300	18.00
Yanzhou Coal	4/1/98	HK/NY	820	0.00	7/1/98	80	8.80

Source: Bloomberg and Wind Information System

Chart 3.2: A to H share price ratio

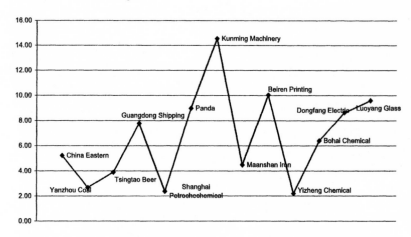

period. The data suggests that investors value the Shanghai and Shenzhen A share markets over the Hong Kong H share market by a factor of over two times. This is not, as concluded before, the result of different outlooks on these stocks, it is entirely the result of the exchange controls which make the domestic markets a virtually closed system. This topic is further explored in Chapter 8.

This discussion need not consider whether the shares are fairly valued, undervalued or over valued. The charts and tables simply compare trading prices regardless of fundamental company performance

Table 3.9: Year-end P/E Ratios by Market

	Shanghai A	Shanghai B	Shenzhen A	Shenzhen B	H share	Red Chip
1990	28.05	NA	NA	NA	NA	NA
1991	81.83	NA	26.71	NA	NA	NA
1992	72.65	17.4	57.52	35.56	NA	NA
1993	42.48	NA	44.21	20.11	NA	NA
1994	29.67	9.94	10.67	7.02	11.61	NA
1995	16.32	8	9.8	6.01	10.05	NA
1996	32.65	14.04	38.88	14.07	10.85	NA
1997	43.43	11.99	42.66	10.67	14.84	NA
1998	34.38	6.04	32.31	5.71	7.11	10.44
30 June 1999	46.51	14.39	48.12	14.39	22.77	157.8

Note: NA indicates unavailable data
Source: Bloomburg, SSE and SZSE Fact Books

and business outlook. While there is no absolutely correct method to determine the 'true' value of a stock, any market price must be compared with other investment choices existent at the same point of time. Based on this, it would seem fair to assume that the H share market as well as other China related shares trading on the SEHK provide a better sense of the true value of a given company than the Shanghai or Shenzhen valuations. International investors have a greater range of trading methodologies, information, levels of expertise and investment opportunities. Overseas markets, in short, are broader and deeper than China's domestic market.

All of this suggests that domestic shares are substantially overvalued. At current market levels the domestic A shares of these 13 companies together with their related non-listed shares have a market value of around US$15 billion. If the SEHK share price is used to value the same company, however, this value collapses to US$5 billion. This outcome validates the conclusions reached in Section 3.1, but from a different perspective. In this case, the excessive valuation is explained by the closed system and trading restrictions. Domestic investors do not have the ability to buy H shares due to the non-convertibility of the Renminbi. This precludes the growing number of funds and other institutional investors in China from participating as well.[17]

A further important factor in this regard is the controlled supply and demand of the domestic market. The Chinese government has been quite successful in raising the profile of the domestic stock markets and encouraging interest in shares. The two exchanges have recorded strong growth in terms of number of listings and numbers of share accounts in recent years. Trading turnover has reached over RMB80 billion a day during the June 1999 market rally. However, the pool of potential investor funds, if one takes about US$700 billion in bank savings into account, has remained far in excess of the pool of tradable shares and new issues. The inherent surplus of demand over supply combined with a scarcity of other investment opportunities has ensured that the domestic markets remain at inflated P/E multiples.

Allowing the Renminbi to be convertible for the capital account should, in the absence of other restrictions, permit domestic investors to participate directly in the Hong Kong market (and other markets as well) and international investors to participate in the domestic markets. It is, therefore, critical for the government to make significant preparation in advance to ensure market stability as a result of the convertibility decision. As things now stand, any move toward convertibility will level out valuation discrepancies for those companies listed domestically and abroad and, given the prominence of some of these companies, any downward valuation could lead to a stampede. Over the longer term, convertibility will compel the domestic markets to develop in line with their international peers.

4
China's Stock Exchanges

Shanghai's beautiful new stock exchange building in Pudong houses one of the most advanced electronic trading centers in the world and is a matched set with that of Shenzhen. Both exchanges give the appearance of long established markets which have just completed a full upgrade in preparation for the next millennium. In fact, China's experience with securities markets does extend back into a long forgotten history of over one hundred years. Before the 1949 revolution China had active stock exchanges in Shanghai, Tianjin and Beijing. The forerunner of the Shanghai exchange was established in 1891 and the other two during the early years of the Republic period, 1910–20. All primarily traded government debt securities. The last of the three, the Tianjin exchange, was closed in mid-1952, marking the start of China's experiment with a Soviet-style planned economy. As time went on the political climate in China grew increasingly hostile to securities and securities exchanges. Even as recently as 1992 investment bankers searched for ways to say 'privatization' in Chinese without saying privatization (*siyouhua*) in deference to their audience. It seemed unthinkable that exchanges could exist without private companies. Of course, eight years later nothing resembling privatization has happened, but Chinese now use the previously forbidden word freely and the state has begun to reduce its demand for absolute majority control of listed companies.

The policy of opening up and reform initiated in 1979 created the positive environment for such changes to gradually happen. This, combined with the needs of economic development and, in particular, the need to develop new ways to finance development, led to experimentation with different forms of ownership, which quickly led, in turn, to the creation of various types of equity shares. Before the decade of the

71

1980s was over, shareholding companies had been established throughout the country and shares were traded vigorously on an OTC basis. Had June 4 not intervened and the direction of the country's development not once again become a subject of sharp political dispute, China's national stock exchanges might have been established much earlier than, in fact, they eventually were. And the whole issue of privatization, apparent or not, might have long since passed into history.

This chapter reviews the emergence of securities markets during the 1980s as a background for outlining the regulatory and organizational structure of China's two national securities exchanges. It also touches briefly on the operating characteristics of the two exchanges. The chapter concludes with a summary of the historical experience of three other types of trading arrangement including the regional trading centers, STAQ and NETS.

4.1   1979–88: over the counter trading

As described in Chapter 2, during the early years of China's equity markets investors acquired securities which paid a fixed dividend and consequently thought these were equities. Investors tended to hold, not trade securities, having invested to obtain the steady dividend cash flow. The ownership of such securities was, moreover, transferable since the market was almost entirely open and unregulated, but, given the original investment objective, little trading took place. From the mid 1980s equity issuance became increasingly frequent. In August 1986 Shenyang became the first to initiate formal OTC trading followed by Shanghai in September. In October of the same year Shenzhen became the first government entity to produce a formal set of procedures governing the establishment of companies limited by shares.[1] On this basis five Shenzhen SOEs offered shares to the public in 1987 led off by the Shenzhen Development Bank, China's first financial institution limited by shares. The issue, however, was not successful as the planned amount of RMB7.9 million was only 4.9 per cent subscribed. Even a 10 per cent dividend at the end of the year could not arouse investor interest.[2]

The Shenzhen government simultaneously approved the formal establishment of OTC trading counters at various financial institutions which, in turn, increased trading volumes. By the end of the decade there were nine financial institutions conducting OTC trades in eleven business offices across the city and one institution providing share registry services.[3] The existence of this market infrastructure later on enabled the government to apply the brakes on the overheated market of 1990.

Aside from the formative experience of 'share fever', the Shenzhen government benefited from the stock markets: trading had grown to such a volume that the government considered stamp duty on ownership transfers and dividends to be a significant source of revenue.[4] From an annual trading volume of only RMB4 million in 1988, equity trading increased to over RMB1.8 billion in 1990 on a year end market capitalization of RMB7 billion as a consequence of people's growing awareness of the capital appreciation potential of shares. In contrast, bond trading had virtually come to a halt in 1989.[5]

Although various kinds of government debt securities were also traded in Shenzhen, local investors came rapidly to prefer what were in essence penny stocks – they were cheaper, more volatile and so offered the upside potential that suited Shenzhen's get rich quick mentality. A further major factor influencing Shenzhen's development as a center of equities was its proximity to Hong Kong. The city government as it began to plan the establishment of an exchange closely consulted the Hong Kong model and experience, as can be seen in the 1986 provisions. As for local investors, the Hong Kong retail investor mentality easily seeped across the border along with Hong Kong hot money during the late 1980s.

There was a similar evolution in Shanghai, although with a slightly different emphasis: government debt securities rather than equities.[6] As noted in Chapter 2, the process leading to the establishment of the Shanghai exchange in late 1990 began in November 1984 with the Shanghai Feile Acoustics share placement but was actually driven by the government's issuance of treasury securities. From an equity viewpoint, however, Shanghai's evolution went through four stages. From November 1984 to the end of 1986 companies predominantly placed shares to their own employees, although there were a few public placements also, as shown in Table 3.2. During this two year period shares began to change hands informally. From January 1987 to March 1988, the budding market began to attract the attention of trust and investment companies. Some applied to the city government for permission to establish OTC trading operations with a primary focus on treasury bonds which were allowed to be traded from April 1988. The first such office was opened by the Shanghai branch of the Industrial and Commercial Bank of China in September 1986. Through 1988 eight trading counters were established without central government oversight.[7] From April 1988 to the opening of the Shanghai Stock Exchange the development of a specialized securities industry began. During this time the Shanghai Branch of the PBOC approved the establishment of a number of securities companies including Shanghai Wanguo Securities, Shanghai Shenyin Securities, Shanghai Haitong Securities and Shanghai Finance Securities, all of which became major industry powers during the 1990s. But, like Shenzhen, the initial share issues in Shanghai met with a yawn: the third issue by Shanghai Vacuum Electronic Device in March 1989 failed, forcing the underwriting syndicate to take 80 per cent of the shares.

The ability to trade treasury bonds (*guoku*) on an OTC basis beginning in 1988, however, was the driving force behind the rapid developments that led to the establishment of the Shanghai Stock Exchange. In contrast, at this time the shares of only eight Shanghai companies were trading over the counter. From almost the start Shanghai took on the nature of a central government sponsored market for debt securities, while Shenzhen was the Wild West of equity shares.

4.2   1989–91: the effort to impose order

From 1989 on the state initiated efforts to impose order on enterprise experiments with shareholding structure as well as share issuance and trading. This was driven by the old political criticism that stocks and stock markets were capitalist manifestations, were leading to privatization and creating social unrest and, therefore, should be eliminated. Many measures were being prepared which did not go through in the aftermath of the June 4 Incident. But in May 1990 the State Council did approve a report submitted by the pro-market State Committee for the Restructuring of the Economic Systems which on its face appeared to limit the equity experiment by proposing: (1) the continuation of experiments wherein only enterprises participated in the share capital of other enterprises, that is, investment by legal persons only; (2) restrictions on the further spread of the sale of shares to employees; and (3) limiting the development of OTC markets to Shanghai and Shenzhen alone.[8] In reality, however, the SCRES report, together with Shenzhen's 'share fever' drove the market forward. In June the State Council gave the go ahead to the establishment of formal securities exchanges.

The opening of the Shanghai Securities Exchange[9] in November 1990 followed shortly thereafter by the Shenzhen Securities Exchange in February 1991 were both extremely symbolic historical events. Both exchanges were heavily promoted by their respective local municipal governments and had the approval of the nominal regulator, the PBOC. Elsewhere in the country OTC trading continued, particularly in the major cities of Shenyang, Wuhan and Tianjin each of which had sought to establish a recognized exchange but had lacked the political clout. It is difficult now to imagine the force of market events in early 1991 even though the scale of the markets was in fact quite small. Unruly crowds of would-be investors teamed to open share accounts with securities houses and the trading floors of the Shanghai exchange made the Chicago Merc seem like a public library by comparison. This was a period when the whole character of China seemed on the verge of changing overnight.

4.3   The '810' Incident

Then, of course, it did change with some finality in early 1992 with Deng's Southern Journey. But the beginning of the end of local dominance over the exchanges started with the Shenzhen Riots of 10 August 1992, or the '810 Incident'. Tens of thousands of would be investors had lined up for over three days and nights at the local PBOC offices to obtain a form which would give them the right to subscribe to shares of an upcoming IPO. But on the day these forms were handed out, 10 August, the prescribed 5 million forms had been used up in less than four hours. That afternoon and evening Shenzhen was the scene of violent rioting as the populace vented its anger against a process which was clearly corrupted by the managing PBOC officials. The next day the government distributed a further 500 000 forms and order was restored. This event led directly to the establishment in October 1992 of the CSRC and the start of the central government's effort to exert control over the development of the securities industry in general and the stock exchanges in particular. Looking back, it is fair to say that this process is now over as symbolized by the adoption of the much disputed Securities Law in 1999.

4.4   Original organizational structure of the Shanghai and Shenzhen exchanges

From their establishment both the SSE and the SZSE shared a similar organizational structure as non-profit organizations run by members through a general meeting which elects a standing executive committee, or Council.[10] The Council is headed by a Director with a separate General Manager selected as the legal representative for the exchange.

In addition, a Supervisory Committee responsible to the members' general meeting was also established.

The degree of independence of the two exchanges differed significantly, however, as summarized in Table 4.1. While both exchanges were subject to the supervision of their respective local branches of the PBOC, the Shenzhen exchange had relatively more independence. For example, the designation of the General Manager for the SSE was subject to the approval of PBOC Beijing, while for the SZSE this remained a local matter. The exchanges worked closely with their respective municipal Securities Commission to which the municipal government appointed representatives from each of the agencies or bureaus responsible for certain aspects of the corporatization and listing process.[11] In practice this meant nearly every government agency was represented. The Commissions, in turn, operated through an executive body, a Securities Administration Office, which was devoted to the administration of the markets, approval of listings, supervision of listed companies and oversight of dispute resolution. The two exchanges were thus well integrated into their local govern-

Table 4.1: Comparison of management structures of the SSE and SZSE

Position	SSE required approval	SZSE required approval
Membership	Exchange followed by PBOC Shanghai Branch review, PBOC Beijing review if a non-Shanghai entity	Exchange followed by PBOC Shenzhen branch review
Council	Nominated by Council followed by PBOC Shanghai branch approval	Director nominated by PBOC Shenzhen branch
General Manager	Nominated by PBOC Shanghai branch and approved by PBOC Beijing	Nominated by Council Director and approved by Council followed by PBOC Shenzhen branch approval
Deputy General Manager	Nominated by PBOC Shanghai branch and approved by PBOC Beijing	Nominated by Council Director and approved by Council followed by PBOC Shenzhen branch approval
Supervisory Committee	Director and Deputy Director appointed by PBOC Shanghai branch	Director and Deputy Director elected by the Committee followed by PBOC Shenzhen approval

ments which, at the outset, managed them for the benefit of companies domiciled in their own jurisdictions.

4.5 The 1993 Provisional Regulations of Securities Exchanges

Following the 810 Incident and the dislodging of the PBOC as the market's regulator in 1992 this cozy relationship began to change. In July 1993 the State Council Securities Commission issued 'Provisional Regulations on the Administration of Securities Exchanges' marking the start of the central government's takeover of the exchanges.[12] The regulations firmly established the right of the CSRC to supervise the respective local government's management of the exchanges. The exchanges were compelled to revise their articles of incorporation accordingly. Of the two revised versions, however, only the Shenzhen exchange made its relationship with the CSRC explicit as below:

- the operating regulations of the exchanges were now to be approved by the local government and the CSRC
- new members accepted by the exchange were to be reported to both the local government and the CSRC
- nominations by the members' general meeting for the Director and Deputy Director of the stock exchange council had to be first reviewed by both the local government and the CSRC prior to submission for voting by the general meeting
- nominations for general manager of the exchange had first to be reviewed by the local government and the CSRC prior to submission for voting by the stock exchange council
- a representative of the CSRC participated in the Listing Committee set up by the exchange council
- the exchange was required to report to the local government and the CSRC on any legal suits or dispute involving its operations or its senior management.[13]

In contrast, the Shanghai exchange made only a general reference to the securities regulator and no direct reference by name at all to the CSRC. For example, after setting out its scope of operations, the SSE's revised articles notes '... or any other capacity as permitted and entrusted by the national securities supervisory organ.'[14] It appears that Shanghai was either not supportive of the national effort to establish an integrated regulatory regime or perhaps believed that the CSRC would not succeed. In fact, the first years of the CSRC's existence were marked by serious disputes between the Shanghai exchange and the CSRC over the latter's focus on listing Chinese companies on international markets and a variety of other issues.[15] Among other things, the Shanghai exchange wanted to know why China's best companies were not being listed in Shanghai and believed if they were the market would develop all the more quickly.

4.6   The 1996 Regulations on the Administration of Stock Exchanges

By 1996 this dispute had been solidly resolved in favor of the SCSC and CSRC and the 1993 Provisional Regulations were replaced by a final version, the 1996 Regulations.[16] This final version removed all uncertainties as to who was the boss of the national exchanges, delegating the authority to the CSRC alone to supervise and administer (*jiandu guanli*) them and their related securities settlement companies. For example, the following issues required the final approval of the CSRC after being passed on by the exchange itself:

- listing of new securities products
- provision of new services
- revision of operating regulations
- revision of articles of incorporation (SCSC approval required)
- any change in an exchange's number of seats
- revisions in the operating regulations of the settlement company

On top of this the CSRC was delegated the unilateral authority to:

- nominate the Director and the Deputy Director of the stock exchange council
- nominate the General Manager of the exchange
- propose the dismissal of the Director and Deputy Director of the exchange council and the General and Deputy General Manager of the exchange
- request the exchanges and their settlement companies to revise their articles of incorporation and operating regulations
- send personnel to investigate the operations, finances or other matters of the exchanges and their settlement companies

There continued, however, to be redundant regulation of non-Shanghai or Shenzhen brokers and trading centers with the PBOC claiming jurisdiction over 'cross region linkages' based on an old 1990 regulation and the CSRC claiming jurisdiction over the actual links with the exchanges based on the 1993 law. This typified the regulatory structure during the 1990s and is discussed in more detail in Chapter 5.

4.6.1 The 1999 Securities Law

The Securities Law devotes an entire chapter to the exchanges,[17] but this chapter is in many ways less comprehensive than the 1996 Regulations. Consequently, as in the case of the Standard Opinion and the Company Law, and most laws in China, the 1996 Regulations and the Securities Law should be seen as complementary. However, the Securities Law has effected a number of changes and, as usual, left certain matters open for further elaboration.

The original legal structure for the two exchanges was laid down in their Articles of Incorporation, which were re-confirmed, although with conforming revisions, by the 1996 Regulations. This structure remains but with adjustments and omissions noted below which further enhance the authority of the CSRC.

Members' general meeting

Under the 1996 Regulations the members' general meeting was the highest authority of a stock exchange. The Regulations also specified the meeting's scope of authority and how such authority is exercized. The Securities Law is silent on these issues, however, so until the State Council enacts further regulations, the 1996 Regulations continue in effect.

The council of the stock exchange

The Council in the 1996 Regulations is defined as the decisionmaking body whose principal function is to implement decisions made by the members' general meetings. The Securities Law recognizes the council but is silent on its powers.

General manager

The most obvious change made by the Securities Law is the provision for the appointment of the general manager. This power was originally placed in the Council with basic veto authority residing in the CSRC. The Securities Law has now taken this power from the Council and the local governments entirely by vesting the power to directly appoint the general manager in the CSRC.

Members

The qualifications for membership are specified in the Articles of Association of each exchange and are not dealt with in either the 1996 Regulations or the Securities Law. Each exchange has somewhat different membership qualifications as shown in the Table 4.2.

Risk fund

The Securities Law mandates the establishment of a risk fund funded by an allocation of the exchange's transaction charges, membership fees and fees for trading seats. The risk fund is to be managed by the stock exchange council. The powers of the council and the uses of the fund have yet to be set out.

4.7 Securities registration and clearing institutions

Currently the two stock exchanges conduct registration and clearing operations through respectively owned subsidiaries, the Shanghai Securities Central Clearing and Registration Company ('SSCCRC') and

Table 4.2: Exchange membership qualifications

Exchange	Qualifications
Shanghai Stock Exchange	• applicant approved by the PBOC Beijing and Shanghai Branch (now CSRC) • more than RMB 5 million registered capital (of which RMB 5 million should be in cash) • positive reputation and operating results • profitable securities operations for two years • minimum membership fee of RMB150,000
Shenzhen Stock Exchange	• legal person registered in Shenzhen • financial institution approved by the PBOC (now CSRC) and authorized to carry out securities operations • at least RMB5 million in capital allocated to securities operations • management structure and personnel must comply with the requirements set out by the exchange • minimum RMB1 million membership fee

Note: Article 8, Shanghai Securities Exchange Articles of Incorporation (Revised), March 1993, Chun *et al.*, *Zhongguo zhengquan fagui zonghui*, Vol. 8, p. 859; and Article 7, Shenzhen Securities Exchange Articles of Incorporation, (Revised), 20 May 1993, Chun *et al.*, *Zhongguo zhengquan fagui zonghui*, Vol. 8, pp. 867–8

the Shenzhen Securities Settlement Company ('SSSC'). Chapter 7 of the Securities Law envisages the establishment of a nationwide centralized operation which will replace the two existing clearing organizations. This focus would seem to be misplaced since the current institutions operate extremely well.

Holders of securities are required to place all securities into the custody of one of these two institutions prior to trading on a stock exchange. The institutions are not permitted to pledge or lend the securities and are responsible for the accurate and complete registry of securities holders, for accurate and complete records of all securities transfers and for the maintenance of correct historical records. As noted, they fulfil these roles in a professional fashion and are critical to the overall performance of the market.

4.8   The growth of exchange membership

The development of the exchanges can be seen in the dramatic increase in the number of members through 1995. There were three categories of members including local Shanghai or Shenzhen brokerages, brokerages domiciled outside of Shanghai or Shenzhen and trading centers, which are discussed in a later section of this chapter and were members of the SSE alone. The regional trading centers were closed at the end of 1998.

The sharp drop of membership in both exchanges beginning in 1997 is largely due to stagnant trading volumes resulting from the govern-

Table 4.3: SSE and SZSE membership trends

Year	Local members SSE	SZSE	Non-local members SSE	SZSE	Trading centers SSE	Total SSE	SZSE
1991	NA	NA	NA	NA	NA	26	15
1992	NA	NA	NA	NA	NA	101	177
1993	46	28	330	398	2	378	426
1994	49	30	501	466	19	569	496
1995	49	34	504	498	24	577	532
1996	45	34	478	508	24	547	542
1997	43	24	424	349	26	493	373
1998	12	15	305	314	0	317	329
3Q 99	11	15	298	303	0	309	318

Source: SSE and SZSE Fact Books

ment's anti-inflationary campaign. Lower volumes drove a consolidation of the brokerage industry which continues through to the present, although for different reasons. The decline in membership is also reflected in the number of seats or trading positions at each exchange. Despite lower trading volumes during these years, the number of account holders grew substantially to approximately 40 million equally divided between the two exchanges.

By the end of 1998 there was a broad geographic distribution among exchange members but significant concentration as well. Twelve provinces and cities accounted for approximately 66 per cent of the total Shanghai exchange membership. The Shenzhen exchange shows the same distribution. Given the rapid development of China's coastal provinces and their relative prosperity, it is not surprising that only seven provincial-level areas including Guangdong, Fujian, Zhejiang, Shanghai, Jiangsu, Shandong and Beijing account for 47 per cent of total membership. The relatively strong representation of Liaoning is accounted for by the fact that Shenyang was a leader from the very beginning in the experiment with shares and shareholding ownership structures and until the end of 1998 was the location of one of the three major regional trading centers. The strong representation of Henan, one of China's poorest provinces, is due to the presence in Zhengzhou of a major commodity exchange.

4.9 Exchange products traded

Unsurprisingly, the exchanges share a similar product mix, although Shanghai continues to be the principal market for Chinese government bonds (CGBs), while the SZSE is dominated by A share trading. The exchanges trade A shares, B shares, CGBs, securities funds, corporate bonds, convertible bonds, and CGB repos. Dual listings, that is, the listing of a company's shares on both exchanges, are not permitted. As Table 4.5 illustrates, A share trading dominates the volumes of both exchanges, while Shanghai dominates bond trading.

Because Shanghai dominates bonds it also leads in CGB repo trading, which requires some discussion given its direct linkage to the equity market. A repo involves the use of a CGB as collateral for a cash loan.[18] Such loans are then used by securities firms to purchase shares for outright trading purposes or to acquire shares at the time of an A share IPO. When new A share issuance is heavy there is a corresponding increase in repo volume and interest charged (the repo rate).

Table 4.4: Trends in number of seats, SSE and SZSE

Year	Local members SSE	Local members SZSE	Non-local members SSE	Non-local members SZSE	Trading centers SSE	Trading centers SZSE	Total SSE	Total SZSE
1991	37	–	–	–	0	–	37	–
1992	144	–	–	–	0	–	284	–
1993	779	–	821	–	47	–	1 647	348
1994	1 280	111	2 025	656	1 010	15	4 315	782
1995	1 465	122	2 082	742	1 353	23	4 900	887
1996	1 467	234	1 963	864	1 803	27	5 233	1 125
1997	1 609	246	1 797	1 069	2 294	28	5 700	1 343
1998		240		1 237	0	28	5 394	1 505
3rd quarter 99		239		1 340	0	0	5 066	1 579

Year	Visible seats SSE	Visible seats SZSE	Invisible seats SSE	Invisible seats SZSE
1997	3 711	–	1 989	–
1998	3 037	–	2 357	–
3rd quarter 99	2 749	–	2 317	–

Source: SSE and SZSE Fact Books; blanks due to incomplete data series

Chart 4.1: SSE A share accounts and exchange members (1991–Sept. 1999)

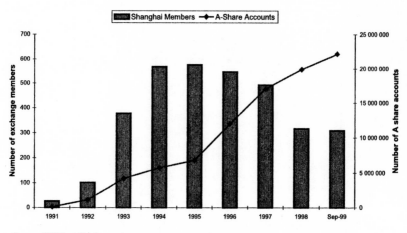

Source: SSE Fact Book

Chart 4.2: Graphic representation of SSE members (1998)

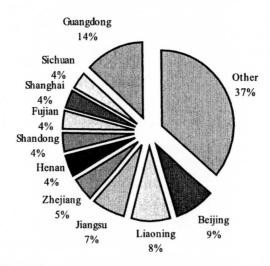

Source: SSE Fact Book

4.9.1 Trading and execution

There are two methods of trading on the SSE and SZSE, the 'visible' seat and the 'invisible' seat as shown in Table 4.4. All products can be traded

Table 4.5: Exchange traded products and trading volume (30 Sept. 1999)

Product	SSE		SZSE	
	Products	Volume (RMB bn)	Products	Volume (RMB bn)
A shares	460	1 480	439	1 241
B shares	54	13	54	12
Securities funds	23	111	14	92
CGBs	5	448	5	.56
CGB Repo	8	868	9	43
Convertibles and other	15	21	5	3.7
Total Products	565	2 941	526	1 391
US$ bn		343		168

Source: Wind Information System

using either method, B shares, however, must be traded through a visible seat. The visible seat refers to an actual physical seat and trader on the exchange floor. From this position the trader manually inputs trades telephoned in from various offices around the country through a computer terminal into the exchange mainframe trading system. In contrast, the invisible seat represents a satellite linkup between a broker's office and the exchange mainframe trading system. Thus, a broker may input a trade from his office directly into the exchange trading system.

The invisible seat has been in operation since August 1995 in Shenzhen and November 1997 in Shanghai. While it provides greater speed, accuracy and capacity than a visible seat, it tends to be less stable operationally. Moreover, it does not allow a broker to see as many price quotes, and so have a better market feel, as a floor trader: a broker can see three bid/offer quotes versus five for the floor trader. Despite this, the direct linkage into the exchange's trading system provides the best solution as trading in China becomes more electronically based and less geographically specific. At this point, the invisible seats have assumed a primary role in trading, while the floor traders provide a needed backup function.

4.9.2 Institutional vs. retail trading

As discussed in greater detail in Chapter 7, institutional investors in China include fund managers, insurance companies, pension funds, securities houses and a huge variety of corporates. Such investors use both the visible and invisible trading system. Retail orders are typically placed at the business offices (*yingyebu*) of the various securities firms.

In these offices the broker provides computers which allow the individual investor to place orders directly to the broker's system which then sends them directly via the invisible trading system to the exchanges. Each business office typically has its own invisible seat which, combined with the computers used by the investor, generally provide sufficient trading capacity to meet demand. To access a computer to place an order the retail investor is issued a computer card with a magnetic strip enabling them to log into their individual portfolio. Retail investors are required to trade on a cash basis only with funds first deposited with the broker.

4.9.3   IPOs on-line

One of the most unique roles of China's stock exchanges is their settlement of IPO transactions. In the United States, for example, orders received from all categories of investors are taken by the lead underwriter, but it is only after final allocation of shares has been done that orders are actually funded by the investors who now know the amount they must pay. Such funds are received by the bank in one of its own designated bank accounts and then passed to the issuer after various fees have been deducted. In China, by contrast, all orders must be backed by funds. During the subscription period orders and funds are transferred to, not the lead underwriter, but the exchange settlement corporation which holds all funds collected until final allocation. Following allocation, unneeded funds are sent back to investor accounts while the final issuing amount is wired to the lead underwriter's bank account for ultimate payment of net IPO proceeds to the issuer. This arrangement has been made to ensure that the massive amounts of subscription funds are not misused by securities firms during the subscription period.

4.9.4   Settlement and clearing

Each investor, whether retail or institutional, must open two accounts. One account is opened with the exchange clearing house and is called the shareholder account. The other account is a cash or, in the case of a retail investor, a brokerage account with a given broker. Once these accounts have been opened and cash deposited in the brokerage account, the investor is ready to trade. Account opening takes only a few days and requires a small opening fee. On its opening the shareholder account is allocated to a specific seat number, that is, broker, and all trades are cleared on a seat basis. Investors, as a result of this requirement, can deal with only one broker at a time.

Settlement for A shares is on a T+1 basis and B shares on a T+3 basis. A shares are settled domestically in RMB, while Shanghai B shares are settled in New York in US dollars and Shenzhen B shares in Hong Kong in HK dollars. A significant difference between Chinese and international market practice is the trading deposit. The Securities Law requires that all investors have sufficient funds in their accounts *before* they trade that is, if an investor wants to buy RMB 1 million of stock he must have at least RMB 1 million of cash in his brokerage account. Once an order has been placed the client's money is frozen and the client is unable to touch those funds until the trade has settled and the securities are placed in his shareholder account. This practice ensures settlement and eliminates settlement risk for the trading parties and is well suited to the China market where the domestic banking infrastructure is poor, as is the understanding of credit risk. However, on days when IPO orders are being solicited, this requirement typically ties up billions of RMB in the banking system as will be shown in a later chapter.

This elimination of risk advantage is somewhat offset by the significant cash balances left on deposit under the control of the broker; such client funds are often used to trade the stock market. This has been a common problem which the CSRC has sought to address, but the blame here lies not with the exchanges but with the brokerage houses. Both markets close at 3 p.m. and about one hour later the exchange sends specific trade and settlement information to each broker using its satellite system. On receipt of the data the broker will check the trades and send out confirmations by fax or some other means. Actual cash payments will not happen until the next day, hence the T+1 payment.

4.9.5 Data systems

As mentioned above, each broker needs a satellite link with the exchange for its invisible seats, but a second link is also required to receive exchange broadcast information. The exchange routinely sends out price and volume information for all securities on a real time basis. This information is reconfigured by various software applications which present the data in a more user friendly format. One such system is *Qianlong*, itself a recently listed company in Hong Kong. Qianlong takes market and securities information and provides a graphic for each stock and the bid/offer price and size for each security. The software also provides historical data and a variety of technical analysis. *Qianlong* also provides news and company information in association with the Wind (*WanDe*) Information System. Other software packages include *HuiJin* and *JianGong* which provide data in much the same style as *Qianlong*. Most trading halls will provide at least two software packages for investors to analyses exchange data, but smaller brokers will likely use only one such program. The exchanges also provide a vast amount of data in both soft and hard copy form. In addition to the daily broadcast information, they produce monthly trading statistics on individual companies and brokers as well as the broader market. Yearly statistics books are also published showing more detailed breakdown of geographical concentration of trading and capital structure of companies. Independent of the exchanges there is a huge range of television programs, newspapers, magazines and books available to provide analysis and discuss the market. Obtaining market information is not a problem in China, although independent and insightful comment is often lacking.

4.10 Other trading arrangements

In terms of equities, the Shanghai and Shenzhen exchanges are now the only functioning securities markets in China. There were, however, other exchanges, the most important of which were the regional trading centers, STAQ and NETS. STAQ, or the Securities Trading Automated Quotation System, was established as an automated OTC market for legal person shares. It is currently moribund, having been created in the early days, but never got off the ground. NETS, or the National Electronic Trading System, was managed by the PBOC and was designed to trade government bonds. The PBOC was compeled to divest it in 1993, whereupon it was merged with the Shanghai settlement company. In contrast, the regional trading centers played a major role in stock market development in China and, in particular, the development of the Shanghai exchange.

4.10.1 The regional trading centers

The trading centers were first established in early 1993 under the sponsorship of provincial governments and PBOC branches. Their growth was largely fostered by the Shanghai Stock Exchange's need to resolve a technical limitation in its trading arrangements. Trading centers also suited the ambitions of other local governments which still hoped to establish securities exchanges of their own. Lagging the SZSE, the SSE did not at first have direct computer links with securities companies (the invisible seat). Hence, securities firms had to buy actual physical seats on the exchange in order to trade. As order volume grew, the number of seats also grew reaching more than 7000 at one time. At the same time, orders coming in from securities firms nationwide jammed the Shanghai telephone system. If the Shanghai exchange was to continue to grow, it needed a solution to these physical limitations. The trading centers provided it. Local brokers could buy seats at the local trading center and transact business on the SSE through the trading center's communications links with the SSE. In short, the trading centers allowed the SSE to decentralize its operations. By late 1997 the SSE instituted its invisible seat system and in 1998 settled into its new building which had the telecommunications capacity to support invisible seats. With this the reason for the trading centers disappeared, at least from the point of view of the SSE. On the other hand, financial scandal provided the reason for the central government to move against the centers. For a customer transacting with a trading center, the associated fees and share prices were the same as if he or she were transacting directly with the SSE itself.[19] There was one key difference, however, his funds remained with the trading center. At its height, the Beijing Trading Center contributed 12 per cent of SSE trading volume. The amount of funds was enormous and all profits went to the local governments. It is easy to see how problems might occur as they did most spectacularly in Wuhan where customer funds were lent to investments promoted by the local government. Unfortunately such investments did not work out and client funds were lost.

At the end of 1998, as part of the larger picture of strengthening market regulation, the government told the centers to either return all customer funds or deposit them with the two exchange-affiliated depository companies.[20] At the same time the trading centers were given until 30 June 1999 to close. Most merged with local securities firms.

Among the many centers three stood out, Shenyang, Tianjin and Wuhan. In addition to trading shares, these three, unlike all other trading centers, had their own local products – funds and debt securities of local enterprises. The success of these centers explains why the proportion of investors from these areas, which are not considered wealthy, continues to be so large on both the SSE and SZSE.

4.10.2 STAQ or Securities Trading Automated Quotation System

STAQ, after a year of preparatory work, went into operation with government approval on 5 December 1990. This automated market system had been promoted by the Stock Exchange Executive Council (the 'Lianban'), a loosely defined organization which continues to exist in a very gray area somewhere between the state and the markets.[21] STAQ was supported by 17 major Chinese entities as founding members of the new exchange. This group included CITIC, China Everbright Group, Sinochem and a variety of national-level 'trust and investment' companies. Structured as a non-profit member sponsored organization along the lines of the Shanghai and Shenzhen exchanges, STAQ was meant to be a fully automated trading market similar to NASDAQ, which traded government bonds and beginning from July 1992, legal person shares. By the end of 1992 there were ten different legal person share issues trading and over 200 members.[22]

This was a promising start, but the total number of shares trading dwindled and in the end amounted only to eight including the Hengtong Group, Hainan Huakai Industrial, Hangzhou Nature Industrial, Hainan International Investment Industries, Changbai Computers, Beijing Five Star Beer, Beijing Central Plaza, and Hainan Provincial Airlines. By 1995 its articles of incorporation had been revised to read '... the basic purpose of the system is: ... to increase the circulation of securities, in particular, government bonds ...'[23] And by 1997 this market had ceased to function as all trading functions for all types of securities were concentrated in the two national exchanges.

4.10.3   NETS or National Electronic Trading System

NETS was established in early 1991 with the direct sponsorship of the PBOC and operated by its majority controlled company, China Securities Trading System Corp. Ltd. ('CSTS'). Other promoters included banks and the four national securities companies. The purpose of NETS was to provide a unified national electronic market for all securities including 'government bonds, municipal bonds, state bank bonds, corporate bonds, shares, investment fund bonds and other securities.'[24] Although this seemed to be a good idea, its timing was unfortunate, coming as it did immediately after the opening of the SSE and just prior to that of the SZSE. Until 1993 NETS primarily carried out government bond trading. The PBOC sought to retain CSTS and the company was then restructured, recapitalized and its operations focused on a small number of major cities.[25] But later the same year, as a part of the effort to bring the two national exchanges under stricter central control, the State Council compelled the PBOC to divest the company and it was thereupon merged with the SSE's settlement company. NETS should be seen as the PBOC's last ditch effort to involve itself as a player in the lucrative securities markets. Like STAQ, NETS was a remnant of the early days of market experimentation which outlived its usefulness.

5
Market Regulatory Structure

Creation of an effective regulatory structure for the securities industry was an afterthought of the experiment with enterprise shareholding structures. As even the most ardent institutional proponent of the experiment, the State Committee for the Reform of the Economic Systems, put it in 1989, 'The purpose of the share system is the share system and not to issue shares to the public.' What SCRES meant here was the purpose was to develop a form of ownership structure which might result in enhanced enterprise efficiencies through greater management autonomy, the elusive goal of separation of government and enterprise (*zhengqi fenkai*). That being the case, the whole affair was simply one of the usual inter-governmental planning and co-ordination, there would be no new industry and no need for a special regulator.

From this it is of no surprise, therefore, that the government's approach to securities markets regulation in the 1980s was extremely haphazard and driven largely by local developments. As discussed previously, Shenzhen and its wide open political and economic environment was the cradle of China's equity markets. But Shenzhen was also the catalyst for China's effort to create a relatively workable regulatory structure as well. This was by necessity given that a securities market had come into being. And the Shenzhen market, in particular, the stock craze of 1989 and 1990, and the riots in August 1992, drove the People's Bank from the scene and gave the industry the CSRC.

The PBOC and other agencies did not fade from the scene easily, however, it took a fight and further market scandals. Through October 1992, the PBOC was the emerging regulatory power in the equity and debt markets. It was responsible for all aspects of the regulation and administration of China's securities industry. And, what's more, it was a player, sponsoring China's first international IPO of a Chinese company in October 1992.[1] Although it has always been called China's central bank, the PBOC for most of its existence has served an entirely different function – that of cashier for the Ministry of Finance. Under Soviet-style planning, the People's Bank functioned as the country's sole banking institution from the late 1950s until the early 1980s. In addition to handing out working capital loans to SOEs, its attractiveness to all levels of the state as a financial partner was enhanced by its control of China's mints. And the PBOC organization was enormous with a branch in every provincial capital and a deposit taking office on nearly every street corner. Its staff numbered in the millions. Until the 1994 passage of the Central Bank Law, the PBOC was the balancer of last resort for the national and, quite likely, many local budgets. So close was its 'co-operation' with the Ministry of Finance that the two were housed in the same building during the 1970s.

So, although it was called a 'central' bank, the People's Bank was, in fact, a very decentralized entity with principal staffing and functions at the provincial level and a small staff of a few hundred in Beijing. Its close relationship with local governments became, at points during its history, entirely intimate since the local party had the right to nominate senior branch staff. Local branches, in short, although reporting on a direct line to Beijing, had strong links to local governments and were willing participants in the corporatization wave which swept across China in the 1980s. After all, if an SOE could get money elsewhere, it meant less pressure on the bank itself. From this background it is clear that the PBOC was hardly an appropriate candidate to act as the national regulator of a rapidly evolving market-based experiment. On the other hand, there was no other suitable candidate to fulfil this function and the government did not foresee such a rapid pace of change.

The establishment of a new bureaucratic entity in China is not easy and the Chinese Securities Regulatory Commission is a case in point. In what is perceived and played as a zero sum game, there is resistance from all sides, particularly if the new organization is designed to take over the roles of more established players. And at times, even the strongest political backup will wilt in the face of a difficult decision. The PBOC was not happy and neither were other agencies including the Ministry of Finance and its panoply of subordinate bureaus such as the State Asset Management and State Land Management Bureaus. And, of course, the securities exchanges and their sponsoring local governments were not happy. Although the CSRC was established in late 1992, it was not solidly established until 1998, a victory memorialized by the Securities Law of 1999, itself, like the CSRC, six years in the making for mostly the same reasons. The story of the CSRC's emergence is a story of how market forces unleashed compelled the government to continue rather than halt the stock market experiment and its required institutional development.

5.1 The PBOC as securities industry regulator: 1986–92

The Chinese government from the beginning of its experimentation with shares viewed them as a part of the financial (*jinrong*) or banking sector. The PBOC's jurisdiction over the securities markets, therefore, was a consequence of this judgement and the fact that it was the sole administrator and supervisor of the financial sector, meaning largely banks and non-bank financial institutions conducting traditional loan and deposit taking businesses. By the mid 1980s experimentation with securities, and debt securities in particular, had grown sufficiently widespread that some sort of regulation was necessary. At the same time, the banking system itself was undergoing a radical restructuring as the government sought to reform the sector after nearly 25 years of nominally Soviet-style central planning. As a part of this, banks which had been closed since the 1950s, for example the Bank of Communications, were being re-established and the PBOC's role shaped to be a true central bank.

Through 1994 the PBOC's authority was founded in the January 1986 State Council document 'PRC provisional regulations on the administration of banks' (the Provisional Banking Regulations).[2] These regulations were the predecessors of the Central Bank Law and the Commercial Bank Law which eventually came into effect eight years later in 1994. The 1986 Provisional Banking Regulations laid out the basis for a national commercial banking system including, almost as an afterthought, the nascent securities industry. The regulations defined the PBOC's role as follows: 'The PBOC is the State Council's organ for leading and administering national financial undertakings and is the State's central bank ...' For the most part, its responsibilities were most directly applicable to commercial banking institutions. But the provisions clearly defined financial organizations as those which, among other commercial banking activity, could provide agented financing through the issuance of securities (*daimu zhengquan*). The PBOC's authority *vis-à-vis* financial institutions was spelled out in three points:

- review and approve the establishment, closure and merger of specialized banks and other financial institutions

- lead, administer, co-ordinate, supervise, audit the operations of the specialized banks and other financial institutions
- administer negotiable securities including enterprise shares and bonds etc. (*sic*), and administer the financial market.

In short, the PBOC was authorized to approve the establishment of 'other financial institutions', which came to include securities companies, specify how the ownership of securities should be registered and transferred, set the price for such transfer, collect data as to market trends and so on. Local governments leveraged this authority with the acquiescence of local PBOC branches in these years moving ahead to establish what might be called securities companies, but what were really just brokerages conducting OTC trading. In response to this and with the backing of the State Council, PBOC Beijing was forced to restate its authorities in 1988.[3] The State Council confirmed that the PBOC '... is responsible for the administration of stocks, debt securities and so on, and for the administration of the financial markets (including the securities markets, the issuance of government bonds, and the circulating (that is, the secondary) markets, and the administration of all credit instruments.' Local governments continued to pursue their own best interests together with the local branches of the PBOC which began to establish securities trading counters in their own trust and investment companies. From this point on, it was clear that the PBOC was at odds with itself.

What the PBOC was not involved in during the early stage of corporatization was the restructuring of enterprises into shareholding companies and the process leading to the issuance of shares. In later years, this was the sphere of SCRES, the institution responsible for defining policy for the shareholding experiment. In the beginning, however, it fell to the local governments with a process typically led by the Bureau of Finance. The first step toward greater central government involvement, at least superficially, came in early 1987 as a result of a State Council notice defining the scope of the corporatization experiment. The notice declared that all securities issuance must first be reviewed and approved by the PBOC.[4] Such issuance was defined by the State Council as excluding all public issue of securities. This exclusion ran directly in the face of the provisional regulations governing equity issuance, including public issuance, and trading of shares which had just been put out by the Shenzhen government in late 1986. It is clear looking back that Shenzhen and other localities, for example, Shenyang, continued their experimentation with the buy-in of local People's Bank branches.

At an unspecified date in 1989 the PBOC Shenzhen branch, basing its authority on the Provisional Banking Regulations, as well as the 1987 State Council notice, took the lead in specifying approval procedures for share issuance.[5] This marked the first time that procedures were formally established with the aim of standardizing the process of enterprise restructuring into shareholding companies. These regulations were likely to have been issued late in the year in response to the equity fever which was taking hold. However, the fact that only the year and not a specific date is referenced suggests that such regulations may never have been enacted at that time.

It took the Shenzhen share craze plus the June 4 incident, previously described, to alter the central government's *laissez faire* attitude toward the shareholding experiment. While political debate slowed the process temporarily, events in Shenzhen put an end to any temporizing over what, after all, had become a practical reality. The awakening of Shenzhen investors to the capital gain potential of equity securities gave impetus to the discussion: rein in the experiment. It is interesting to note the lack of importance assigned by the PBOC to the regulation of share issuance and trading: none of the various regulations enacted by local branches of the central bank were included in the PBOC's annual compilation of laws and regulations until 1990. Apparently the PBOC did not consider such local events of national importance. The May 1990 State Council circular referenced in Chapter 4 initiated the regulatory effort by limiting the legal bounds of the trading experiment to Shenzhen and Shanghai and inter-company investment to legal persons only.[6] But the second half of 1990 marked the true start of the central government's attempt to impose control over the entire process. With the decision to establish the Shanghai Securities Exchange taken in July, a variety of measures were issued in preparation.

This began with the People's Bank August 1990 prohibition of all banking institutions from directly participating in the securities markets via branches or subsidiaries.[7] Henceforth, separate entities independent of the banking system would be required. This too was largely ignored and it was not until 1994, as part of a strong effort to reform the banking system, that a wall was effectively built between the banking and securities sectors. In October 1990 the PBOC issued the first national regulations governing the establishment of purely securities companies.[8] Based on these regulations, securities companies could only be established with the approval of PBOC Beijing; local branch and government sign off was no longer sufficient. The scope of security company operations was limited to within the given administrative area of the sponsoring local government, as a result national securities companies were prohibited. Indicating the active role local PBOC branches had played, the regulations permitted them to retain their ownership of existing securities companies which they had capitalized and established. Thus, the PBOC continued, as before, to be both regulator of and active participant in (and beneficiary of) the securities markets.

In recognition of the fact that the securities industry was creating a national as well as a local market, the PBOC in the same month set out the rules for trading between regions.[9] The measures called for the local governments and PBOC branches to strengthen control over securities trading activity between local securities entities and those elsewhere in the country. The securities defined included government, enterprise and bank debt securities as well as shares. Securities companies had to receive PBOC approval to establish trading links with counterparts (and, by extension, exchanges) elsewhere in the country.

To ensure prices between regions were standardized the bank also initiated a national reference price list to be published by PBOC Beijing at the start and in the middle of each month. This list enabled local branches to 'carry out inspection of and appropriate intervention in local securities prices.' Trades made without reference to this price were illegal. Judging from this, the PBOC had yet to emerge from the days of a planned economy. This approach shows that the organization had absolutely no understanding that markets do not stop to wait for bi-weekly price quotes. Shortly afterward, in November and December 1990, the Shanghai and Shenzhen securities exchanges were formally approved and established. The articles of incorporation of both exchanges clearly specify the role of the PBOC as overall market regulator. China now had the basic infrastructure supporting the development of its securities industry. On the other hand, it still lacked a regulatory structure and philosophy suited to the market's development. Even worse, unless the state revised or rescinded the May 1990 regulations and again approved the issue of securities to the public, the two exchanges would have little business other than to provide a centralized trading place for securities already issued publicly. In fact, the first five companies listed on the SSE were listings by way of introduction, that is, the shares were already traded over the counter and their listing on the exchange was purely an administrative affair involving the raising of no new funds.

So the exchanges came into being against an unfavorable political background and without the hope of listing significant amounts of new securities product. Their existence was based on the argument that centralized trading locations would give the state greater control over an experimental activity. This activity, the development of shareholding companies, might not be one which the state chose to further develop and, even if it did so, the public listing of shares was not seen as the final objective, since such trading had a demonstrated capacity to produce serious social unrest. This was the reality in late 1990. What was important was that the exchanges existed.

The intent to exert full control is again shown in early 1991 when the State Council required all companies (outside of those already properly approved for public listing in Shanghai and Shenzhen) which local governments had approved to issue shares to the public to resubmit applications for issuance approval by the central government.[10] SCRES and the SAMB led the process. After a submission received the approval of these two agencies, the company then applied to the branch of the PBOC in its locality and, after receiving approval, applied to PBOC Beijing for approval. If it received all four approvals, the company's previous issuance of shares was legal. The involvement of the three ministries indicated the seriousness of the state's intent and, indirectly, its lack of faith in the integrity of the PBOC.

This reapproval process, however, was a one-off situation and did not apply to listings going forward. In April 1991 PBOC Beijing recognized this as an opportunity and proposed to the State Council that it take the lead in establishing a specialized Securities Market Office which would ensure co-ordinated central control over the industry.[11] This was approved and the PBOC established the function which was meant to be a co-ordinating body including all key organs of the state planning bureaucracy. The list of representatives is a Who's Who of state planning and worth noting in full to illustrate how cumbersome and, therefore, how little changed the nature of the regulatory process was likely to be. Bodies represented included the State Planning Commission ('SPC'), the Ministry of Finance ('MOF'), the State Administration for Foreign Exchange Control ('SAEC'), the State Tax Bureau, the State Asset Management Bureau ('SAMB'), the State Council Office for the Economy and Trade, the Ministry for Foreign Economic Relations and Trade ('MOFERT') and the State Bureau for Industrial and Commercial Administration. With no clearly designated senior leader, and there was none as most participating entities were bureaucratic peers, this gathering of ministry-level organizations did not represent much of an improvement over the previous situation.

In recognition of this, the Office established a smaller, more manageable working group responsible for the actual day-to-day work including the review of enterprise listing applications, oversight of the operation of the two stock exchanges, as well as the co-ordination of the various bureaucracies whose approvals would be needed to get things done. But before this regulatory structure could be institutionalized, Deng Xiaoping's early 1992 Southern Journey blew the doors wide open. During 1992, 40 companies listed shares on the two exchanges, nearly seven times as many as in 1991. An additional 3800 issued shares through private placements. In response to this, the PBOC's authority was again significantly enhanced in June 1992 when the State Council gave it sole oversight of China's securities markets. At the same time, the State Council moved the just created Securities Market Office to its own jurisdiction recognizing that such a group needed a firmer hand than PBOC could provide as well as direction by a senior level. This special securities office became the immediate predecessor to the SCSC. These moves made the State Council securities office responsible for inter-agency co-operation, leaving the PBOC alone responsible for day-to-day operations.

Social unrest, in the end, terminated the PBOC's role as market regulator and led directly to the formation of the SCSC and the CSRC in October 1992.[12] The Shenzhen riots in August 1992 and memories of June 4 unleashed a fury of bureaucratic effort and much of the critical national legislation on the markets came out in 1992 and 1993 having been pending since 1989. The complicity of the PBOC Shenzhen branch in catalyzing the riots finally brought home to the central government the reality that the bank as an institution was unsuitable to act as market regulator. There was simply too large an internal contradiction between controlling and participating in the market.

5.2 The CSRC as securities industry regulator: 1992–present

The State Council's decision to establish the Chinese Securities Regulatory Commission, which everyone calls the 'CSRC', did not create the clear cut regulatory structure the outside world might have thought at first sight. And the Securities Law, which was designed to produce the strong regulator the industry actually needed, was delayed for years until its passage by the National People's Congress in December 1998, only going into effect in July 1999. This delay was simply due to the continued struggle over control of the industry. It was not in the self-interest of other government agencies to see the lucrative securities sector controlled by any single entity. So it was not immediately clear at the outset that the CSRC would emerge as the dominant regulatory body. Given past practice, there was a higher probability that little would change and the combined SCSC/CSRC would perform in ways similar to the PBOC given the conflicting goals of market participants and the overwhelming search by local governments and enterprises for access to financing. And in fact, the CSRC and its limited initial staff of 80 faced severe opposition as they sought to establish themselves in China's competitive bureaucracy.

First of all, and unlike the PBOC, the CSRC was merely a vice-ministerial entity with offices only in Beijing. Its actual status was reflected in the poor office space its budget afforded, on the sixth floor of Beijing's oddly designed Poly Plaza which was accessible by only one trundling elevator. The CSRC reported directly to the former special securities office, now renamed the State Council Securities Committee, a ministry-level entity. Similar to the Equity Market Office, the SCSC consisted of a Chairman, two Vice Chairmen and thirteen representatives from every potentially securities related bureaucracy in China.[13] Representatives, all of whom were vice-ministers themselves, came from SCRES, the PBOC, the SPC, the State Council Office of Trade and the Economy, the MOF, the SAMB, the State Bureau of Industry and Commerce, the State Tax Bureau, MOFERT, the State Administration for Exchange Control, the Ministry of Supervision, the Supreme Court, and the Supreme People's Inspectorate. This group was given the sole policy authority for the industry, drafting laws and regulations based on appropriate research, drafting a development plan for the industry as a whole, co-ordinating central and local governmental bodies with regard to the securities markets and managing the CSRC. Given the exalted position of each representative and his responsibilities, it is not surprising that real authority devolved gradually to the CSRC. Vice Premier Zhu Rongji was the SCSC's Chairman and Liu Hongru, the first Chairman of the CSRC, one of the two Vice Chairmen. The other original Vice Chairman, Zhou Daojiong, became the CSRC's second Chairman after Liu was ousted in late 1994.

The CSRC was designed to be the implementing apparatus for the SCSC. Established as a quasi-governmental organization (*shiye danwei*: so it could pay its senior staff relatively high wages and benefits and, therefore, attract well-qualified people), the CSRC was responsible for drafting various detailed regulatory measures, overseeing and supervising entities involved in the securities business, supervising companies involved in issuing securities both domestically and internationally and compiling the requisite statistics and market analyses so as to be able to advise the SCSC on policy matters. The first group of CSRC department directors under Chairman Liu were all extremely international and professional. Despite the CSRC's ability to influence, authority continued to be highly dispersed among various other government agencies. In its 'Notice on further strengthening the macro-administration of the securities markets', the famous 'Document 68' of late 1992 empowering the SCSC and CSRC, the State Council clearly delineated the functions of all agencies involved in the corporatization process in an effort to strengthen the two new agencies.[14] This was the first ever attempt by the central government to impose co-ordinated action among the various agencies responsible for the corporatization and securities listing process. For example, Document 68 confirmed that the SPC was responsible for preparing a comprehensive Securities Plan specifying the amount of securities financings for a given five-year period and that the PBOC was responsible for the licensing of all financial sector participants.

But what could the CSRC do if it determined that a particular firm, or people within a firm, were violating whatever securities regulation or market practice? The same problem existed with regard to lawyers, accountants and asset appraisal companies which were licensed respectively by the Ministry of Law, the Ministry of Finance and the State Asset Management Bureau. As another example, SCRES remained responsible for policies and regulations governing the structure of corporatization and the selection of the specific companies involved in listing and the Shanghai and Shenzhen Municipal Governments remained in control of their stock exchanges. So even though its own scope of authority was defined, the CSRC continued to be unable to exercize authority without the acceptance of other agencies.

Even more important as the later situation attests, Document 68 did not seek to extend the jurisdiction of the CSRC over the local governments. Beginning in 1993 provincial governments each established securities offices which co-ordinated securities-related matters within the province, for example, the selection of listing candidates, frontline supervision of futures brokerages and markets, training and transmission of important notices. Although such offices became in some ways correspondents of the CSRC, they were a part of the respective provincial government's staff and in no way were under the CSRC's control.[15] The SCSC and CSRC were, therefore, isolated in Beijing with no formal way to extend their authority to ensure the implementation of whatever measures were passed.

To make matters more difficult, the CSRC's own position as a quasi-governmental vice-ministerial entity made it impossible to communicate directly with these other ministry-level organizations other than through the SCSC. Consequently, and entirely similar to previous

Table 5.1: Document 68 distribution of interagency responsibility

Entity	Responsibility
SPC	• Formulation of a securities fund raising plan • Formulation of securities industry development plans based on recommendations of the SCSC
PBOC	• Licensing of and administrative jurisdiction over securities institutions
MOF	• Administrative jurisdiction over accountants and accounting firms with review by the CSRC of those engaged in securities-related work
SCRES	• Formulation of regulations concerning shareholding pilot projects and co-ordination of the implementation of the shareholder system
SSE and SZSE	• Under the administrative jurisdiction of the local governments but subject to supervision by the CSRC; any new exchange subject to the review of the SCSC and approval of the SC
Local shareholding companies	• Conversion of locally owned enterprises into shareholding companies subject to the joint review of the CSRC and the local government
Central shareholding companies	• Conversion of centrally owned enterprises into shareholding companies subject to the joint review of the industry regulator and SCRES

experience, real regulatory action out of this galaxy of bureaucracies required a disaster which could not be shuffled away, for example the scandal arising from the US$37 billion February 1995 Shanghai Shenyin Securities ('SISCO') bond futures scandal.[16]

5.3 The internationalization of the CSRC

Given this complex domestic bureaucratic environment, it is understandable that the CSRC from the outset tended to focus its efforts on

Figure 5.1: Chinese securities industry regulatory framework (October 1992–July 1999)

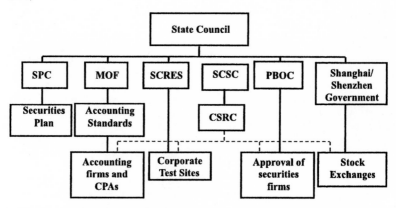

overseas listings, and the organizations and institutions involved with them: here it had real influence and could extend it single-handedly. This international emphasis stemmed from the logic that China's own markets were too young and undeveloped to exert an influence on the major SOEs which the government wished to expose to a strict regulatory environment as part of the reform process (or, for that matter, to provide financing in the amount the state expected). In fact, Chairman Liu had been working on a plan for overseas listing in 1992 while he was still at SCRES and prior to his assignment to the CSRC.[17] But it was also, in the short term, a good strategy to make the SOEs comply with its regulations. No CSRC approval, no overseas listing, no money. The alliances struck up with the international exchanges assured that its word would stick.[18] In the meantime, the CSRC could wait for events to develop.

The Chinese did not have to push the idea of internationalizing the corporatization experiment. This was an idea which had long been promoted by the SEHK. In the wake of June 4 and the 810 Incident the idea began to make sense to the Chinese government: export potential social unrest by listing Chinese companies elsewhere. In 1991 the SEHK made a suggestion to the Chinese government that it consider listing Chinese enterprises in Hong Kong. Coming so early in China's experiment with corporate equity listings, the government had given little previous consideration to the merits of such a proposal and determined to follow up with an unofficial study group. Consequently, in December 1991 a small team of 'specialists' went to Hong Kong as guests of China's unofficial embassy, Xinhua News Agency.[19] This group included four members, all from SCRES, and was led by Liu Hongru, then Deputy Director of SCRES. The purpose of their visit was to form the basis for a report to the State Council concerning the feasibility of listing Chinese companies in Hong Kong. This report, as might be expected, concluded positively, stating that listing Chinese companies in Hong Kong would: (1) support Hong Kong's economic stability and development (a nice point in consideration of the then long awaited handover scheduled for 1997); (2) be of great assistance in raising much needed capital for Chinese companies; and (3) promote the internationalization of Chinese companies. The report also noted some negative points: (1) the existing joint venture strategy provided Chinese companies with advanced technologies which listed companies would have to procure directly and at a potentially higher price; (2) companies to be listed would have to be profitable and have a solid profit outlook; the listing of such companies would mean giving up a piece of the profit to foreign investors; and (3) listing in Hong Kong might conflict with the state's effort to support the development of the Shanghai and Shenzhen stock exchanges. Overall, however, the report concluded that the benefits of a Hong Kong listing outweighed the negative points and proposed that the practical aspects of listing Chinese companies in Hong Kong be actively explored. The decision of the State Council, however, was to continue to prioritize the development of the two domestic exchanges. The idea appeared to have been effectively shelved.

5.2.2 The Stock Exchange of Hong Kong succeeds at the top

But stonewalls can be jumped in China. Having won over the working team to the idea, the SEHK then focused its strategy on the key decisionmaker, Vice Premier Zhu Rongji, who was then responsible for overseeing the Chinese financial sector. In April 1992 the Chairman of the Stock Exchange, Charles Y.K. Lee of Hong Kong visited Beijing and met with Vice Premier Zhu. During the meeting, Li brought up the idea of Hong Kong listings and actively pushed their positive aspects. Premier Zhu, having heard Li out, suggested the selection of up to ten companies as experimental listing candidates and agreed to the idea of establishing a formal working group to establish the basis for such listings. Premier Zhu's proposal was afterwards approved by the State Council and working groups were then established with ten members and two secretaries from the two sides. The Chinese team was composed of Liu Hongru (SCRES), Sun Xiaoliang (SCRES), Jin Jiandong (PBOC), Chen Baoying (State Council Office on Hong Kong Macao

Affairs), Li Qingyuan (SCRES) and Nie Qingping (SCRES) as the secretary. Many of these people would later on play significant roles in the corporatization process. The Hong Kong side was represented by senior staff from the SEHK.

The first meeting of the working group was held in mid July 1992 at the State Guest House in Beijing. Over the next eight months the group met eight times alternating in Hong Kong and Beijing and established the basis for settling the legal, accounting and technical listing methodology for Chinese companies seeking a direct listing on the SEHK. In the meantime, the CSRC was established with Liu becoming its first Chairman. With this, there was no doubt that Hong Kong would turn out to be a well-promoted 'experiment'.

The work of the two groups was, in fact, already a success in October 1992 when a list of nine Chinese SOEs designated to list in Hong Kong was announced. But the details were formalized by a Memorandum of Understanding with the SEHK signed on 19 June 1993, and put into actual practice on 29 June 1993, when Tsingtao Beer became the first Chinese state enterprise to list directly on the SEHK, raising approximately US$115 million. This deal was a blow out since even most Americans (and the fund managers, in particular) had had at least one bottle of 'Tsingtao' beer at their local Chinese eatery and, therefore, were pretty well acquainted with the brand name. Things got off to a strong start on the international side of the CSRC's equation.

5.4 The CSRC's domestic development

The CSRC's accretion of power domestically was a more extended process and came in three stages: (1) 1992–93 marked the establishment and consolidation of authority over the securities and future markets and extension of investigatory and enforcement powers; (2) 1996 marked the CSRC's assumption of full control over the two securities exchanges; and (3) 1998 the SCSC was dissolved and the CSRC became a full ministry-level organization empowered by the 1999 Securities Law. As discussed in Chapter 4 the CSRC assumed significant supervisory control over the two securities exchanges via the direct appointment of their senior managers in 1993. By this move the State Council overrode the PBOC's existing supervisory authority over financial institutions, which included securities exchanges and regional trading centers. The PBOC's involvement in the securities sector was virtually terminated in 1993. Later in 1993 the SCSC authorized the CSRC to investigate and enforce regulations relating to the issuance and trading of shares.[20] This authorization gave the CSRC an extremely broad scope to enforce securities laws and regulations as shown in Table 5.2. The CSRC was authorized to impose fines or other penalties on the violators unilaterally unless the revocation of the given violator's securities license was at issue, in which case the CSRC had still to obtain the PBOC's agreement.

Although the CSRC was given great authority, the reality was with a limited staff in one office in Beijing, it could do very little enforcement work. In an effort to increase its efficiency, during the course of 1993

Table 5.2: Acts violating securities issuance and trading

Violating Entity	Type of violation
Shareholding company	● Issuing shares without approval ● Illegally obtaining approval to issue and trade shares ● Issue shares in an unregulated manner or outside of the proper scope of issuance (e.g., selling state shares to individuals)
Securities company	● Issuance of shares at unapproved time, by an unapproved manner ● Unapproved distribution of share purchase applications ● Loan client shares to third parties or the use of client shares as collateral ● Charging of unreasonable fees ● Use of client names to conduct own trading ● Misuse of client guarantee deposits ● Sharing of gains/losses with clients or guaranteeing clients against trading loss ● Provide financing for share trading
Insiders	● Insider trading or provision of insider information to third parties
Any organization or individual	● Trading securities outside of established exchanges ● Release of false information or rumors during the issuance or trading of shares ● Conspiracy to manipulate share prices at issuance or during trading ● Short selling ● Unapproved share or index options or commodities trading ● Provision of false regulatory required reports ● Falsification of stock issuance and trading records

the CSRC sought to reach co-operative pacts with other government agencies directly involved in the share market, for example, the Ministry of Justice, the State Asset Management Bureau, the MOF, the State Tax Bureau, the Office of the Audit and so on.[21] In each case, these agreements indicated that the relevant license or approval would be jointly extended. This effort was based on, and was at least procedurally successful, due to the State Council's strong support evidenced in Document 68 published in 1992. These pacts, at a minimum, improved the co-ordination among the various departments even at the risk of losing efficiency. As any SOE will testify, the story of obtaining listing approval is a story of chasing down elusive bureaucrats to chop documents. And finally, at the end of the year, the State Council placed the SCSC and CSRC in charge of the futures markets and their participants, terminating oversight of the Ministry of Internal Trade and State Bureau of Industry and Commerce.[22] In short, 1993 was a year during which the government significantly strengthened the two central securities regulators at the expense of the power of local governments as well as other central government agencies.

The next major centralization of authority came in 1996 when the SCSC further expanded its jurisdiction over the exchanges by extending the CSRC's power over the securities exchanges and the securities registration and clearing companies.[23] This effectively removed local governments from administrative involvement in the exchanges which they had at the start initiated, established and promoted. The dissolution of the SCSC in mid 1998 and the elevation of the CSRC as a ministry-level organization presaged the passage of the long awaited Securities Law in early 1999. The Securities Law signified the end to the war for bureaucratic turf in the securities industry with the CSRC emerging as the sole winner. China's regulatory situation has been finally clarified by consolidating the jurisdiction of the securities industry in the hands of the CSRC.[24] The CSRC has now replaced the PBOC as the regulator of record for securities firms and has the power to approve the establishment of new firms and the expansion plans of existing firms.

In addition to its function of approving the issue and listing of securities, the CSRC's oversight over all professional entities engaged in the securities business, including law firms and accounting firms, has been strengthened. The second half of 1999 marked a major relicensing effort of all securities companies operating across the country. Such oversight also involves the formulation of specific qualification and conduct standards applicable to persons and firms engaged in securities

Figure 5.2: Chinese securities industry regulatory framework (from 1 July 1999)

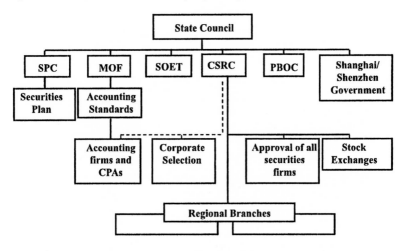

business. It is responsible for investigating and sanctioning any conduct which violates the Securities Law, has the authority to enter into places to investigate illegal activities and collect evidence, conduct interviews, examine trading records and other documents, and review the securities accounts of persons concerned and can apply to the courts to freeze such accounts. In the event that illegal activities are discovered, the CSRC can transfer the case to the judicial system. However, despite strengthening the CSRC's regulatory hand, intermediary organizations such as lawyers, accountants, asset and land appraisal companies and so on continue to be licensed and regulated in their non-securities business by their original approving government agencies.

The most significant structural change has eliminated the CSRC's isolation in Beijing. In mid 1999 the CSRC took over the functions of all provincial Securities Regulatory Offices from the provincial governments. The CSRC since then has begun to establish ten regional branches located in the major cities of Tianjin, Shenyang, Shanghai, Jinan, Wuhan, Shenzhen, Chengdu, Xian, Beijing and Chongqing. As a result the CSRC will have a central/regional organizational structure similar to the PBOC, both with the same objective – the reduction of local influence. At the same time, this new structure should enable the CSRC to control implementation of central government policy over the markets and market participants. Although the CSRC has emerged as the sole regulator of the securities industry and markets, the

Figure 5.3: Organizational structure of the CSRC (1999)

Source: CSRC

Securities Law also marked a shift in the philosophy of the regulatory process. For example, the Law makes no mention of any listing candidate quota system, implying that the CSRC will review each application as it is submitted. This, in itself, marks a dramatic shift in the entire listing process from being a component part of a State plan to one which is more market oriented and driven by companies and investment banks. This will be treated in more detail in the next chapter.

Second, prior to the enactment of the Securities Law, the CSRC had complete discretion over the approval of share issuance and listing. This discretion was based largely on the protection of the State's interests in a legal and regulatory environment which was complex and in many ways incomplete. The Securities Law, by limiting the CSRC's power over approval, indicates that the government is more comfortable with a process it may feel is clearly documented in regulations and laws which are final and not 'provisional'. At the same time, there has been a clarification of risk and responsibilities which shifts to the issuing enterprise full responsibility for the results of its operations and to the investor the consequences of his investment decision.[25] The Securities Law has shifted toward removing the government, and the CSRC in particular, from being the focus of any potential investor discontent due to scandal, a market crash or even the poor performance of a listed company.

In all past documents, public offerings are described as requiring the CSRC's approval (*pizhun*). The Securities Law has introduced three slightly different approval procedures for share issuance: verification and approval (*hezhun*), examination and approval (*shenpi*) and approval (*pizhun*). The Securities Law requires that all domestic public issues conform with the Company Law and receive the 'verification and approval' of the CSRC. The CSRC's role in the listing process has, therefore, been changed significantly with the implication that the Securities Law's intent is for domestic share issues to be approved if they meet the required conditions. For domestic corporate bond issues which must satisfy the requirements not only of the Company Law, but also a number of PBOC regulations, the Securities Law describes the CSRC's approval as 'examination and approval'. And for overseas share issues, the CSRC continues to have full authority to approve or disapprove such issues.

In 1993 the CSRC established a Public Offering and Listing Review Committee (*Faxing weiyuanhui*) whose existence has been confirmed and required by the Securities Law. The Committee, which is an extension of the Public Offering Supervision Department, is composed of CSRC staff and, if necessary, outside experts who do not have voting rights.[26] The Committee has two working groups each of which must be composed of at least seven members. After hearing the case for a particular listing, the committee reaches a final decision through a secret ballot with decisions based on a simple majority. The greater transparency of this process is to be welcomed.

On 1 July 1999, the Securities Law came into force marking the end of a 15 year process and established the most definitive regulatory structure China's increasingly important securities markets have had to date. The history of trial and error and bureaucratic turf battles which delayed the enactment of the Law by nearly seven years, have left many past compromises yet to be brought into line. Nonetheless, 1999 marked a major development and very positive progress for the industry as a whole. All that remains is that the regulator must decide how it will proceed to regulate now that it is empowered at last to do so.

6
The Issuers and the Listing Process

By the end of the 1990s over one thousand Chinese companies had completed initial public offerings and a few dozen more had tried and failed internationally. As could be expected from the foregoing chapters, listed Chinese companies are not particularly comparable. Generally speaking there are four broad categories of listed companies: the A shares, the B shares, the H shares and the Red Chips. But there are also a handful of NASDAQ shares, which seems likely to increase given the hi-tech market fad, and British Virgin Island holding companies for issuers like China Telecom. There has been a deliberate screening by the government as a result of which what it considers the best companies have been offered on international markets, while smaller ones, or those which have failed at an international listing, list domestically.

The A share companies have tended to be small and unfocused with a wide variety of businesses under their corporate umbrella. Typical A share IPOs have been in the US$50 million range representing a 25 per cent ownership interest. Disclosure, both at the time of listing and on an ongoing basis, tends to be extremely poor. The B shares represent a continuing headache to the Chinese government since international investors have abandoned the market. While the B share companies are larger and subject to listing requirements similar to overseas listed transactions, ongoing transparency is only somewhat better than A share companies. Deal sizes tend to be somewhat larger with the largest being around US$250 million. The H share companies are Chinese SOEs which have gone through major restructuring designed to complete an international IPO, one leg of which is almost always in Hong Kong. Transaction sizes generally have ranged between US$100 and 600 million. In contrast to the A share companies, H share companies represent focused businesses which have strong positions in China's domestic economy. These companies have been selected by the government to complete listings as part of the overall state enterprise reform effort. The Red Chips are Chinese controlled companies domiciled in Hong Kong with the majority of their operating assets located in China. They tend to be conglomerates in which the Hong Kong entity is used as a funding vehicle for its Chinese operations or for the further acquisition of Chinese assets.[1]

The listing process for international Chinese issues is similar to that of all internationally listed companies. Domestically listed A shares, however, are not subjected to the same quality of due diligence nor is there consideration given to their future prospects when it comes time to price the shares. Despite this, the approval procedures an A share company goes through prior to listing is comparable to that of the international Chinese issuers. The principal difference lies in the fact that internationally listed companies must meet the requirements of the respective overseas regulatory authority as well as the ultimate acceptance of their offering by investors.

6.1 The selection process for listing candidates

The effort first to become a company limited by shares and then achieving the opportunity to restructure once again into a company approved to offer shares, either domestically or internationally, is an extremely complex undertaking in China. The process begins when the State Planning Commission lays out its annual financing plan for state enterprises. Although this ties into the overall enterprise production

Table 6.1: Trends in Chinese company IPOs, (30 June 1999)

	90	91	92	93	94	95	96	97	98	99	Total
H shares	0	0	1	8	12	2	6	17	2	1	49
Red Chip	2	0	5	8	11	2	2	9	0	1	40
International	2	0	6	16	23	4	8	26	2	2	89
Shanghai A	8	0	22	73	68	15	103	85	53	20	447
Shanghai B	0	9	13	13	2	6	8	2	0	0	53
Sub-Total	8	9	35	86	70	21	111	87	53	20	500
Shenzhen A	0	6	18	52	42	9	100	121	51	19	418
Shenzhen B	0	0	9	10	5	10	9	8	3	0	54
Sub-Total	0	6	27	62	47	19	109	129	54	19	472
Domestic	8	15	62	148	117	40	220	216	107	39	972
Total	10	15	68	164	140	44	228	242	109	41	1061

Source: Bloomberg and Wind Information System

and sales plan, the proceeds from the sale of securities is also considered *vis-à-vis* commercial bank borrowing and foreign direct investment, on the one hand, and the state's monetary policy and foreign exchange reserve balances on the other. After the calculations and political balancing, a total figure representing capital to be raised by all listings is entered into the State Plan. Once in the Plan, this figure becomes reality, regardless of market conditions. In the process, the SPC considers which industrial sectors should be the beneficiaries of equity financing. Its considerations are based on such questions as which sectors are the current strategic focus of the state, which are open (or closed) to foreign investment and so on. Until recently, the SPC co-ordinated with SCRES for such decisions.[2] This top down approach is balanced somewhat by the active lobbying of the SPC by ministries and provincial governments wanting to ensure financing for their favorite companies.

At this point it becomes clear once again that the non-state sector, since it was never included in the Plan and was explicitly excluded by the Standard Opinion, has not been included in the thinking about which enterprises should be enabled to finance through the sale of securities. To date, equity financing for Chinese companies via either the domestic or the international markets, has been for SOEs alone.[3] This is the reality notwithstanding the original statement of principal by the SPC and SCRES that '... the appropriate development of other economic entities should be permitted and encouraged ...'[4] And Sino-Foreign Joint Venture enterprises were forbidden outright in the beginning to establish shareholding companies. For those which had already succeeded in doing so, the foreign shareholdings were either frozen as 'Overseas Legal Person' shares, which could not be listed or traded, or with approval could be issued as B shares.

The second step in the process involves the disaggregation of the national quota, a decision taken by the State Council itself. The CSRC then allocates the listing quotas among administrative agencies or regional governments across the country. For central government enterprises, quotas are distributed among the various industrial ministries. For locally owned enterprises, quotas are distributed to the provincial governments. Quotas for domestic and international listings in the past were defined in different ways. A share quotas have been distributed in terms of the number of shares to be issued. For example, a province might receive a quota for 100 million shares. The responsible government entities then allocated this out to one or more enterprises. This, in part, explains why the average IPO size on the A share primary market has been so small. For H shares, the quota was defined in terms of simply the number of candidates. Thus, a ministry might be allocated one or two positions which it could fill from its system of enterprises across the country. In contrast to the A share methodology, this did not limit the size of the potential transactions from the outset.

Once the CSRC had distributed the quotas, extremely active lobbying on the part of the enterprises and their respective government owners begins. Here again the State Plan has an impact. Investment funds are designated in the Plan for a five year period and then disaggregated into annual amounts. These amounts are further divided between the central and provincial-level governments. The central government has tended to invest large amounts in what, therefore, became large enterprises. Provincial-level governments have tended to spread their money more widely within their jurisdictions so that the size of local enterprises was somewhat smaller. Local governments, with less investable funds, established what became known by default as 'small and medium size' enterprises.

The success of an enterprise in obtaining a listing quota and, particularly an H share quota, therefore, depends to a large extent on which part of the 'state' is its owner: the local, the provincial or the central government. Stacking the odds even more against local enterprises is the fact that provincial governments held the final quota approval authority for non-central government enterprises (of course, subject to CSRC and the regulating Ministry review and agreement). Since provinces generally held only one quota for international listings and a limited number of A shares at a time, it was clear from the start which enterprise would be favored: the central and provincially-owned enterprises. This also makes clear why non-state enterprises are extremely unlikely to have the opportunity to list. They do not belong to the state, but the quota does.

6.2   The listing approval process

After the listing candidates are selected, each company goes through a similar work process aimed at obtaining an extensive list of approvals. Approval documents for different aspects of the work constitute the bulk of the supporting documentation to be sent to the CSRC for review and final listing approval.[5] This is the company's responsibility, as is the selection of the various intermediaries whose assistance it will need to successfully complete the listing process. The CSRC has, in the past, played a significant advisory role in this regard, particularly during the early years when companies were less knowledgeable.

6.2.1 Domestic listings

As noted previously, the Securities Law deals almost entirely with domestic securities and does not include internationally listed securities within its scope. For domestic A share listings the Securities Law specifies the required documentation to be submitted as follows:[6]

- a listing report (similar to a feasibility study)
- a shareholders' resolution approving the listing application
- the company's articles of association
- the company's business license
- the audited financial reports of the company for the previous three years or since the establishment of the company
- a legal opinion and a recommendation by a securities company
- a draft prospectus.

In addition to this documentation, the company itself must meet the following basic requirements:

- at least RMB50 million equity capital post-listing
- at least 1000 individual shareholders with at least 1000 shares a piece
- shares offered must represent at least 25 per cent of the company's expanded equity base
- must have a record of three years of profitability prior to offering
- one exchange member must act as Sponsor for the listing

Until 1999 the CSRC had complete discretion over the final approval decision. This made it the focus of intense lobbying. The Securities Law, as noted previously, has now limited its authority to one of verification and approval (*hezhun*) indicating that the company will be approved for public listing so long as the required conditions are met.[7] Once the CSRC has reviewed the documentation and agreed, the issuer submits the verification and approval documents and other relevant documentation to the designated stock exchange and then waits in line. The stock exchange is required to arrange for the shares to be listed within a six month period.

On notification that the stock exchange has approved its listing, the company must publish a notice making public its approval to list. This notice must include such information as the date of the offering, the names of the top ten shareholders and the number of shares held, and the names of all senior management and the number of shares they hold. This public notice usually serves as a prospectus to the public since it includes a description of the company, the number of shares offered and their price, a description of its business and risks to its business, and financial information.[8] The publication of prospectuses similar to those in the overseas markets is not required, but is sometimes done for public relations purposes. Article 43 of the Securities Law provides that the CSRC may at some future point authorize the stock exchange to verify and approve applications for listings 'in accordance with conditions and procedures as prescribed by law.' This is unlikely to happen in the near future as this would mark a dramatic shift of power back to the exchanges and a corresponding loss by the CSRC. What was gained with such difficulty just a few years ago, will hardly be given up lightly. In this regard, the stock exchanges have their own listing application requirements.[9]

The 1995 B share Provisions continue to be the governing procedures for B share issues.[10] These companies follow the general procedures as listed below:

- the promoter seeks the sponsorship of that agency of the government which 'owns' the company
- the government agency then sponsors the company's application to the CSRC
- the company must provide:
    an application (similar to a feasibility study)
    documents verifying the promoter's ownership of the company's shares
    a document evidencing the decision of the promoter(s) to list the company
    documents evidencing the government agency's approval to list
    sponsorship letters from the government agency
    draft articles of incorporation
    prospectus
    a feasibility study on the proposed use of proceeds including project approval documents from government agencies if the funds are to be invested in fixed assets
    three years audited financial statements
    an asset appraisal report
    a proposal on how the issue of shares is to be structured
    any other documents required by the CSRC

As can been seen simply from this list, the CSRC has set much higher standards, at least in terms of documentation, for shares to be sold to foreign investors. In addition, the CSRC has issued a number of regulations with regard to the required contents and quality of the information to be provided in the application materials. But the principal difference with A shares is that B share companies are the result of deliberate asset restructuring whereas A share companies need not be. For international offerings to succeed it is extremely unlikely that the entire company can be incorporated and offered to international investors as is. The same is true for the H shares. Unrestructured, the company would remain an SOE and, consequently, not present an even remotely attractive investment opportunity.

6.3 Overview of corporate restructuring for international listings

The problem confronting the banker in China is to identify an SOE which has the potential to complete an international offering. The difficulty lies in the reality of an SOE: it is so tightly intertwined with the state that it is hard to know where the enterprise leaves off and the state begins. There is a close symbiotic relationship between the two wherein the state provides the SOE with goods and capital and the SOE in return provides goods as well as social services. Some potential transactions, for example, Wuhan Iron and Steel, were notable because in the end the two could not be pried apart without threatening the viability of the SOE itself. The relationship of an unrestructured SOE with the state is illustrated in Figure 6.1

In the beginning of the overseas listing experiment restructuring was relatively simple.[11] Guided by the investment bank's view of the market, companies carved out the productive tip of the SOE, established it as a 'company', leaving the uneconomic remainder to the 'parent' company. This was a major issue for the first major H share deal in 1993, Shanghai Petrochemical. Here the central government owned the company, but the Shanghai government was compelled for policy reasons to assume responsibility for all social security-related liabilities associated with the company's retired worker population. This approach worked once, but not twice. For example, in the case of Maanshan Steel the bankers and company management created a fairly lean steel company by excluding tens of thousands of redundant workers in preparation for the listing. These workers were left in the parent holding company, which, after the listing of the productive company, had limited cash flow to support them. In contrast, before the listing, the cash flow of the 'good' company was sufficient to support them all at a certain survival level, but of course at the expense

Figure 6.1: An unrestructured state-owned enterprise

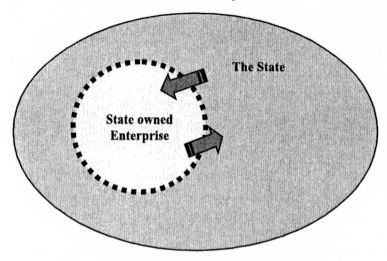

of profitability by non-Chinese standards. Beginning just after the listing, these redundant workers began slowly migrating back to what by then had become the listed company. The results were predictable: the company's expenses swelled and, combined with a poor market for steel products, drove the listed company into years of extremely poor profitability and losses. But at least the people had something to eat.

This general problem, which is illustrated by Figure 6.2, quickly became evident to the people responsible for putting up the money to buy SOE shares: they did not like it since the value of their investments decreased. But it was also evident to the Chinese authorities themselves, and they did not like it either: it caused social problems. Consequently, the challenge became more complicated for the bankers suggesting a restructuring. Not only did they have to sift through an enterprise's business to find the most profitable part, bankers had to ensure that the parent itself had sufficient cash flow to support what was left behind. This sort of balancing act was not easy and accounts in part for the high failure rates in the Fourth Batch.

It is not surprising, therefore, that the so-called infrastructure companies became a fad during the mid 1990s, since they satisfied the pressing needs of both the Chinese government and investment bankers. First of all, the Chinese had few good companies that increasingly sophisticated investors would plunk their money down for. Second, the bankers for the same reason, had run out of deals. There

Figure 6.2: Schematic diagram of a state-owned enterprise

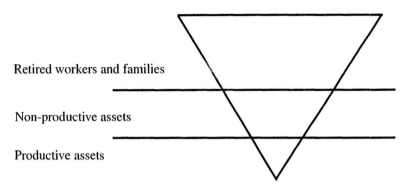

Retired workers and families

Non-productive assets

Productive assets

had to be something new, and there was: toll roads and then infrastructure companies. Anywhere else in the world such projects would have been financed by debt, whether from banks or the bond markets. But in China, the banks could not or would not lend enough, and project financing was a non-starter for a variety of reasons not least of which was the government's concern that loan or bond principal might not be repaid. The only financing alternative left was equity, whether from joint venture investors or from the equity markets.

There were only two problems: there were no companies as such to start with, only the Provincial Bureaus of Communications, and, in many instances, there was no profit either. But both problems were easy to solve: create a new company to hold a group of assets. These assets, for example, highways, could become tollways, in which case the toll revenues over a ten-year period could be easily projected, and investors sold a notional chunk of toll revenue. What remained to be done was to concoct a tariff structure. This assumed, of course, that the roads were used and, if used, people actually paid (or collected) the tolls. Compared to the social engineering challenges of a real SOE, however, this was clearly easier work for the banker and all others involved in the process. These deals, illustrated by Figure 6.3, were similar to the power company transactions that were attempted in the early days of the listing experiment.

The key to making this collection of assets profitable was the tariff structure applied to it. This structure defined the fees associated with usage of the asset whether it was a road, a power plant or a water treatment facility. The tariff was basically a contract between the 'company' which was formed to manage and operate the assets and

Figure 6.3: The notional infrastructure 'company'

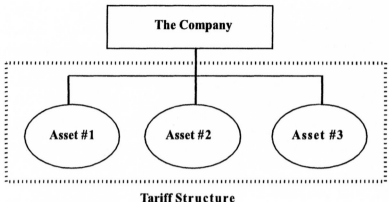

Tariff Structure

the governmental agency which had built the same assets and transferred them into the company. Once this tariff formula was agreed to, it became a simple matter of engaging a proper consultant who would develop believable projections of traffic volumes, multiply by the tariff and figure out how much revenue the new company would earn; no need for social engineering at all. There was one problem with this approach: since prices and costs change due to inflation, the tariff formula should also change to ensure profitability. But such changes, as well as the original tariff structure, were subject to the purview of the State Price Control Bureau whose role was to stand on the side of the 'people' to ensure that the market economy did not gouge them. If the Price Control Bureau did not agree to a proposed structure or increase, then there was no structure or increase. As a rule Price Control Bureaus did not like, nor did they accept, anything resembling a fixed formula which could be used to calculate a tariff for anything beyond one year. This is what killed power company listings.

Prior to this equity financing experiment, tolls and costs were of course charged to users for water or power, but such prices were not calculated in relationship to the possibility of a defined sets of assets earning a profit. With a formalized tariff structure in place and the company's shares offered to investors at a price reflecting a future projection of revenue and earnings, the Price Control Bureau could wreak havoc by refusing to adjust tariffs in accordance with expenses. This would have less impact on a bond price (as long as interest and principal were paid on time), but would kill share prices since they reflect expectations of earnings growth. In short, the infrastructure company, unlike the true SOE, was nothing more than a tariff structure wrapped around a number of related or even non-related assets masquerading as a company. Infrastructure equity financing was simply municipal bonds by another name (and without the principal pay back). By the Fifth Batch in late 1998 some municipal governments desperate for money, and short on viable assets, had thrown in everything but the kitchen sink – heating plants, ring roads, ports, water treatment facilities, breweries – and called it 'XYZ City Infrastructure Development Co. Ltd.' In fact, these so-called companies were little more than hived off divisions of local governments. There was no true differentiation between the company and the state planned economy. In contrast, the traditional SOE, at least, was some kind of company with much more independence of the state.

Already, at this early stage it was clear that the original policy motivation for international listings had not worked out. The idea that international markets could pressure the reform of SOEs might be true, but the restructuring of SOEs was a difficult social issue. The overseas listing process thereafter was revealed for what it was: an opportunistic funding vehicle for State infrastructure projects.

6.3.1 How to 'package' an SOE

Restructuring an SOE into a shareholding company with the hope of listing its shares internationally is a lot of work. This is an understatement. In this work bankers are not alone in their effort to sort out what a company is going to be. There are lawyers (domestic and international) representing the 'company', on the one hand and the bankers on the other. Then there are the accountants, the asset appraisers (again, domestic and international), a public relations firm, a legal printer and maybe a domestic financial adviser, all of whom are hired by the company, but orchestrated by the banker. The Chinese call this lot 'intermediary organizations (*zhongjian jigou*)', which suggests that these professionals are viewed by the government as little more than shysters.

The critical part of the work, as noted above, is to identify the assets which are meant to comprise the new company. To do this, enterprise management and the bankers sit down together to create the new company, starting by reference to what sort of operations a Western company in the same industry would own. The easy part is carving off schools, hospitals, police and fire departments, courts, tourism and hotel management operations, and dormitory areas for the workers and staff and any other entities which do not relate directly to the company's operations. Some of these functions could be directly passed over to the local government without objection since they belong there in the first place. There were always surprises in this process. In addition, the responsibility for the pensions of retired workers, who with their dependents could number in the tens of thousands, was also largely left in what would become the Parent Company. The local government did not want this obligation. This stage of the process is always described as 'packaging (*baozhuang*)' and its final product is illustrated in Figure 6.4. As soon as the banker and the company agree on a 'package', everyone else goes to work. A highly detailed, and usually highly unrealistic time schedule coordinating everyone's work, is put together by the banker. The touchstones of this schedule are the completion of a draft audit of the proposed company and an expected date of listing. The draft audit is the make or break event of a deal. It is then that it becomes clear whether the assets chosen to be packaged were, in fact, productive and profitable, or whether they are like the rest of the company, not so productive and not so profitable. Despite all the wiggle room for 'creative' accounting which accounting principles provide, many deals blow up when the draft audit appears, unable to go forward due to irremediable lack of profitability.

Figure 6.4: Schematic diagram of 'packaged' company

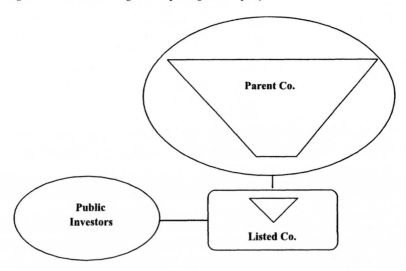

The asset appraisal draft result is a critical part of the audit work as well, since it sets the accounting or book value of the fixed assets (property and equipment) and, therefore, depreciation. Asset appraisal results are the object of intense negotiation. The company always wants to hold down the adjustment, minimize depreciation and so report higher net income and receive more IPO proceeds. But the State Asset Management Bureau must also be satisfied and for it assets can only appreciate. The appraisal and the audit work go on simultaneously. From a market viewpoint, this work is completely unnecessary. An asset appraisal provides no useful information to investors or anyone else (including the state) on true asset value. The question is not how much assets are worth, but how the assets are used to produce products which can be sold at a profit. A company may have a beautiful plant which is poorly operated and creates no value at all. In fact, there are any number of these littered across the Chinese landscape. On the other hand, if the State Asset Management Bureau requires an asset appraisal, arrangements are made to provide one. The Bureau takes the report seriously even if no one else does.

As discussed in Chapter 3, the concept of value contained in an asset appraisal report represents the replacement cost of the assets. This approach assumes that today's ten-year-old, mostly depreciated machine, is worth the price of a brand new machine and that is the price used in the company's book. The result of such an appraisal will always be to inflate the value of the company's fixed assets by definition with a similar increase in the company's capital account. This outcome is satisfying to the SAMB: through its dedication, the state's assets always show increases in value. Under its strict guidance, the write-down or write-off of the value of any machinery is absolutely impossible in China, no matter what the reason might be. Asset values can only go up, never down. Aside from the impact on operations, this would all be of little importance except for a related restriction on the price at which a company's shares can be sold.[12] By regulation shares must be priced at a level exceeding the company's net asset value per share. The higher the appraised value of the fixed assets, the higher the net asset value per share and, consequently, the higher the price must be set to sell the company's shares. If the company can not be sold at this price after all share orders are received, the deal will not be approved by the CSRC. There is, therefore, great pressure on the company and its hired help to find a balance that satisfies the State Asset Management Bureau's quest for increases in the value of state assets, while holding the increase to a level that allows the company to attempt the offering in the opinion of its bankers.

This outcome is largely the result of negotiation before the asset appraisal is submitted to the Asset Management Bureau, but there are a few things that can be done to create an acceptable outcome. For example, no listed Chinese company ever owns the land it sits on: this would gross up the value of its assets so high that a listing would be impossible. Also, no one in China has any idea what land is really worth. In the absence of a real property market for industrial property, there is no objective basis by which to value it. Land values are simply set by, what else, the State Land Management Bureau (SLMB) or its authorized representative at the local level. The bigger issue is left behind with the parent company to deal with at some later date. The new company simply rents the 'land use rights' from its parent based on a rent schedule which can be designed to boost bottom line profits: little or no rent in the early years, increasing rent in the later years. Such arrangements are outside the control of SLMB and are perfectly legal. Between playing with land use rights and running scenarios on fixed asset value, it is an understatement to say that domestic asset appraisal companies are extremely practical in their work.

The draft audit sometimes requires great flexibility from the banker and the as yet notional parent company. If the audit shows the bottom line still insufficient to produce a successful listing, everything is up for grabs again in the new company's design. Without going into excruciating detail, the bankers, company and the accounting firm comb through the prospective balance sheet and income statement to identify items which might produce a large negative impact on profitability. This might include such things as a product line with low profitability, unproductive fixed assets creating large amounts of depreciation, too many employees, too much debt, excess taxes (taxes can sometimes be negotiated) and so on. Once such pieces are identified, the question arises of whether they can be got rid of. Usually the answer is: stuff them in the parent company.

Participants in this work cannot be accused of shortchanging the state (or even investors) since they seek ways to create value out of an SOE. With all due respect to the state, what is the value of an SOE? It most certainly is not what the balance sheet suggests before or after completion of a state approved asset appraisal. And it is doubtful that any responsible state leader believes that it is. The SOE's value is what the market will give for it and nothing else. If the shares can not be sold, then the company has no market value, only a book value which represents the results of a set of arbitrary accounting decisions as directed by the state owner. This, unfortunately, is the status quo and its consequence is that the state, as ultimate owner, has no objective idea whether or not any given company is operating successfully and therefore worthy of continued investment. For example, Baoshan Steel in Shanghai is China's most modern steel maker, as everyone knows. But even senior officials in the State Planning and Development Commission have no clear idea of what steel products the company makes or if the company is truly profitable. This is the true problem of SOE reform in China: no one is sure of whether even the best companies are capable of reform if that means a rapid restructuring in preparation, whether for increased global competition or just an international IPO.

6.4   A case of international listing approvals

For the years 1992 through 1997 candidates for overseas listings were approved by the State Council in groups or 'Batches' with the First Batch announced in October 1992 and the last, or Fifth Batch, in 1998. After the failed Fifth Batch, the state has taken a more *ad hoc* approach, approving candidates which it wants reformed as a matter of policy. Companies that attempt international listings are subject to the Overseas Listing Rules and the same requirements as B shares.[13] The CSRC defers, of course, to the given overseas regulatory body and stock exchange with regard to the various listing requirements, standards of disclosure, provision for shareholders' rights, and the legal obligations of the various intermediary organizations. All this is spelled out in the memorandum the CSRC concludes as a matter of practice with each overseas regulator.[14]

This hardly means that the Chinese bureaucracy is passive in an overseas listing. Listing candidates must still run the entire gamut of the domestic approval process at the same time as they work on completing all requirements for an international listing. As a consequence, the process calls for extensive coordination, all of which is provided by the investment bank involved. Organizing the workflow of two to three sets of lawyers, two asset appraisal companies, one auditor, a Chinese financial adviser, and a disorganized Chinese enterprise is not an easy task, to say nothing of finally securing all necessary state approvals on a relatively timely basis.

The approval process in China rapidly escalates into a race, on the one hand, with time and market conditions and, on the other, with a bureaucratic process that is outside of both time and market conditions. Every transaction has its stories of how domestic approvals were finally obtained. The general procedure involves a company representative literally camping out at the office of the particular approving agency ingratiating himself with the official involved and ensuring that the application papers are not placed at the bottom of the official's inbox. More activist measures can also be taken to improve the speed of approval. Tables 6.2–6.5 below are based on an actual transaction and show a somewhat generalized set of approvals required for an overseas IPO. Comprising 23 major approvals and numerous subapprovals the tables give an indication of just why the approval process is discouraging to all enterprises but the most politically connected, determined, or in the most dire financial straits. They also serve as an indication of why increasing numbers of companies elect to list on the domestic markets for which the process is simpler, less expensive and with a near 100 per cent guarantee of listing success. As domestic enterprise managers say, A share IPOs are 'a bit easier to manage (*haoban yixie*)'.

Steps 1–3 take place following the distribution of listing quotas as companies are notified and decide internally whether to seek listing approval. The word goes out that the CSRC is entertaining applications for overseas listing candidates, ministry or provincial quotas are handed out and company managements begin to think about applying. By the third step, a new batch of listing candidates has been formed by the CSRC, approved by the State Council and the companies included informed. This part of the process can take up to a year and did in the case of the Fourth and Fifth Batches.

By the time a project arrives at the point when its tariff structure and asset appraisal are submitted for formal approval, the draft audit has been produced, the asset appraisal result found acceptable to all involved, and sufficient profitability found to make an offering possible in the bankers' opinion. While approvals of a tariff and the appraisal are pending, work goes on to finish the audited financials with the aim of submitting a preliminary prospectus to the overseas regulator (for example SEHK) and prepare marketing plans for the IPO. This does not mean domestic approvals are complete. While investment bankers work on finalizing the international prospectus and seek regulatory approval overseas, the domestic legal counsel and financial advisor prepare a Corporatization Plan which includes an explanation of shareholders' interests both before and after the proposed listing. If the Plan is agreed to by the Ministry then it is submitted to SCRES for

Table 6.2: Steps 1–9 in the international offering approval process

Item	Approving entities	Comments
1. Corporatization proposal	Ministry/Prov. government	Preliminary approval to go forward
2. Corporatization plan	Ministry/Prov. Government	Detailed plan showing: 'company' designed for listing and rationale for listing
3. Overseas listing approval	1. Ministry 2. CSRC	Based on quota, if Ministry advances a given company, it will usually get CSRC okay
4. Project proposal	Ministry	The final packaging proposal developed with the investment bankers
5. Initiate asset appraisal	1. Ministry 2. SAMB	The formal asset appraisal requires approval to begin
6. Initiate land appraisal	1. Ministry 2. SLMB	Only appraised if the land use rights remain in the packaged company
7. Approve asset appraisal	1. Ministry 2. SAMB	SAMB was required to give a formal response (but not necessarily approval) in three weeks.
8. Approve land appraisal	1. Ministry 2. SLMB	SLMB is also meant to reply in three weeks.
9. Tariff structure (if needed)	1. Ministry 2. SPCB	Formulas are not possible; the tariff is reviewed each year.

review and approval. With SCRES approval the new company can formally proceed to establish itself as a Chinese legal person in Step 16. Steps 17, 18 and 22, involving approvals to establish an independent legal person company limited by shares with approval to sell shares (*shehui muji gongsi*) are the critical part of the process. The only more difficult approval is Step 20, the review of the share valuation which reflects the investment bank's best estimate based on analysis of comparable listed companies, investor sentiment and market conditions. Prior to this, company management, the bankers and the domestic financial adviser seek approval of the prospectus and offering plan. The key part of the offering plan is the amount of shares to be offered to international investors or, conversely, the percentage to be controlled

Table 6.3: Steps 10–23 in the international offering approval process

Item	Approving entities	Comments
10. State ownership interest plan	1. Ministry/Provincial Government 2. SAMB	State ownership cannot be less than 51%
11. Corporatization plan	1. Ministry 2. SCRES	Corporate charter, shareholder breakdown and issuance plan
12. Use of IPO proceeds	1. Ministry 2. SPC 3. State Council	To insure that projects to be funded by IPO proceeds are included in State Plan
13. Valuation analysis	Ministry	Ministry knows the price it wants regardless of the quality of the company and the market
14. Feasibility study	Ministry	Provided by domestic financial adviser
15. Roadshow material review	1. Ministry 2. CSRC	To ensure roadshow materials conform with state policies
16. Incorporation of company	1. Ministry 2. SCRES	Actual formation of the designed company as a legal entity
17. FX account opening	Ministry	To receive IPO proceeds
18. Company registration	1. Ministry 2. Bureau of Commerce and Industry	Business license
19. Prospectus review	1. Ministry 2. CSRC	To make sure 'Risk Factor' section is not insulting
20. Offering and listing plan	1. Ministry 2. CSRC	Provides an opportunity to negotiate pricing range
21. Offering and listing plan	State Council	Ministry/CSRC joint submission
22. Transformation to company limited by shares	1. Ministry 2. SCRES 3. CSRC	The corporation becomes a company limited by shares and approved to issue new shares to foreign investors
23. Application for JV status	1. Ministry 2. MOFTEC	Gives the company a tax break for three years

by the state subsequent to the offering. If this is approved, the company can then seek approval to transform itself into a company limited by shares in Step 22. If the process is well organized, the receipt of final state approval should dovetail with the final submission of the prospectus to the overseas regulator. At this point, the process enters the final stretch and is usually complete within one month.

6.5 Pricing

The entire issue of pricing involves a general explanation of how equity shares are (or should be) valued. As discussed in Chapter 3, the value of a company's equity reflects the value of its *future* profit potential. If a company has exceptionally strong growth prospects, its shares should be worth more than a company with low growth prospects, all things being equal. The process of arriving at a judgement on future profit potential involves an understanding of the markets, the industry, the company, its management and so on. A financial model of the company incorporating this understanding is built, projecting its operation out three to five years into the future.

Based on this and a comparison with similar companies whose shares are already listed and trading, a prospective P/E ratio is arrived at. Potential investors are then asked to consider an investment in the company based on this ratio (typically expressed as a price per share range) and to place orders for the shares. The point is that the value of equity lies in how management directs the company's future performance and in how investors view the company's prospects. The past, while useful as a reference, is history. The approach, briefly described here, is the one used for overseas listings of Chinese companies, including B shares. It is also the overwhelmingly predominant approach to equity valuation in use throughout the world's markets. Until recently Chinese practice was significantly different.

6.5.1 A shares

In stark contrast to the aforementioned, the Chinese adopted administrative pricing from the start. From the beginning A share pricing, for all intents and purposes, was based on a formula which applied a 15 times P/E ratio to the average of the company's past three-years profits.[15] Although the intention was to avoid excessively high valuations based on overoptimistic projected earnings by overly optimistic bankers, there are many things wrong with this approach. Reliance on past performance, first of all, is obviously no guarantee of future performance. For example, earnings may have declined from a high to a low level during the three year period, suggesting that the company was encountering difficulties. Second, a mandated 15 times price provides equal treatment for all companies, but companies are not equal.

Beginning in late 1997 the CSRC experimented by adjusting the pricing mechanism to place a 70 per cent weighting on the earnings of the most recent financial year and 30 per cent on projected earnings.[16] Then in late 1998 the CSRC encouraged domestic underwriters to use a P/E ratio higher than the figure resulting from the 1997 formula if the company's performance justified it. This was done for the first time in early 1999 with the IPO of China World Trade Center on the Shanghai exchange. Priced at nearly 20 times, the company's shares traded up only 15 per cent in the days following the listing in contrast to the 30–70 per cent plus jumps in price of typical A shares. In short, in this case the issuer enjoyed a higher price and larger proceeds, while less was left on the table for investors to profit from.

Following this, on 28 July 1999, the CSRC announced the experimental adoption of the international approach to pricing domestic IPOs and the selection of the Konka Group Ltd. as the pilot issuer.[17] These new rules apply only to potential issuers with more than RMB400 million in total equity capital. For issuers with less than this amount the 1997 pricing method still applies. Like international practice, the 1999 regulations allow the underwriter to set a price range and seek investor bids based on it. A final price is set based on the strength and price level of investor demand as shown in an order book. In theory, this should bring pricing in line with market demand which, in turn, should reflect a more accurate valuation of the company's prospects. Given the Chinese situation, however, this may not be the result, at least in the near term. For this approach to work properly, investors need to be able to arrive at their own judgement of the company's value. At present, neither the few institutional investors nor the average Chinese retail investor have this capability.

The 'new' approach adopted for Konka dovetails with the CSRC's effort to make Chinese securities firms, accountants and legal advisers assume greater responsibility as defined in the Securities Law. While in the past, it had, in effect, assumed all responsibility based on its final approval authority, the CSRC now will assume a more passive role. What effect this will actually have on valuation and how the market will react is as yet undetermined. Even after Konka's successful subscription it remains unclear, for reasons discussed in the next section, whether this new methodology will continue in use.

6.5.2 Konka case study: China's first bookbuilding experiment

The Konka Group is China's second largest manufacturer of white goods and the largest exporter of such goods, and listed A and B shares in 1992 on the Shenzhen exchange. The CSRC selected Konka based on its profitability and presumed future prospects. In order to raise funds for expansion, Konka planned to offer 80 million new shares, not as a rights offering, but as a secondary offering of shares. Thus, investors were not limited to existing shareholders. China International Capital Corporation (CICC) was selected by the CSRC as the lead underwriter for this ground breaking transaction based on its international experience with the bookbuilding process, something which no domestic securities company could claim. On the other hand, no institution had ever attempted to use international pricing methodologies in China's domestic market and it was highly uncertain at the outset how Chinese investors would respond.

In designing an offering structure based on bookbuilding CICC had to consider the characteristics of potential investors. New share financings have a negative impact on the secondary market price of existing shares given that increased share holdings dilute existing investor interest. This was typically dealt with by offering a rights issue at deeply discounted prices to existing investors so that on balance these investors benefited. Hence, the large number of rights offerings in the Chinese markets. CICC and the CSRC hoped that by directing marketing efforts at new, potential shareholders the discount to the secondary market price could be significantly reduced, thereby benefiting the issuer, Konka. At the same time, a reduced discount would also benefit existing shareholders, particularly if sufficient demand could be stimulated to drive the share price up following the offering. Thus, the focus of the marketing effort was on new shareholders and particularly institutional shareholders who might be expected to hold the shares for a relatively long time.

Like international offerings, CICC arranged the first ever domestic roadshow in Beijing, Shanghai and Shenzhen. The roadshow included the traditional investor luncheon presentations and one-on-one meetings with all 15 securities investment funds and their managers. Unfortunately, this plan was disrupted when the State Council suddenly ordered a three month lockup on investments by corporations.

The effect was to significantly reduce corporate interest in the transaction. The roadshow, therefore, was turned into a purely media event to which reporters from journals, newspapers, and television stations from across the country were invited (and fêted). The roadshow team, which included Konka's senior management, was followed constantly by television camera crews. The intent was to drum up as much interest as possible among retail investors in the belief that the institutional side would fail to participate. Of course, in the developed markets the participation of even one reporter in a roadshow meeting or luncheon is against the law. In China there is no such law.

In the meantime, CICC and the company were flooded with questions about the offering and pricing process. The media was again used extensively in an effort to educate potential investors about how the process worked, what its merits were and, of course, why they should participate. In spite of this effort, the company and CICC received death threats by phone and by fax during the course of the offering! Fortunately, nothing came of them.

Two hours before the close of the ten-day offer period directed at institutional investors, CICC had received orders for just 10 per cent of the offering. But then a flood of orders poured in. At the end of the day orders for just over 80 million shares, or a bit more than 100 per cent, had been received. The variety of bidding investor was amazing, ranging from rural credit unions to electric power bureaus and from municipal 'development' companies to collective and private enterprises from all over the country.

Compared to a typical A share, the subscription level was not very exciting. Nonetheless, the orders provided a broad enough price range with sufficient order concentration at a discount of between four and seven per cent to market. A satisfactory price range for the on-line retail offering could, therefore, be set. The on-line offering was a success with an over-subscription rate of 6.3 times the number of available shares or, adding in the institutional subscription, a total demand of 7.3 times the 80 million available shares or 584 million shares with corresponding upfront cash deposits of approximately RMB9 billion. After much internal discussion CICC recommended that Konka accept, and it did accept, a per share price of RMB15.5. This represented a five per cent discount from the average of the previous twenty days daily closing price. In comparison, the average discount for rights offerings completed in 1999 was 34 per cent. In short, the company left perhaps 29 per cent less on the table for investors to gain from. The overall strategy seems to have been a success judging from the post-listing performance of Konka's shares. In the few days after the listing of the new shares, Konka's price edged up slightly in contrast to the overall market which fell nearly one per cent. Also a positive sign, the volume of shares changing hands settled down after the first day to a range of 1.5 to 2.5 million per day.

The market, however, was not satisfied, judging from a number of critical comments made in the financial press.[18] First, the Konka offer was judged to be too risky, meaning that little upside remained for investors. Second, the subscription rate to the Konka offering was among the lowest in years for similar issues and marked 'the rejection by over 90 per cent of investors of the bookbuilding methodology'. Third, people subscribed only in the belief that 'The first time [the government] tries something new, it cannot fail.' Fourth, old shareholders could not understand management's strategy in not giving them cheap shares in a rights offering. Fifth, should other companies attempt to use this approach the end result will be that no companies will succeed in issuing new shares: people will not buy. Sixth, how new shares are sold is not as important as the Party's current policy of using the market to finance companies and, in fact, the bookbuilding approach conflicts with the Party's policy. Similar comments and criticisms penetrated the CSRC as well and it is uncertain when or whether this experiment will proceed.

6.6   Analysis of listed companies

A review of the past seven years of listings indicates that the screening process described in Section 6.1 has in actual practice been effective in streaming Chinese companies, so that the larger and more prominent national companies have listed shares overseas, while the smaller, locally owned companies have listed on domestic markets. To illustrate this point, through mid 1999 there have been 47 H share offerings raising US$15.7 billion or an average of US$332 million per offering. In contrast, there have been 865 A share offerings raising US$24.3 billion or an average of US$28 million per offering. The scale is similar for B shares for which there have been 107 offerings raising US$3.9 billion or an average of US$37 million per offering.

6.6.1   International issuers

There have been two groups of international issuers: (1) Chinese companies which have listed their shares directly on overseas markets, that is H shares and the like; and (2) the so-called 'Red Chips', which are

Hong Kong registered companies into which Chinese assets have been injected, usually in a share for asset swap. The asset injection comes both prior to, or as part of the listing, and might continue thereafter with minority shareholder approval. Red Chips are, therefore, holding companies with typically little specialization in any one industry and, for the most part, are rather low quality in terms of management and earnings. Many of the Red Chips are the result of so-called 'back door' listings in which a non-listed Chinese company acquires a relatively dormant SEHK listed company and then injects mainland assets. In short, from the time of the first 'backdoor listing' by Capital Steel in 1993 until the frenzy stirred up by Shanghai Industrial and later on Beijing Enterprise on the eve of the Hong Kong handover, the Red Chip sector has not reflected government policy *vis-à-via* SOE reform. It does, however, reflect the pressing demand for capital of Chinese organizations. Nonetheless, after every city in China began working on Red Chip listing plans in 1997, the CSRC squelched the whole idea. Yet these sort of under the table listings do get done here and there still and might be called 'Pink Chips'.

For all these reasons, it is difficult to identify which Hong Kong listed companies are, in fact, Red Chips other than by reliance on the Hong Kong Red Chip Index. Hence, this discussion on international issuers deals only with those Chinese companies which have been directly listed on overseas exchanges. Since 1992 there have been five groups, or batches, of candidate enterprises for overseas listings total-ing 86 companies. Given that listing candidates are selected in part based on the importance of certain sectors to the State Plan, it is not surprising that the largest number of candidates have come from the infrastructure (largely highways and ports) and power (25) sectors fol-lowed by transportation (9), petrochemicals and chemicals (9), and steel (6), which, taken all together, account for 57 per cent of the total. Of this group 58 per cent successfully completed a listing. The owner-ship of these entities reflects the planned investment environment

Table 6.6: Completed H share and Red Chip IPOs (30 June 1999)

	90	91	92	93	94	95	96	97	98	99
H-shares	0	0	1	8	12	2	5	16	2	1
Red Chip	2	0	5	8	11	2	2	9	0	1
Total	2	0	6	16	23	4	7	25	2	2

Source: Bloomberg and SEHK

Table 6.7: H share listing candidates by industrial sector

Industry	Number of candidates	Number listed	Success rate %
Infrastructure	13	6	38
Power/Power equipment	12	7	58
Transportation	9	5	56
Petrochemicals/Chemicals	9	6	67
Consumer products	7	5	57
Steel	6	3	50
Building materials	5	3	60
Agriculture/Foodstuffs	5	2	40
Pharmaceuticals	5	2	40
Machinery	5	3	60
Real estate	2	1	50
Energy	2	1	50
Non-ferrous metals	2	1	50
Other	4	2	25
Total	86	47	55

described previously: of the 86 entities 28 were owned by the central government, 40 by provincial governments and 15 by local governments (three companies are of unknown ownership), or about two for each provincial-level government. For the most part, the central government has invested in and, therefore, 'owned' all the major power plants, steel companies, airlines and car makers, while provincial governments have had a difficult time, especially in recent years, finding candidates of an economic scale sufficient to interest international investors.

Reviewing the composition of each batch by industrial sector and considering the element of time over which the batches came out brings out a number of interesting points. First, although power and transportation were heavily favored by government policy in the first two batches, both sectors were failures in later groups. This reflected a dearth of appropriate candidates in the case of transportation (trucks, planes and railways) and a significant lack of investor interest in power, even though the government continued to push it in the Fourth Batch. This lack of interest reflected the unpredictability of government policy regarding what should be a steady, predictable industry. Petrochemical and chemical companies were steadily represented in all batches but the failure rate was significant later on again as investors became wary of the volatile regulatory environment of the

Table 6.8: Listing candidate batch composition by sector

Industry*/date of batch	10/92	1/94	9/94	12/96	12/98	Total
Petrochemicals/ Chemicals	3 (3)	2 (2)	0	4 (1)	0	9 (6)
Machinery	2 (2)	1 (1)	0	2 (0)	0	5 (3)
Steel	1 (1)	2 (0)	0	3 (2)	0	6 (3)
Consumer	0	1 (1)	3 (3)	3 (1)	0	7 (5)
Power/Power Equipment	1 (1)	6 (6)	0	5 (0)	0	12 (7)
Transportation	0	7 (5)	1 (0)	1 (0)	0	9 (5)
Building Materials	0	3 (2)	0	2 (1)	0	5 (3)
Pharmaceuticals	0	0	2 (2)	3 (0)	0	5 (2)
Infrastructure	0	0	1 (1)	5 (4)	7 (1)	13 (6)
Energy	0	0	0	2 (1)	0	2 (1)
Agriculture/ Foodstuffs	1 (1)	0	0	2 (1)	2	5 (2)
Real estate	0	0	0	2 (1)	0	2 (1)
Non-ferrous metals	0	0	0	2 (1)	0	2 (1)
Other	1 (1)	1 (0)	0	3 (1)	0	4 (2)
Totals	9 (9)	22 (17)	7 (6)	39 (14)	9 (1)	86 (47)

* Number of successful listings in ()

sector. Consumer related enterprises grew over time but experienced significant failure in the Fourth Batch as the government selected companies which were makers of commodity computer and television components. Following the listing of the Shenzhen Expressway in 1995 local governments China-wide concluded that highways, ports, and whatever else a city or province might call 'infrastructure' could be put together in a 'company' and successfully listed. There was, thus, an explosion of follow-on deals, accounting for the high number of infrastructure candidates.

There were plenty of lessons in what the market seemed to like at first, but then had enough of. But misinterpretation of what the market wanted, the momentum of the process itself and a continuing feeling that anything can be sold, all combined to make possible the Fifth and last Batch (last because the government has now, in large part, stopped attempting to second guess the preference of the market). This group of nine companies consisted of seven so-called 'infrastructure' companies and two 'agriculture' concepts, conceived after the unexpected success of First Tractor in early 1997. The abrupt failure in early 1999 of a group of farms in Heilongjiang Province which were cobbled together put a quick end to this 'concept'.

The monolithic character of Fifth Batch companies was indicative of a number of key problems with the entire state orchestrated process. First, by the end of the decade nearly all major companies in the favored policy sectors had been selected as candidates: there simply were no more 'good ones' to choose from. Second, international investors had been burned so often by listed companies failing to deliver on their promises that they had lost all interest in what was, after all, an SOE reform effort, especially when it boiled over into agricultural reform. Finally, Chinese companies themselves had lost interest in the process: it was too difficult and frequently did not deliver the expected money while preparatory expenses piled-up. Instead, they were turning their sights to the domestic A share markets where listings could be done with far less difficulty and fewer questions were asked.

The geographic location of each of these candidates underscores the point just made. A quick review shows a preponderance of candidate enterprises from China's more prosperous coastal provinces and cities. It is only somewhat surpr..ing that the country's capital, Beijing, accounted for 14 per cent of the total number of candidates followed by Guangdong with 12 per cent. This is probably explained by the municipal government's proximity to the State Council and the central government's ongoing effort to make Beijing a showcase. Taking them all together, the coastal provinces (excluding the Northeast) accounted for 49 per cent of total candidates. Contrariwise, the Northeast accounted for only 12 per cent despite its heavily industrialized character, leaving the interior provinces at only 39 per cent, or 30 per cent if Sichuan is excluded.

Although the oil and gas industry located in the Northeast and Far West was not yet permitted to seek listings in the period up to 1998 (and, in any event, is centrally-owned), the geographic breakdown described above only partly reflects the failed government policy to reduce the economic gap between China's East and West. The rest is economic reality. Take the Northeast, for example, although it is highly industrialized, most of the enterprises are in the heavy industrial sector, have outdated plant facilities and would not make a profit even under Chinese accounting practices consistently applied. Jilin, for example, receives the majority of its tax revenues from First Auto Works (FAW). At the time FAW's name came up as a potential listing candidate every investment bank in the world beat a path to its door. But no amount of work by even the best investment banks (and everyone gave it a try egged on by an anxious Ministry of Machinery) could come up with an idea which would result in a successful listing of even

Table 6.9: Listing candidates by geographic location of incorporation

Province	No. of candidates	No. listed
Beijing	12	11
Guangdong	10	7
Shandong	7	5
Sichuan	7	5
Shanghai	4	3
Anhui	4	3
Liaoning	4	1
Zhejiang	3	1
Jiangsu	3	3
Henan	3	2
Tianjin	3	1
Jilin	3	1
Heilongjiang	3	1
Hebei	3	0
Hubei	3	0
Yunnan	2	1
Jiangxi	2	1
Other (one each)	12	1
Total	86	47

one part of the company. There simply was nothing there of interest to international equity investors. FAW later on listed part of its operations on the A share market.

The Northeast is China's rust belt and until the economy there is turned around, or new industries emerge, it is simply impossible to use publicly raised international capital to finance its enterprises. This is true even for A and B shares listings which have lower approval standards: less than 11 per cent of all companies listed on the Shanghai exchange come from the Northeast. So despite appearances, identifying appropriate listing candidates for the international market has been an extremely difficult task which is getting no easier. In the interior provinces, large-scale enterprises are few and far between. Even Sichuan, which has been fairly successful in getting candidates approved, could not come up with a single enterprise to promote during the run-up to the Fifth Batch in 1998 although in the Fourth Batch it was represented by a highway, two steel companies (one centrally owned) and a chemical fertilizer plant. And if Shanghai could come up with only five candidates during this six-year period, the difficulties elsewhere are easy to imagine.

6.6.2 Domestic issuers

There have been two periods of intense domestic market activity as illustrated in Table 6.10. The 1992 to early 1994 period was given over to the initial excitement of the experiment. China's burst of enthusiasm stemming from Deng Xiaoping's Southern Journey was the principal stimulus restoring China's confidence in the future after the darks days of 1989. As discussed later, the markets were extremely quiet from the second half of 1994 and all of 1995 due to high interest rates and other administrative measures aimed at controlling inflation. Such measures included a near halt in approvals for new IPOs given their potentially inflationary impact. The markets rebounded in 1996, as the country emerged from the danger of hyper inflation, and 1997, due to the enthusiasm generated by Hong Kong's restoration to China, with both years recording almost one IPO per day.

As Table 6.11 indicates, the top ten provinces of incorporation for the two exchanges represent a total of only 14 provinces and these have contributed 63 per cent of the total number of listed companies. Selecting only the coastal provinces and cities from this list of 14 yields nine which have contributed 49 per cent of the total. These nine provinces represent less than one third of the total provincial-level regions in China and about 25 per cent of the population. This result is similar to that of the H shares and reflects the reality of China's development, despite the long term policy to narrow the gap between the coastal and interior regions.

Shanghai Stock Exchange

At the end of September 1999 there were 474 companies listed in Shanghai of which 52 were B share companies. Of these, 60 per cent

Table 6.10: Trends in domestic A and B share listings (June 1999)

	Type	90	91	92	93	94	95	96	97	98	99
Shanghai	A	8	0	22	73	68	15	103	85	53	20
	B	0	9	13	13	2	6	8	2	0	0
Sub-total		8	9	35	86	70	21	111	87	53	20
Shenzhen	A	0	6	18	52	42	9	100	121	51	19
	B	0	0	9	10	5	10	9	8	3	0
Sub-total		0	6	27	62	47	19	109	129	54	19
Total		8	15	62	148	117	40	220	216	107	39

Table 6.11: Sectoral representation of listed companies (30 Sept. 1999)

Sector	Shanghai exchange	%	Shenzhen exchange	%
Industry	282	59.5	340	69.0
Commerce	49	10.3	39	7.9
Utilities	39	8.2	32	6.5
Real estate	9	1.9	21	4.3
Finance	0	0.0	3	0.6
Conglomerates	95	20.0	58	11.8
Total	474	100.0	493	100.0

Source: SSE and SZSE Market Facts

were industrial, 10 per cent commercial, 2 per cent property, 8 per cent utility and 20 per cent classified as other.

The Shanghai exchange was originally established solely for the benefit of enterprises incorporated in the Shanghai administrative region. Since 1993, however, enterprises from elsewhere in the country have also been able to list there. At the end of 1998 each of China's provinces (even Tibet) and four directly administered cities was represented by at least one listed company. Shanghai, however, remained the best represented, accounting for 27.4 per cent of a total of 438 listed companies, followed by neighboring Zhejiang at 7.1 per cent and Sichuan at 5.7 per cent. The top ten provinces or cities account for nearly 72 per cent of the total listed companies, again illustrating the poor representation of the country as a whole.

Table 6.12: Top provinces of incorporation of Shanghai companies (FY1998)

	A share	A and H share	A and B share	B share	No. of Companies	% Total
Shanghai	79	2	33	6	120	27.4
Zhejiang	29		1	1	31	7.1
Sichuan	24	1			25	5.7
Jiangsu	20	2		1	23	5.3
Shandong	20	2	1		23	5.3
Beijing	18	1			19	4.3
Fujian	19				19	4.3
Liaoning	17			2	19	4.3
Hubei	17		1		18	4.1
Heilongjiang	15		1		16	3.7
Total	270	8	37	10	313	71.5

Source: SSE Market Statistics

Shenzhen Stock Exchange

By third quarter 1999 there were 493 companies listed on the SZSE of which 54 were B share companies. From a sectoral viewpoint, 69 per cent were industrial, 8 per cent were commercial, 6.5 per cent were utilities, 4.3 per cent real estate, 0.6 per cent financial and 11.8 per cent classified as other. Like Shanghai, the Shenzhen exchange was originally established for the benefit of local companies and Guangdong continues to be best represented on the exchange. Other than this obvious geographic difference, the Shanghai and Shenzhen exchanges are remarkably comparable in terms of the origin of the listed companies. This is not particularly surprising and strongly suggests the influence of the planning process at the CSRC in the selection of listing locale.

In summary, China has permitted a bit more than 1000 state enterprises to enter the equity capital markets whether domestic or international. The selection of these enterprises reflects a policy screening for favored sectors and an economic screening for those allowed to raise capital internationally. Because the number of successful international issuers has been few, the original sectoral policy grip has been relaxed so that enterprises from nearly all but the most sensitive industries can seek an international listing. Domestically there is an almost endless supply of potential issuers from the state-owned sector, but they represent more of the same thing: SOEs as commodities. The only area

Table 6.13: Top provinces of incorporation of Shenzhen companies (April 1998)

	A share	A and H share	A and B share	B share	No. of companies	% Total
Guangdong	69		28	4	101	26.4
Liaoning	21	2	2	1	26	6.8
Sichuan	24				24	6.4
Hubei	17		1	1	19	5.0
Shandong	15	1		3	19	5.0
Hainan	14		2		16	4.2
Hunan	15				15	3.9
Jiangsu	11		2	2	15	3.9
Fujian	14			1	15	3.9
Jilin	13	1			14	3.7
Total Top 10	213	4	35	12	264	69.1

Source: SZSE Market Statistics

which has not yet been explored remains the non-state or private sector. The addition of such companies may be the only way that the domestic exchanges can offer a true equity product to their investors.

7
Investors and Other Market Participants

China's equity market development to date has made the concept of investor somewhat of an oxymoron. The reality for the past decade is that market participants were 'players' and that the vast majority of players were individuals with the securities houses added in to stir the soup. In the years of the 1990s this picture has begun to change somewhat as the government has sought to build a base of so-called 'institutional investors' who, presumably by holding shares for the long term gains sound management might provide, would attribute greater stability to the markets. As a consequence, market participants have become somewhat more diverse. Yet the overwhelming fact is that retail investors account for 99.6 per cent of total A share account holders at the end of 1999.

Investors are normally categorized as professional, or institutional, and retail. Retail investors are individuals investing their own funds, as opposed to a professional investor, a category representing a variety of entities using institutional, that is, other people's funds to invest. It is generally considered that retail investors have very short term time horizons and are speculative in their investment strategies. This is particularly the case in China as well as in other emerging markets. In contrast, although certain types of institutional investors are professional speculators, there are many others who manage client money for long term returns.

In spite of these developments, the Chinese markets continue to be dominated by retail investors and this accounts in part for their volatility. In China professional investors were until recently represented by the proprietary trading departments of securities firms and various other non-bank financial institutions, such as trust and investment companies. Corporate investors, too, have played the markets from time to time when regulations permit. All of these entities contribute to market volatility. In addition to the securities firms, China has always had a number of 'securities investment funds'. The number of such funds has grown rapidly since 1998 in line with the government's hope that they will eventually provide a true institutional investor base. But despite double digit annual growth in the past year, institutional accounts at the two exchanges are still a small percentage of total accounts as shown in Table 7.1. Other than individuals, securities firms, corporates, and the investment funds, no other organizations or institutions are permitted to purchase shares directly in China at this point of time.

7.1 Retail investors

The two exchanges have equal numbers of accounts, approximately 22 million apiece. Without question there is some overlap, so perhaps in total there are only 30 million individuals and others with share accounts across China, or 2.5 per cent of the total population. But this is an extremely important 30 million since they represent citizens living predominantly in China's developed and wealthy coastal provinces. Nearly 33 per cent of the total Shanghai population hold A share accounts on the SSE and the SZSE. After Shanghai comes Beijing with more than 12 per cent followed by Guangdong with 9 per cent. Second, from an exchange perspective, Shanghainese, not unexpectedly, are by far the largest group of account holders on the SSE at 15 per cent, followed by Guangdong at 8.8 per cent, Sichuan at 8.6 per cent, Jiangsu at 8.4 per cent and Shandong at 6.7 per cent. The regional character is similar for Shenzhen, where Guangdong accounts for 23.9 per cent, followed by Sichuan at 8.5 per cent, Shanghai at 8.2 per cent, and Jiangsu at 7.2 per cent. Overall, the top ten provinces record of account holders in both markets account for over 70 per cent of all accounts and the same provinces compose the top ten for each market. This is not surprising since these ten provinces or cities are among the most prosperous in China, representing nearly 25 per cent of China's population and half of the country's GDP.

Recent efforts to enliven the markets have clearly been based on the government's conclusion that the great bull market performance in the US had created a 'wealth effect' that has led to the heroic consumption binge by US citizens in recent years. In China, however, this kind of analysis suggests that those who get rich from playing the markets are those who are already relatively well off. This portion of the populace may be the largest potential consumers and so have a major impact on

Table 7.1: Monthly growth in retail and institutional A share accounts (1999)

Month	Individual	Shanghai institutions	% Institutions	Individual	Shenzhen institutions	% Institutions
12/98	19 860 500	55 600	0.28	18 924 659	86 244	0.45
1/99	19 939 900	56 300	0.28	19 022 416	86 630	0.45
2/99	19 963 700	56 400	0.28	19 044 512	86 744	0.45
3/99	20 078 500	57 100	0.28	19 208 273	87 444	0.45
4/99	20 182 600	57 600	0.28	19 306 064	87 898	0.45
5/99	20 277 700	58 100	0.29	19 481 237	88 270	0.45
6/99	20 757 400	54 400	0.29	19 967 397	89 221	0.44
7/99	21 360 100	61 000	0.28	20 522 463	91 830	0.45
8/99	21 754 100	62 700	0.29	20 895 262	94 704	0.45
9/99	22 122 000	67 500	0.30	21 227 221	98 786	0.46
Growth %	11.4	21.4		12.2	14.5	

Source: SSE and SZSE Market Data

the national economy. Given the distribution of accounts, however, it does not appear that boosting the markets will have a significant effect on the interior provinces (except Sichuan) other than to further widen the gap between the two regions.

7.2 Corporate investors

As shown in Table 7.1, in late 1999 there were around 170 000 non-retail accounts which might be thought to fall largely into a corporate bracket. By corporates, it is meant legal entities, the main business of which is not the management of capital. Corporate, therefore, excludes pension funds, insurance companies and so on. China's economy over the past 20 years has given rise to a great diversity of corporates many of which are active in the stock market. For example, in a recent IPO the following distinctions were made: SOEs, SOE holding companies, private companies, foreign-invested companies, rural credit unions and 'other', which included such entities as 'investment' or 'development' companies, but in fact were most likely to be money managers. For obvious reasons, the state has imposed restrictions from time to time on the participation of corporates, especially SOEs. SOEs traditionally have not been permitted to trade any shares until recent new regulations allowed them to subscribe to IPOs subject to holding restrictions (or a 'lockup') of six months for a so-called strategic holding or three months for a common investment. Listed companies have also been restricted from share trading but these regulations are typically skirted by going through a related party. Smaller firms make use of an individual account to trade as internal control is often lacking and money transfers are more easily done.

The corporate investment mentality is not dissimilar to that of the individual – short term gain rather than long term investment. As indicated in Table 7.1, the 1999 rally encouraged many corporates to enter the market in the hope of offsetting poor operations, but results were no doubt mixed due to poor controls and procedures. In short, in the overall structure of Chinese investors, corporates are located somewhere above individual accounts, by virtue of being able to invest more money, but below the mutual funds and securities houses.

7.3 Insurance companies

The number of insurance companies in China has increased rapidly over the past several years. At the end of 1997 there were 25 insurance

Table 7.2: Regional composition of SSE and SZSE A share accounts (31 December 1998)

Top ten	A share SSE a/cs	A share SZ a/cs	Population (000)	% Pop. Sh A a/cs	% Pop. Sz A a/cs	% Pop. all a/cs
Shanghai	3 150 345	1 563 047	14 570	21.6	10.7	32.3
Beijing	820 296	723 450	12 400	6.6	5.8	12.4
Guangdong	1 760 631	4 549 502	70 510	2.5	6.5	9.0
Jiangsu	1 663 655	1 359 891	71 480	2.3	1.9	5.2
Liaoning	1 172 714	779 089	41 380	2.8	1.9	4.7
Fujian	706 814	554 412	32 800	2.2	1.7	3.9
Zhejiang	967 442	725 255	44 350	2.2	1.6	3.8
Sichuan	1 713 019	1 623 812	114 720	1.5	1.4	2.9
Hubei	729 684	973 426	58 730	1.2	1.7	2.9
Shandong	1 328 819	896 865	87 850	1.5	1.0	2.5
Top 10 a/cs	14 016 419	13 748 749	304 450			
Total	19 916 090	19 010 903	1 223 200			
% of Total	70.4	72.3	24.7			

Source: SSE and SZSE Market Statistics

companies in China of which three were Sino-Foreign Joint Ventures. By the end of 1998 insurance companies held RMB199 billion in assets.[1] This group of investors is often seen as the key to the establishment of a strong institutional investor base for China's markets. Through mid 1999 the bulk of their money was invested in CGBs, Policy Finance Bonds (RMB bonds issued by China Development Bank, Export-Import Bank or China Agricultural Bank) or bank deposits, as these were the only permitted types of investment product. Recent changes in early 1999 allowed insurance companies to invest up to 2 per cent of their assets into high credit quality corporate bonds. Corporate bonds, however, continue to suffer from extremely poor secondary market liquidity caused by conflicting tax treatments and unrealistic yields set by administrative means. Given the extremely poor returns on capital characteristic of these types of investments, the insurance industry in China faces significant difficulties meeting its obligations in the future unless new investment products are permitted.

The first word that insurance companies might be allowed to invest in shares leaked into the markets during the summer rally when the word was that up to 2 per cent of their assets could be so invested. Then, in October 1999, regulators agreed to permit them to invest up to 5 per cent of their assets in A shares indirectly through the purchase of fund participations.[2] This decision has been received with varying degrees of enthusiasm, domestically owned firms have been very positive, while the JV entities more cautious, as they consider the likelihood of long-term returns. It is understandable why the authorities have been slow to grant insurance companies the ability to invest in equities. On the other hand, permitting only indirect investment through funds will not enable the insurance companies to develop their own internal management expertise. The immediate impact on the market should be limited. Insurance companies are likely to take a go slow approach to investing, by subscribing less to new CGB issues, waiting for existing bond holdings to expire and only then investing in equity funds. In the meantime, they will investigate the expertise of the various fund management companies.

This approach makes sense given the state of China's fund industry as discussed later. Investment in securities funds would have the insurance companies entrusting their equity money to fund managers who in most cases have little, or no, experience and no proven track record given the short history of the industry. This unproven fund manager then makes the investment decisions in place of the insurance company. In addition to assuming management risk, the insurance company will also be subject to the highly volatile discount/premium swings typical of closed-end funds, especially those listed in China. The same stocks bought directly in the market are, in fact, characterized by less volatility. On the other hand, investment by insurance companies may assist in the professionalism of the fund industry. In theory the funds should benefit as they have more sophisticated clients who will demand better returns and management. On the other hand, the funds are already well oversubscribed upon issue through strong retail demand, which has been less demanding. In short, this partial entry into the A share market seems to be of limited benefit to the insurance companies and will likely create further problems as the market develops.

7.4 Pension funds

Unlike pension funds in developed markets, Chinese pension funds are not yet permitted to invest in the stock markets either directly or indirectly. There are two broad categories of pension fund in China: Social, which are operated by local governments, or Corporate, which are managed by individual companies. Both fund types are only allowed to invest in Chinese government bonds or cash deposits. The emerging problem is easy to see. Annual fund contributions at present are not much more than annual payments to retirees, leaving the funds with little investable cash. The current state pension fund balance is approximately RMB6–70 billion or only four-months payments. With China's aging population and a tradition of providing generous support to retirees, the government will have to liberalize regulations to enable the funds to invest in financial instruments with greater rates of return. Interestingly, however, the lack of funds and lack of developed capital markets were recently cited at a pension fund conference in Beijing as two reasons why the funds are *not* pushing to enter the equity markets. Pension funds and other social security matters have just begun to be topics of political and economic discussion and there is, as yet, no consensus as to how to proceed. But there are many different types of experiments. Until this strategic issue has been addressed pension funds are unlikely to play a significant role in the equity market.

7.5 Securities investment funds

The securities investment funds *per se* are more properly a traded product than a market participant, however, by looking at these funds the effort is to see through them to the strategies and performance of the fund managers behind. At the start, investment funds were a product created by the regional trading centers in the early 1990s.[3] The first fund established, The Wuhan Securities Investment Fund, was approved by PBOC Wuhan Branch in October 1991 and raised RMB10 million. A year later the first specialized fund management company in China was established in Shenzhen, the Shenzhen Investment Fund Management Company. Through 1996 a total of 75 investment funds were established which taken together raised some RMB730 million (or US$88 million), an extremely small amount which, if averaged out, comes to only a bit more than US$1.2 million per fund. Of these 27 were listed on the two national exchanges (including 15 local funds which traded electronically in Shanghai and Shenzhen) and 63 were listed and traded on the various regional trading centers. In terms of approvals, only four funds had received approval from PBOC Beijing, while the remainder were all signed off on by local PBOC branches. The rapid growth of fund establishment led to a halt in their approval in late 1994 and this was not lifted until the end of 1996 on the eve of the enactment of standardized measures regulating the industry.

Fund management companies generally managed only one fund and with poor results. Due to their limited available capital, the funds themselves had little stabilizing impact on the markets, particularly since many also invested in real estate and the like. This reflects the fact that, aside from 'oversight' by local governments and branches of the PBOC, funds were entirely unregulated. Table 7.4 also illustrates the fact that the management structure for most of these original funds was entirely self-conflicted. Frequently, the fund promoter and manager were one and the same legal entity, or the promoter and custodian were the same. Clearly there was a need for national regulation if the industry was to develop beyond this early stage.

Such legislation was provided by the adoption of the 'Provisional Measures for Managing Securities Investment Funds (the "1997 Fund Measures")' in late 1997.[4] The 1997 Fund Measures affirmed the important contributions funds could make to the markets if their operations

Table 7.3: Trends in fund establishment (1991–1999)

	1991	1992	1993	1994	1995	1996	1997	1998	3Q 1999
Funds	2	57	10	6	0	0	0	5	10

Source: Cao Fengqi, p. 224

Table 7.4: Illustrative role definition in the management of investment funds

	Fund promoter	Fund manager	Custodian
Banks	9	1	18
Trust companies	51	34	30
Securities companies	20	13	3
Insurance companies	3	0	1
Enterprises	17	17	0
Government	1	0	0
Totals	101	65	52

Source: Cao Fengqi, p. 233

were properly managed. Together with supplementary measures,[5] they clarified and standardized the structure of funds, as well as the obligations of fund managers, trustee banks and investors and placed all approval, regulatory and supervisory authority with the CSRC. With the passage of the 1997 Fund Measures a base was established for the organization and promotion of new funds. In 1998 five new funds were organized and listed followed by ten more through the third quarter of 1999. These 15 funds are closed-end in character and range in total contributed funds from RMB2.0–3.0 billion, and in all raised some RMB35 billion or US$4.2 billion. Each fund has tended to have joint promoters with the fund manager being affiliated with one of them. Fund performance and principal investments are posted on a weekly basis by the exchanges and their activity is closely watched by the investing public given their combined market weight. With daily trading volume in, for example, Shanghai of around RMB4.5 billion, fund managers can have an impact on the market as well as on individual company shares. This was, for example, especially evident when both the SSE and SZSE experienced the famous government sponsored 60 per cent run-up during the period 19 May to 30 June 1999. Table 7.5 illustrates for 10 August 1999, the weightings of certain shares in fund holdings to illustrate this point.

7.5.1 Securities fund performance, 1997–October 1999

Since the standardized securities funds are being seen by the regulators as a less dangerous path into the A share market for such sensitive industries as insurance, a quick look at their performance may provide a better understanding of things to come. As at 30 September 1999, there were 8 Shanghai listed funds and 7 Shenzhen listed funds with the oldest established in April 1998. Analysis here focuses on NAV and closing price

Table 7.5: Summary of 1997 provisional fund measures

Item	Description
● Type of fund	Open or closed-end
● Promoter	Securities companies, trust and investment companies and fund management companies
● Promoter qualifications	3 years or more of securities investment experience
	RMB300 million or more of capital (excl. fund management companies)
	Sustained profitability
● Closed-end fund:	Investment held by Promoter determined by CSRC as % of total fund
	Fund life of at least 5 years
	Minimum size of RMB200 million
a) Subscription period	3 months from date of CSRC approval
	Establishment approved if 80% of planned amount is raised
b) Listing	Promoter and trustee can apply on approval of establishment
● Open-end fund:	Minimum size of RMB200 million
a) Subscription period	3 months from date of CSRC approval
	If subscription fails, the promoters are liable for all costs
	If subscription fails all funds must be returned to subscribers with interest
● Fund management company	Establishment approved by CSRC
a) Promoters	Securities companies and trust and investment companies
	3 years of profitable operations
	RMB300 million in capital
b) Capitalization	Minimum of RMB10 million
c) Scope of business	Fund management; fund promoter
● Fund investment restrictions	Not less than 80% invested in shares and debt securities
	Not more than 10% of one fund invested in the shares of one company
	A fund manager managing more than one fund cannot invest more than 10% of the total of all funds in the shares of one company
	Not less than 20% invested in Chinese Government Bonds

since all funds are closed-end. This means that after the initial subscription period, when an investor buys or sells fund units on the market the fund manager does not receive or redeem them. The units simply trade on the secondary market as shares of the fund itself. Consequently, the secondary market price of fund units can vary significantly from the actual value of the funds assets. This price discrepancy is called either the premium or discount to net asset value or 'NAV'. The premium or discount is driven, in part, by NAV performance, that is, by how well the fund manager does his or her job. And it is also, in part, driven by sentiment and supply and demand considerations. Since the standardization of funds in 1997, fund performance can be divided into three periods: pre-June 1999 rally, post-June 1999 rally period and the post-October 1999 period as defined by insurance company involvement.

The pre-June 1999 rally period was a time of high premiums based on very little underlying share performance. This tells more about the investor mentality toward this new product class than anything about how the funds were managed. The first two funds opened at premiums of 100 per cent above their NAV, but there followed a year of continuous premium contraction as investors gained a better understanding of the linkage between NAV and closing prices. NAVs showed little change as the fund managers remained cautious in outlook and the stock market itself was stagnant. The initially large premium and its gradual decline can be attributed to the retail investor expectation of IPOs in general. In other words, it appears that investors did not fully understand how securities funds should be valued. It was an expensive lesson for those who bought in that first year and did not get out. As more funds were listed, few were able to distinguish themselves among the pack and all funds traded with similar premiums. By mid May 1999, however, most funds were trading around NAV and this coincided with the rally in the stock market.

Propelled by the June 1999 rally, the funds generally performed well, at least in terms of NAV, with a number out performing the Shanghai A share index. These NAV gains failed to correspond to equivalent gains in unit closing prices, consequently, the funds began to trade at a discount to NAV. This can probably best be explained by the dominance of direct stock trading. When investors poured into the market, they bought up favorite names rather than go through the securities funds. This is not to say that the funds were not oversubscribed upon issue or that their absolute returns were not good; many showed returns of over 20 per cent in a 3-month period. It merely shows the problems of closed-end funds as an investment vehicle.

A new phase has begun since October 1999 when insurance companies were allowed to enter into the market indirectly via the funds.

Table 7.6: Major holdings of funds (10 August 1999)

Company share	Fund	Fund holding as % of free float	Fund holding as % of fund capital
Eastern Electric	Anxin	11.8	3.0
Huanbao Shares	Anxin, Antai	17.5	4.5
Youth Travel	Anxin, Anshun	25.7	9.6
Shiyi Shares	Anxin, Anshun, Xinghua	26.4	7.0
Fenghua Technology	Yuyang, Yulong	31.5	8.4
Dongda Er-pai	Yuyang, Xinghua	13.7	4.7
Shenzhen	Yuyang, Jinghong,	10.0	2.5
Technology	Jintai, Hansheng		
Taiji Group	Yuyang	15.8	4.0
Lekai Film	Yuyang, Yulong,	27.7	10.2
	Puhui		
Tongjunge	Yuyang, Yulong,	37.5	9.1
	Puhui, Anxin, Tongyi		
	Kaiyuan, Jinghong, Hansheng		
Shenzhen Airport	Kaiyuan	19.5	6.5
Xifei International	Kaiyuan	14.6	5.2
Nanjing Technology	Kaiyuan	10.7	4.0
Shanghai Sanmao	Kaiyuan, Jinghong	41.6	14.2
Eastern Telecoms	Kaiyuan, Taihe	15.5	1.6
Tongren Tang	Xinghua, Puhui, Anxin	31.5	7.9
Hunan Investment	Xinghua	10.5	4.5
Guofeng Plastics	Xinghua	22.6	7.6
Fuxing Industries	Xinghua	20.4	6.1
Yue Kaifa	Puhui	20.9	7.7
Yongan Forestry	Puhui	7.9	2.2
ST Shen Huabao	Puhui	7.9	2.2
Guangzhou Holdings	Puhui	6.0	0.9

Source: China Securities Daily, 10 August 1999

Table 7.7: Chinese fund management companies profiles

Name	Date established	Shareholders	Capital (RMB MM)
Hua-An Fund Mgmnt Co.	6/4/98	● SITIC, 60% ● Shenyin Intl, 20% ● Shandong Sec, 20%	50
Southern Fund Mgmnt Co.	3/6/98	● Southern Sec ● Xiamen ITIC ● Guangxi TIC	50
Huaxia Fund Mgmnt Co		● Huaxia Sec ● Beijing Sec ● China Sci-Tech ITIC	70
Shenzhen Investment Fund Mgmnt Co.	10/8/92	NA	100
Shenzhen Peninsula Investment Fund Mgmnt Co	3/94	NA	100
Shenzhen Lantian Fund Mgmnt Co	12/92	● SZ Non-Ferrous Metals Finance, 51% ● CITIC Ind. Bank, 20% ● ICBC, 20% ● SZ SEZ Dev Finance, 9%	50

Source: China Securities Yearbook 1998, pp.140–1

This phase looks set to be another period of excessive speculative activity. For example, a newly listed fund, which had been established in 1992, began trading on 28 October 1999. The fund consisted of 200 million units valued at an NAV of RMB1.09 per unit and its opening trade the day of its listing was RMB2.45. In other words, investors paid RMB2.45 per unit versus RMB1.09 per unit NAV which represented the actual value of shares they could buy directly in the market themselves. The unit price then traded to a high of RMB10 and closed the day at RMB6.2. Trading volume was nearly 500 million RMB for a fund whose NAV was only RMB218 million. Why did the market trade like this? The only possible answer is that such behavior highlights how irrational exuberance – how else can this be explained – still plays a powerful role in the fund market. Interestingly the fund in question was suspended from trading the day after its huge run up when the manager made a public announcement warning investors of the potential risks of stock trading. Having covered himself in this way, the manager then announced a rights issue of RMB1.3 billion! The trading in the other more established funds has remained more restrained.

The interaction of insurance companies, securities funds and the market, will determine whether the government's apparent plan to use the funds as a vehicle to broaden market participation will go forward. At the end of 1999 funds have been used to include retail and now insurance funds and there has been talk about using the funds to revive the B share markets. If all that were to go well, it could be that the funds would be used to channel foreign capital participation in the A share market. But all this is well in the future and depends heavily on the professional development of Chinese fund management companies.

7.5.2 Fund investment characteristics

At present most funds have rather similar mandates and investment strategies, although two funds, Xinghe and Pufeng, are so-called index funds which invest most of their assets in the Shanghai and Shenzhen blue chips indices. Even these, however, are required by regulation to maintain 20 per cent of total assets in CGBs. The general lack of differentiation will likely disappear over time through survival of the fittest and specialization. At the end of 1999, however, this market segment is young: putting aside the old 75 funds, only five funds established under the 1997 regulations have a history of over one year. The concept that long term performance should be a key measure of fund performance is virtually non-existent, so selecting a fund manager is very difficult. As more time passes a clear picture of good fund managers will emerge and this natural ranking should drive the ability of firms to launch additional funds. As for specialization, perhaps the demands of insurance companies for better products will incent different firms to specialize in different market sectors. A 'hi-tech' or 'telecoms' only fund would not be surprising nor would more conservative utility or property orientated funds. If structured well, each would offer a different level of risk and potential return and allow the insurance companies, individuals and eventually pension funds to better allocate their resources.

7.5.3 Case study: Hua-An Fund Management Co. and the Anxin Fund

The Hua-An Fund Management Company was one of the original five pilot fund management companies established under the 1997 Fund Measures. Based in Shanghai, Hua-An now runs two funds, the Anxin Fund (Market Code: 500003) launched in June 1998 and the Anshun Fund (500009) launched in June 1999. The company has a registered capital base of RMB50 million. Its principal shareholders are Shanghai International Trust and Investment Company (RMB13 million), Shenyin Wanguo Securities Company and Shandong Securities Company with each of the latter two firms contributing RMB10 million. Details of the Anxin Fund are shown in Table 7.8. Of the 2 billion fund units, 1.94 billion were sold to the public and the other 60 million sold were sold to the fund sponsors. The public portion was 52 times over subscribed and one might wonder why.

All funds provide a close of business Friday net asset value figure which is widely distributed in the press, internet and exchange-based systems (for example the *Qianlong* system). The funds also provide a breakdown of their bond and stocks holdings on a quarterly basis. Table 7.9 illustrates how Hua-An has allocated funds between equities and bonds over the past year in the Anxin Fund to give a feel for how this fund, and its recently listed sister fund, have been managed. Chart 7.1 shows how the same fund has traded since inception.

As mentioned before the premium or discount of Chinese funds has proven to be a significant risk given volatile markets. Table 7.10 lists the premium or discount for each of the 15 existing funds as of 8 October 1999. While there is on average a slight discount, the three funds with the largest premiums include the two 'index' funds, Pufeng and Xinghe, and the Tianyuan fund which invests in only Blue Chip equities and bonds. It is, therefore, perhaps not surprising that they are leading the fund market. The 15 funds have a simple average discount to NAV of 3.45 per cent, although the range of premiums and discount is quite wide. As an asset class, the securities funds seem set to become an increasingly important force in the equity markets. With over RMB35 billion already invested over the past year and maturities of 15 years, their returns and development will become a matter of concern for all domestic equity watchers.

In addition to these domestic funds, there are 26 international funds dedicated to China and managed by well-known professional fund

Table 7.8: Terms and conditions, the Anxin Fund

Terms	Description
Fund type	Closed-end
Offering date	16 June 1998
Placement	200 million units
Face value	RMB1 per unit
Investment scope	Bonds and shares listed in China
Investment objective	LT capital appreciation via investments in treasury bonds and stocks listed in China
Investment restrictions	● 20% net assets must be in CGBs ● Not less than 80% of net assets in stocks and CGBs ● Investment in 1 company must be less than 10% of net assets ● Investment in 1 company not more than 10% of company's total capital
Maturity	15 years
Buyers	Natural persons residing in China
Management fee	2.5% per annum
Distribution policy	Not less than 90% of net earnings
Custodian	ICBC

Table 7.9: Asset allocation, the Anxin Fund

Period	Anxin Fund %		Anshun Fund %	
Quarterly	Equity	Bond	Equity	Bond
3Q 98	47.8	49.7	–	–
4Q 98	66.8	34.3	–	–
1Q 99	64.9	35.4	–	–
2Q 99	79.1	21.2	–	–
3Q 99	78.8	21.5	78.8	21.2

Source: Wind Information System

Chart 7.1: Anxin Fund closing price versus NAV per unit

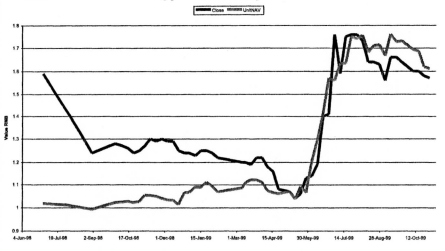

Source: Wind Information System

Table 7.10: Premium/discount status of funds (8 October 1999)

Code	Fund name	Price close, RMB	NAV, RMB	Premium/Discount
4688	Kaiyuan	1.31	1.4678	-10.75%
4689	Puhui	1.25	1.384	-9.68%
4690	Tongyi	1.23	1.3568	-9.35%
4691	Jinghong	1.18	1.2732	-7.32%
4692	Yulong	1.11	1.1237	-1.22%
4693	Pufeng	1.06	0.9884	7.24%
4698	Tianyuan	1.05	0.9891	6.16%
500001	Jintai	1.25	1.3543	-7.70%
500002	Taihe	1.14	1.1544	-1.25%
500003	Anxin	1.6	1.6938	-5.54%
500005	Hansheng	1.21	1.3089	-7.56%
500006	Yuyang	1.48	1.5526	-4.68%
500008	Xinghua	1.33	1.4996	-11.31%
500009	Anshun	1.12	1.0925	2.52%
500018	Xinghe	1.08	0.9937	8.68%

Source: Wind Information Systems

managers, for example, Templeton. The total value of these mostly closed-end funds as of 22 November 1999 was US$632 million or an average fund size of about US$24 million, which is quite small.

7.6 Securities companies and the Chinese Glass-Steagall Act

The securities firms, however, remain the principal players in the Chinese equity markets at the present. Over the past several years, and particularly as the reform of the banking system was pressed beginning in 1994, the government's effort has been to create a Glass-Steagall-like segregation between securities firms and banks, whereby banks were prohibited from owning securities firms. The first step in this process was the separation of the PBOC branch system from all economic entities including securities firms.[6] In December 1993, the State Council issued a further decision aimed at separating out and making independent each entity of the banking system, the securities industry and industrial enterprises.[7] Although the State Council permitted banks and industrial enterprises to invest in financial institutions including securities firms, it prohibited securities firms from investing in any sector but the securities industry. In 1994 the PBOC severed the MOF and local government finance departments from involvement in ownership of securities firms. In 1995 the State Council prohibited the major banks from owning trust and investment corporations, which, in turn, usually either owned a securities firm or had their own internal securities department.

The Securities Law confirmed this segregation in Article 6.[8] The same article also states that securities firms shall be established independently of the same three sectors. On the passage of the law the CSRC announced that it would review all securities firms and only then reissue their business licenses.[9] This was meant to have been completed by 1 July 1999, but the CSRC encountered practical difficulties as it sought to sever existing relationships which ran foul of this article.[10] As of the end of 1998 a survey estimated that there were 90 securities firms and 237 securities trading units controlled by trust and investment companies.[11] Of these, there are seven with capital of over RMB1 billion (US$120 million), while the average capital of the typical firm is RMB30 million. The best capitalized company, Shanghai Shenyin Wangguo, has capital of RMB1.4 billion and is one of the industry leaders. But thin overall capitalization characterizing the industry has increasingly become a matter of concern and 1999 has witnessed a surge of industry consolidation in order to suit the requirements of the Securities Law.

The Securities Law establishes two categories of securities firm: (1) comprehensive securities firms; and (2) brokerage firms. The two are subject to different regulation and receive different licenses. The principal difference between the two is their scope of business and minimum registered capital. A comprehensive firm must have a minimum of RMB500 million in capital, whereas a brokerage needs only RMB50 million.[12] In terms of business scope, as might be expected, the less capitalized brokerage firms can only carry out brokerage business. In contrast, comprehensive firms may broker securities, conduct proprietary trading, act as securities underwriters and seek approval for other securities business from the CSRC.

Given the relatively large capital requirements for comprehensive firms, the first half of 1999 witnessed frenzied efforts among industry participants to merge and, thereby, meet the new capital requirements. The CSRC to date has not approved such mergers[13] and it has delayed issuing new licenses while the government considers how to address the situation. It can be expected, in any event, that the number of large securities firms will decrease significantly and that, therefore, the volume of trading in the market will decline correspondingly.

Consideration is also being given to ways to finance the comprehensive firms. Without access to bank credit, securities firms have had only the repo market for government securities as a financing tool. Thought is now being given to permitting the use of shares as loan collateral and allowing participation in the interbank government bond market.[14] By year end 1999 11 securities firms have been permitted access to the first level interbank market and it is expected that the use of shares as collateral for loans will be permitted in the near future.

Now that China has effectively established a US-style industry, the recent decision by the US government and Congress to do away with the restrictions of Glass-Steagall is worth keeping in mind. Having spent several years and made a significant effort to creating a banking system similar to that of the US under Glass-Steagall, some senior Chinese officials are now pondering whether or not the universal banks of Europe might not be better models for China going forward.

7.7   Investor base for overseas listed Chinese shares and B shares

The preceding discussion has dealt with the current investor base for China's A share market. Obviously, the investor base for China's internationally listed equity securities is significantly different. Looking into the investor base for international securities is the realm of the Equity Capital Markets ('ECM') Departments of the world's investment banks. ECM personnel are responsible for knowing the likes of all investors

Table 7.11: Top 20 securities firms by underwriting and total assets (FY1997)

Name	U/W amount	Trading volume RMB MM	Total assets	Total assets US$ MM	Net profit RMB MM	Net profit US$ MM
1 China Southern	12 782	205 230	15 528	1 875	273	33
2 Shenyin Wangguo	10 555	215 807	16 732	2 021	501	61
3 Guotai	9 539	145 122	51 008	6 160	298	36
4 J&A	8 641	212 200	17 565	2 121	741	89
5 Guangfa	7 898	195 685	69 057	8 340	245	30
6 CITIC	7 818	NR	41 190	4 975	498	60
7 Guoxin	5 348	75 337	45 425	5 486	381	46
8 Huaxia	5 298	253 252	11 060	1 336	216	26
9 Haitong	4 185	160 360	10 267	1 240	304	37
10 Hubei	3 268	53 217	24 461	2 954	NR	NR
11 Guangda	2 937	80 338	31 239	3 773	220	27
12 Dapeng	2 813	61 645	40 337	4 872	105	13
13 China Merchants	2 780	74 321	29 824	3 602	185	22
14 Beijing	1 586	NR	25 285	3 054	NR	NR
15 Jiangsu	1 431	144 400	48 110	5 810	141	17
16 Gansu	1 330	NR	NR	NR	NR	NR
17 Fujian Xingye	833	81 661	NR	NR	278	34
18 Guangdong	706	126 365	40 628	4 907	130	16
19 Shanghai Finance	NR	NR	56 760	6 855	205	25
20 Hunan	NR	52 972	NR	NR	199	24

Source: Handbook of Chinese Securities; NR signifies Not Ranked

and then tailoring an equity product which can successfully suit investor taste, that is, be sold. Such information is extremely proprietary, it goes without saying. In the following sections, the intention, therefore, is simply to touch on this topic.

H shares

Investors in the H share market are relatively easy to identify and anyone with access to Bloomburg or Dow-Jones can see who has invested in whom on a slightly time-lagged basis. H shares represent large and significant Chinese companies and their offerings have on average been well in excess of US$100 million. When distributing such shares, the investment bank leading the underwriting typically reserves about 10–20 per cent of the offering for the Hong Kong retail market (individual investors) while the remaining 80 per cent is marked for placement to a variety of professional investors in Asia, Europe and the USA. Such professional investors include specialists in emerging market equities, hedge funds and specialist industry groups. The specialists may work at small hedge funds, major pension funds, and mutual fund companies. The major point is that all such institutional investors are professionals, are typically supported by large internal staff groups and have clearly defined investment parameters. In contrast, retail or individual investors generally make investment decisions based on current news, market fads and so on, but without the sort of analysis a professional typically uses. This is not to say, however, that professionals do not get caught up in current news and fads. In fact, the review in the Chapter 8 of the market performance of Chinese shares illustrates the extent to which Chinese equities (as a subset of emerging market equities) have at times swept all before them.

Red Chips

In contrast to H shares, the Red Chips share great similarities with the B and A share companies and markets, since they represent investment opportunities with a common characteristic: the issuing companies are long on sentiment and 'concept' but, in the great majority of cases, short on fundamentals. Having said this, there are distinctions in the investor base for each of these three types of equity securities as well as between, for example, Shanghai and Shenzhen A shares.

As with the H shares, data is available from the major wire services in relation to the top ten minority shareholders of a given Red Chip, but this does not really get at the question of what type of investors make the market in this type of shares. The definition of a Red Chip, however, sheds some light on the likely investor base. The SEHK has defined Red Chips with a great deal of preciseness as Hong Kong-listed companies with significant equity controlled by entities in mainland China:[15]

1. the company should have at least a 35 per cent shareholding directly held by either:
   a. mainland entities which are defined to include state-owned organizations, provincial or municipal authorities in mainland China; or
   b. listed or privately owned Hong Kong companies (Hong Kong or overseas incorporated) which are controlled by (a) above;
2. the company should have been listed for at least 12 months on the SEHK;
3. the company should have at least a 12-month trading record after having satisfied criterion (1) above;
4. the company should not have more than 20 trading days without turnover during the past 12 months, excluding days when the company was suspended from trading;
5. the company must not be a constituent stock of the Hang Seng China Enterprises Index (the H share Index).

The combination of points 1 through 3 above strongly suggests that Chinese government organizations, through their Hong Kong companies, are significant participants in the Red Chip secondary market. In addition, Hong Kong retail investors are unquestionably active. Finally, international investors have participated strongly in this market at times, particularly during its massive run up in late 1997. A list of the constituents of the Red Chip Index is included in the Appendix.

B shares

The investor base for Shanghai and Shenzhen B shares differs due to the geographic location of the two cities. Shanghai is a relatively more domestic market as compared to Shenzhen, which increasingly represents a vibrant mix of southern China and Hong Kong. Many legal residents of Hong Kong live, shop and work in Shenzhen. Border crossings are made easily by directly connecting trains and efficient immigration services. The HK dollar is widely used among Chinese residents in Shenzhen and throughout Guangdong province and Renminbi is easily available to anyone. In short, Shenzhen B shares (and A shares as well) are highly permeable to investors other than those clearly defined in Chinese regulations.

There is evidence to support the conclusion reached above. For example, the *Shanghai Stock Exchange 1998 Fact Book* carries data that show that over 66 per cent of B share account holders opened at brokerages in Shanghai are of Chinese nationality. Because Shanghai is more of a true 'mainland' market, it should be the case that there would be fewer Chinese-owned B share accounts and this is, in fact, the case if one considers that a good proportion of Shenzhen Hong Kong accounts belong to mainland Chinese. Combined, Chinese and Hong Kong accounts represent nearly 90 per cent of all Shenzhen B share accounts.

As this review suggests, the first part of China's experiment with equity markets was the easy part – restructure a few enterprises and list their shares. The focus is now changing to the second stage of market development. First with the investment fund rules of 1997 and then the more recent decisions to permit insurance companies to invest in shares indirectly, specific steps are being taken to broaden the market. China's participation in the WTO may hasten this process since the government has agreed to permit foreign involvement in the A share markets through joint ventures in the asset management industry. The success of this stage is critical if China's markets are to develop away from their current emerging market status.

Table 7.12: Ownership of Shanghai B share accounts by country (1998)

	Shanghai		Shenzhen	
Nationality of A/C Owner	Number of Accounts		Number of Accounts	
China mainland	51 712	66.3%	50 501	47.5%
Hong Kong	8 981	11.5%	44 988	42.3%
USA	5 032	6.5%	2 932	2.8%
Taiwan	2 253	2.9%	998	0.9%
Japan	1 868	2.4%	305	0.3%
Macau	295	0.4%	1 415	1.3%
United Kingdom	1 200	1.5%	971	0.9%
Canada	1 133	1.5%	612	0.6%
Australia	1 109	1.4%	629	0.6%
Others	4 386	5.6%	2 998	2.8%
Total	77 969	100%	105 909	100%

Source: China Securities and Futures 1999 Statistical Yearbook, p. 78

8
Market Trends and Performance

Like emerging markets elsewhere, China's equity markets have proven quite cyclical and, in the midst of that cyclicality, extremely volatile. The market's character reflects the influence of two factors: (1) investor sentiment about the country's overall economic performance; and (2) government policy. In spite of the rollercoaster ride of the years since 1992, the experiment with shares and stock markets has long since ceased being an experiment. Almost all market regulations are no longer 'provisional' and market infrastructure and institutions have a feeling of permanence. Equity ownership is now not only a firmly entrenched part of Chinese policy, it is, for better or for worse, the principal direction of the government's financial and corporate reform efforts. By some measures, China's domestic markets now rank as the second or third largest in non-Japan Asia in terms of market capitalization. By discussing market cycles, volatility, capital raised and overall market performance this chapter assembles all the pieces of this ongoing experiment with equity ownership without privatization to illustrate how they have fit together in the marketplace.

8.1 A closed, isolated system

The basic fact of China's domestic markets is that they operate in a closed system. Any influence from either the Asian region or elsewhere in the world, including the US, is fairly muted, if not smothered altogether. This reality is highlighted by a comparison of the performance of the Shanghai A share market, Hong Kong Hang Seng Index and the Dow Jones Industrials. Chart 8.1 covers the two years from the beginning of 1998 to early November of 1999. This period witnessed

Chart 8.1: Shanghai A shares, Hang Seng and Dow Jones Industrials

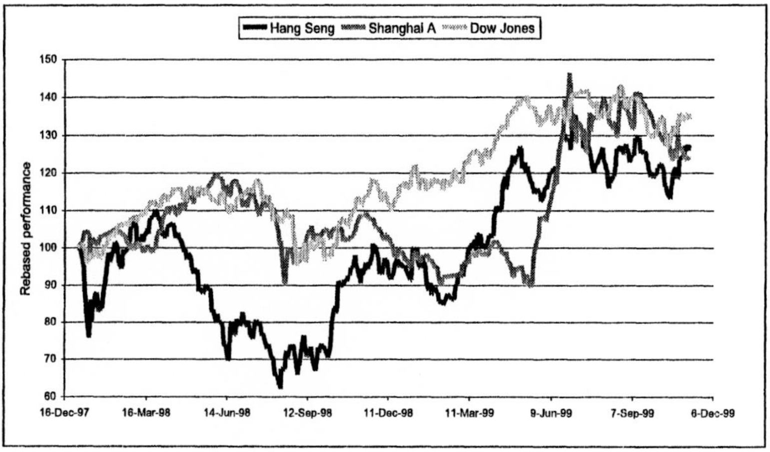

Source: Bloomberg and Wind Information System

extremely significant events in each of the markets: the meltdown of the Asian financial markets in the first weeks of 1998, the late summer 1998 Russian default and the near collapse of Long Term Capital Management (LTCM) in the USA. On the Chinese side, the period covers the spectacular rally in the early summer of 1999. Despite these major events, which could be expected to impact all markets more or less equally, the Shanghai, Hong Kong and New York markets performed, at times, in strikingly different ways.

The early 1998 sell off in Asia hardly affected Wall Street or the Chinese markets. Wall Street and the Hang Seng suffered the most from the Russian debacle and the Shanghai and Shenzhen rallies failed to impact either Hong Kong or Wall Street despite a 60 per cent climb in May and June of 1999. The interrelationship between these three markets, or the lack of it, can be further illustrated by correlation analysis (see Table 8.1).[1] At 10 per cent the correlation between Shanghai and the Dow is so small as to be nearly meaningless. And even the relationship between Shanghai and the Hang Seng at 19 per cent is quite weak. The same relationship, or lack of one, between the two international markets and the Shenzhen market also holds. This shows how successful Chinese government restrictions have been at isolating the domestic A share markets. The non-convertibility of the Renminbi, of course, is perhaps the major determinant of this isolation, but it is by no means the only one. Even if an international investor is determined to find

Table 8.1: Inter-market correlations, Shanghai, Hong Kong and Dow Jones

Index	Hang Seng	Shanghai A	Dow Jones
Hang Seng	100%	19%	54%
Shanghai A	19%	100%	10%
Dow Jones	54%	10%	100%

Source: Bloomberg and Wind Information System

channels to gain local market exposure, and some have, it is not easy to achieve sufficient size to have an appreciable impact.

Since bond markets and equity markets are closely linked internationally, a quick comparison of US markets with China's domestic government bond market may be useful. Here again the lack of correlation is true. Although not directly covered in this book, the domestic bond market and the falling interest rate environment prevailing since 1996 have been major factors driving the stock market rise.

The Chinese government bond (CGB) issued in June 1996, known as CGB 696, is listed on the Shanghai exchange and has until very late in 1999 been the principal bellwether of the domestic bond markets given its relatively large size and liquidity. The lack of correlation between US Treasuries and this CGB is obvious as shown in Chart 8.2. When the US bond prices rose sharply as a consequence of the Russian default in the summer of 1998, Chinese domestic yields hardly changed. And as China's interest rates have ratcheted down to head off deflation, those in the USA have headed in the other direction to head off inflation. The conclusion here is that China is not yet a part of the global village. This does not mean, however, that the CGB market has no linkage with domestic equity markets. It most certainly does just as international bond markets are linked with international equity markets.

In short, China's domestic securities markets are effectively isolated from world financial markets and events. This reality is unlikely to change in the near future even with the country's accession to WTO. Both the Mexican financial crisis of the 1980s, as well as the recent Asian crisis have left a deep impression on a government that, for historical reasons, is extremely sensitive about control over its financial and banking markets.

8.2 Market cycles

China's economic development since 1979 has been characterized by exceptionally high real GDP growth rates. For the decade of the 1980s

Chart 8.2: Performance of CGB 696 versus the 10-year US Treasury Bond

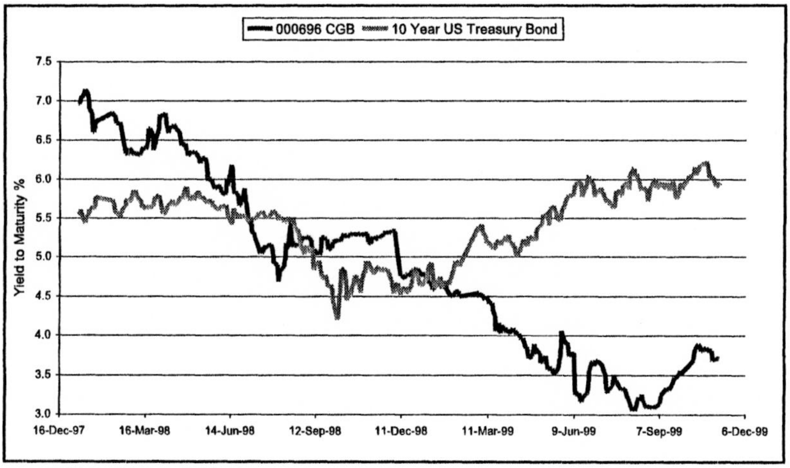

Source: Bloomberg and Qianlong

average real GDP growth was over 9 per cent and the 1990s have maintained approximately the same level in spite of a deflationary trend at their end. Given the size of the country, its population and transitional economic structure, it is not surprising that there have been periodic economic dislocations typified by high inflation rates. One such period occurred in the late 1980s. Efforts to cool inflation led to a period of economic and political stagnation that extended into the 1990s. Back on track again, China's economic development shot ahead from 1992 to 1994, but this again induced extremely high rates of inflation which peaked at the end of 1994 at 21.7 per cent. Measures to control inflation were successful, somewhat unexpectedly, but have since driven the economy into a period of seemingly unstoppable deflation in 1998 and 1999. This story by now is very well-known.

China's domestic equity markets have shown the strong influence of these two major economic cycles which are clearly illustrated in Charts 8.1 and 8.3. Looked at more closely, however, these two cycles can be broken down into four shorter cycles in the equity markets – two booms and two busts, three of which are complete and the fourth ongoing.

Cycle 1: the time of the H shares: 1992–94. The first cycle turned out to be the longest, if not the largest, in terms of number of issues and amount raised. Driven by the sheer enthusiasm of both domestic and

Chart 8.3: China inflation and GDP growth trends (1990–99P)

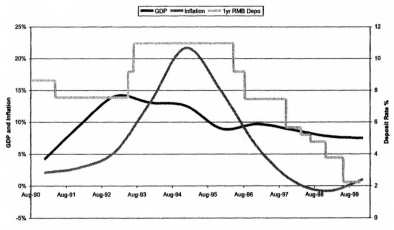

Source: China Statistical Yearbook

international investors, it was touched off by Deng Xiaoping's Southern Journey during which he confirmed that the stock market experiment was 'good' and should be continued in a 'determined fashion'. This gave everyone involved the political cover needed to proceed at the fastest pace possible in case the 'window' closed. During this two-and-a-half year period Chinese shares were in extremely heavy demand by investors everywhere from Milwaukee to Wuhan. Any security even remotely Chinese could be sold, including B share companies. In October 1992, the State Council announced the first batch of Chinese companies designated to offer shares on the SEHK. This was the era of Barton Bigg's unforgettable pronouncement that he was 'maximum bullish on China'. The agonized listing of Huaneng International Power Development on the New York Stock Exchange in October 1994 marked the end of this cycle.

Cycle 2: macroeconomic control: late 1994–96. The second cycle was a prolonged market downturn reflecting an extremely overheated domestic economy. The macroeconomic controls put in place in mid 1994 by then Vice Premier Zhu Rongji involved not only interest rate hikes, but also various administrative measures limiting credit and investment project approvals. Inflation peaked in late 1994, when the national consumer price index increased by 21.7 per cent, then began a gradual month-by-month decline through 1995 and 1996. One of the anti-inflation measures included a virtual halt to the approval of new equity listings both domestically and internationally. This, plus the concern investors, and particularly international investors had with regard not just to the economy's future, but also that of the country itself, explains why B share issues dropped from 23 in 1993 to seven in 1994, while A share issues declined from 125 in 1993 to 36 in 1995. This cycle bottomed out in 1995 when there were only 40 domestic issues in total in both markets. Similarly, overseas shares in 1994 recorded only two issues in the second half of the year and only two for the entire year of 1995. These were difficult years for investment bankers specializing in China.

Cycle 3: the Red Chip craze: 1996–97. By the end of 1995 inflation rates were clearly trending down and in early 1996 the government began efforts to develop a fourth group of H share IPO candidates, which was announced at the end of the year. This was also the start of the run up to the Hong Kong handover. The domestic A share markets recovered and a total of 203 issues were completed as inflation declined to below 5 per cent while GDP growth remained at nearly 10 per cent. It seemed that China's economy had indeed achieved a soft landing. This result propelled Zhu Rongji into the premiership, an appointment which was welcomed by everyone. The IPO markets continued strong into 1997 when a further 206 companies listed in Shanghai and Shenzhen. The H share market mirrored this trend with six IPOs completed in 1996 and 16 in 1997. The period was characterized by the frenzied high point of the Red Chip listings, including the largest China IPO to date, China Telecom, completed on the eve of the Hong Kong market crash in mid October 1997. China Telecom's IPO for all intents and purposes was both the high point and the end of the third cycle.

Cycle 4: waiting for China Unicom: 1998 – present. The fourth cycle to the end of 1999 has not provided a welcoming market for equity issuance, except for China Telecom. This was a function of two factors. First, China has not been wholly immune from the Asian financial crisis, its export growth has shrunk drastically and committed foreign direct investment growth turned negative for the first time since the early 1990s. Now, two plus years after its outbreak in 1997 the crisis had bottomed out in several Asian countries, yet China's economy continues to be characterized by a deflationary trend. Sentiment toward China, therefore, is directionless. The second factor relates to

Chart 8.4: Number of Chinese IPOs, all markets (1990–3rd quarter 1999)

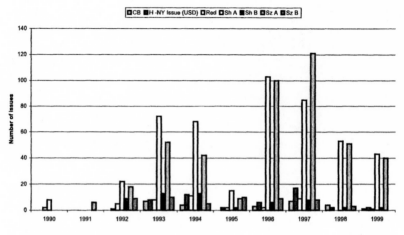

Source: Bloomberg and Wind Information System

uncontrolled, and perhaps uncontrollable, overinvestment during the early 1990s. This created what one person has called 'a big, dumb economy' with significant oversupply of most consumer goods, for example white goods and commodity markets. Overinvestment, in turn, was a result of the incomplete nature of SOE reform. Added to that, the SOE and government agency reform measures of 1998 created a serious threat to state sector employment, causing people to fear for their jobs and, therefore, halt all discretionary consumption. This, the oversupply and consequent sharp consumer goods price competition, all had a negative impact on the non-state sector as well.

Domestic and international equity issues have been severely impacted by this uncertain economic environment. In 1998 there was a total of 107 issues (and only three B share issues) domestically and two internationally. The first half of 1999 has seen only 39 A share issues, no B share issues and only one H share IPO – a leftover from the Second Batch of 1994, Shandong International Power. In the second half, ever reliable China Telecom completed an acquisition of three additional provincial mobile phone companies for US$6 billion of which US$2 billion was easily raised internationally. Marring this success was the failure of the China National Offshore Oil IPO in October 1999. This failure was a poor omen for the much publicized government effort, expected in the year 2000, to list an entire industry, oil and gas, and thereby accomplish the reform of a major part of the state sector in one fell swoop. Should this bold plan fail it may have severe implications for the government's approach to SOE reform. Then there is China Unicom, the nation's second telecom company and the GITIC of the sector. The point is that after eight years of SOE reform through public listing, there seems at the end of the decade very little left to choose from except perhaps the financial sector and a budding internet industry.

8.3   Funds raised

Even though the corporatization effort has been relatively successful, at least from the point of view of fundraising, nonetheless, the absolute amount of financing remains relatively small compared to, for example, commercial bank loans. Over the decade of the 1990s total funds raised through share offerings amounted to US$49 billion of which the A share markets accounted for 65 per cent, or US$32 billion equivalent (at current at issue exchange rates). International investors have contributed the remainder with US$13 billion in the H share and other markets and US$4 billion in the B share markets. This clearly points out the critical importance, both strategic and tactical, of China's domestic markets to the corporatization effort. While the international markets are used to tame the big companies, the local markets are used to promote smaller and perhaps less attractive companies.

8.3.1   Domestic offerings

Both Shanghai and Shenzhen are comparable in terms of the number of A and B share IPOs as well as the total amount of funds raised. This should not come as a surprise given the discussion in Chapter 6 about the planned nature of the listing process. Both exchanges experienced particularly heavy amounts of A share issuance in 1997 and 1998; Shanghai raised US$7 billion over the two years and Shenzhen US$9 billion. Issuance of B shares showed a slight increase by both exchanges, although not to the levels enjoyed in 1992 and 1993 when they reached the peak of their popularity. The amount of funds raised in B shares, however, pales in comparison with both A shares and overseas issuance. During these two years, Shenzhen listed 11 B shares, raising US$600 million, while Shanghai offered 10 issues raising US$900 million. Over the ten years in which shares have been offered to China's public over US$32 billion has been raised in the A share

Chart 8.5: Value of all Chinese issues, all markets (1990–1st half 1999)

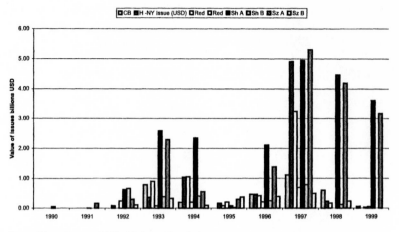

Source: Bloomberg and Wind Information System

market versus only US$4.6 billion in the B share market. This amount of money is significant and has allowed the offering size to grow almost to the size possible in Hong Kong as shown in Table 8.2. As noted previously, the average Chinese H-share IPO is around US$330 million, but only around 15–20 per cent, or US$60 million, of this on average is raised from the Hong Kong retail market, the remainder being placed internationally.[2] In contrast, the largest A share IPOs in 1997 and 1998 were well over US$200 million in size showing the potential strength of Chinese retail demand in the primary market. Although it does not like to be reminded that it was a medium-size regional exchange prior to 1993, and to a great extent still is, it must be said that the development of SEHK has come about largely on the back of Chinese company listings. As recently as 1993 the largest trans-actions ever done in Hong Kong were only US$100 million in size and there had only been two. China's exchanges, including Hong Kong, have come a long way very quickly.

8.3.2   Implications of the fundraising capacity of China's markets

The data on amount raised, the low penetration rate of share account holders and the basic absence of institutional investors suggest that each of the two markets is able to absorb at most about US$4–5 billion a piece annually. It also bears repeating here that, as of mid 1999, the combined A share market capitalization was approximately

Table 8.2: Funds raised via Shanghai A and B share issuance (1990–1st half 1999)

(000)	Shanghai A shares			Shanghai B shares		
	IPO (RMB)	Rights (RMB)	Total US$	IPO (RMB)	Rights (RMB)	Total US$
1990	261 000	0	31 522	0	0	0
1991	0	11 000	1 329	0	0	0
1992	3 617 000	0	436 836	654 680	0	654 680
1993	14 978 000	0	1 808 937	384 560	0	384 560
1994	19 896 000	0	2 402 899	406 830	0	406 830
1995	640 502	0	77 355	22 947	0	22 947
1996	13 046 000	4 495 000	2 118 478	212 000	39 000	251 000
1997	27 857 000	13 100 000	4 946 498	748 000	39 000	787 000
1998	23 069 000	13 924 000	4 467 754	118 000	0	118 000
1999	8 709 333	0	1 051 852	0	0	0
Total	112 073 835	31 530 000	17 343 460	2 547 017	78 000	2 625 017

Source: Shanghai Stock Exchange Market Statistics

Table 8.3: Funds raised via Shenzhen A and B shares issuance` (1990–1st half 1999)

(000)	Shenzhen A share RMB			Shenzhen B Share USD		
	IPO (RMB)	Rights (RMB)	Total, US$	IPO (HK$)	Rights (HK$)	Total US$
1990	0	0	0	0	0	0
1991	869 500	0	105 012	0	0	0
1992	1 736 300	0	209 698	870 080	0	112 413
1993	13 271 740	0	1 602 867	2 529 230	0	326 774
1994	4 687 770	0	566 156	714 260	0	92 282
1995	442 659	2 048 910	300 914	2 857 240	37 600	374 010
1996	8 873 850	2 594 870	1 385 111	2 789 880	207 450	387 252
1997	37 480 640	3 409 450	4 938 417	3 252 330	528 780	488 516
1998	18 639 110	16 064 480	4 191 255	1 766 650	48 470	234 512
1999	8 561 050	2 844 960	1 377 537	0	0	0
Total	94 562 619	26 962 670	14 676 967	14 779 670	822 300	2 015 758

Source: Shenzhen Stock Exchange Market Statistics

US$350 billion, of which two-thirds, or US$200 billion, is not listed and is as yet nontradable. All things being equal, it would, therefore, take around ten years to simply bring ownership to a 50:50 split between state and non-state investors and 40 years to eliminate the overhang entirely. To achieve something like this, however, would mean doing nothing but selling down state and legal person shares to the exclusion of bringing new companies to market. It appears, therefore, that the only solution is for the government to make a strong and consistent effort over time to develop and enlarge the markets in terms of the number and type of participants and amount of available capital. To fail to do so will not only limit the amount companies can raise, but also will condemn the market to remain speculative in character.

8.3.3 International offerings

There have been 47 offerings overseas by Chinese companies direct and four indirect listings of a majority foreign interest in Chinese joint ventures. These issues have raised in total approximately US$12.6 billion. For the most part these companies have been listed on the SEHK. However, when the scale reaches a certain amount, typically US$200 million and above, the investment banks will structure the offering as a 'dual listing'. To date, the vast majority of such dual listings have used the New York Stock Exchange as their second market. The CSRC, however, has reached agreements to list Chinese companies with the London Stock Exchange, the Tokyo Stock Exchange and the Singapore Stock Exchange and NASDAQ (and maybe a couple more here and there). The Hong Kong–New York axis, nonetheless, remains the principal listing structure of choice for large Chinese state-sponsored offerings. Similar to the domestic markets (and for much the same reasons), the peak year for international listing was 1997 when US$7.4 billion was raised. However, US$4.2 billion came from one issue alone, China Telecom

In addition to the initial public offerings, the CSRC has experimented with convertible bonds by permitting certain listed Chinese companies to issue either domestically or into the international markets. Convertible bonds combine the characteristics of debt and equity through the provision of an option to investors to convert the principal of the bond into equity of the issuer at a pre-defined share price within a defined time period. If the price of the company's shares increases above this pre-set price during the specified period, the issuer pays in shares not in cash. While this has the effect of diluting the original shareholders of the company, it does not affect the company's

Table 8.4: Top 10 IPOs in size, SSE and SZSE (1997–98)

	Company	No. of shares (MM)	Price per share (RMB)	Issue size (US$ MM)
Shanghai				
1999	Pudong Development Bank	320	40.0	483
1997	Handan Steel	350	7.5	317
1997	Shanghai Auto	300	7.02	254
1997	Gezhouba Hydropower	190	6.0	138
1997	Guangzhou Holdings	100	7.87	95
1997	China Eastern Airlines	300	2.45	89
1998	Hongqiao Airport	300	6.41	232
1998	Qilu Petrochemical	350	5.0	211
1998	Shanghai Construction	150	6.67	121
1998	Shanghai Bell	112	6.53	89
1998	Lianhua MSG	90	7.01	76
Shenzhen				
1997	First Auto Passenger Cars	300	6.8	246
1997	Angang New Steel	300	3.9	141
1997	Tangshan Steel	120	9.22	134
1997	Guangdong Fudi	120	7.75	112
1997	Saige Samsung	150	6.45	99
1998	Yangze Petrochemical	350	4.2	178
1998	Wuliangye Wine	80	14.77	143
1998	Taiyuan Steel	250	4.32	130
1998	Yunnan Copper	120	6.26	91
1998	Shenzhen Airport	100	6.38	77

Source: Wind Information System

cashflow. Nor does the company have to repay the bond principal unless the shares fail to perform. Of course, all such issuers' shares have failed to perform and, indeed, one frequent issuer has gone bankrupt, Guangdong Investment. With a maturity schedule concentrated in 2003 and 2004, it appears that many issuers will be forced to make thoroughly unwelcome cash principal repayments. Through the first half of 1999 there have been 27 convertible bond issues raising nearly US$3.5 billion.

8.3.4 Implications of international market capacity

Relatively speaking, the segment of the international market dedicated to investment in Chinese companies is quite small but it is, nonetheless, extremely important. China's domestic markets may continue to develop in scope and depth, but they are currently limited in their ability to absorb a major share issue. As the world knows, Chinese bank

Table 8.5: Number of overseas listings and amount raised (US$ 000)

Year	No. of listings	HK primary listing	Secondary listing	Total US$ issuance
1991	0	0	0	0
1992	1	0	80 000	80 000
1993	8	899 146	367 796	1 266 942
1994	12	1 050 478	1 033 080	2 083 558
1995	2	83 375	166 830	250 205
1996	5	568 213	216 790	785 003
1997	16	7 363 796	394 410	7 758 206
1998	2	167 757	232 470	400 227
1H 99	1	15 627	0	15 627
Total	47	10 148 392	2 491 376	12 639 768

Source: Bloomberg

savings have reached somewhere around US$700 billion, but too little is dedicated to equity investment. In the absence of adequate social security and medical insurance systems, the risk is perceived by most Chinese to be too high.

In contrast, China Telecom alone raised US$4.2 billion in its IPO in 1997, representing almost a full year's issuance for either the Shanghai or Shenzhen exchanges. The market capacity most definitely exists internationally for the right investment opportunity. The government's determination to corporatize and modernize the country's oil and gas industry at almost one go is a clear indication of the significance the international capital markets now have for China. It gives pause to

Table 8.6: Convertible bond issuance by Chinese companies

US$	No. of issues	Amount raised, US$
1990	0	0
1991	0	0
1992	0	0
1993	4	470 750 000
1994	6	596 000 000
1995	0	0
1996	2	263 250 000
1997	7	1 282 500 000
1998	6	642 270 530
1999	2	241 159 420
Total	27	3 495 929 950

Source: Bloomberg

consider the extent to which the Chinese government has exposed itself and its reform policy to the whims of international investors in these transactions.

8.4 Market capitalization and liquidity

The market capitalization of the Shanghai and Shenzhen exchanges at the end of June 1999 was equivalent to nearly US$360 billion, up over 50 per cent since the start of the year. All of that increase came after 19 May when the markets were boosted into orbit by the 15 June *People's Daily* editorial stating that the market turnaround (which had begun based on rumors of government intervention) reflected the long awaited fundamental upturn in the economy. This figure makes the two combined markets at the time the largest in Asia after Tokyo and Hong Kong. In contrast, the market capitalization of the New York Stock Exchange alone at the same time was approximately US$11 trillion.

The A share market capitalization represents the total value of all company shares tradable and nontradable valued at the market price per share. However, the accurate valuation of companies which have listed both domestic A shares and foreign currency denominated shares is difficult due to foreign currency inconvertibility. The question this situation poses is: what value should the 70 per cent nontradable shares for such companies be assigned. The exchanges have been unable to come to a conclusion. Consequently, for such companies the domestic market capitalization figures include only the value of A shares and nothing else, a treatment similar to the Stock Exchange of Hong Kong's treatment of H share market capitalization.

Liquidity is equally important as an indicator of a market's strength. Liquidity represents market depth by inferring capital availability for the purchase or sale of securities based on trading volume flows. This is important since strong liquidity will ensure greater pricing accuracy, enhance the willingness of investors to take larger positions (and greater market risk) and permit larger transaction sizes.

The market liquidity of Shanghai and Shenzhen is nearly as strong as that of Hong Kong taken as a whole. Daily Shanghai A share market turnover in 1998 was on average about US$565 million as compared to US$818 million on the SEHK. This was still better than the H shares which had a daily average turnover of US$38 million in 1998. As for B shares, the average daily turnover in 1998 of US$2–3 million is a good indication that this is a retail market. More than any other indicator, this shows that foreign professional money managers have deserted the

Table 8.7: SSE, SZSE and H share index market capitalization trends

(000)	Mkt cap RMB Shanghai A	Mkt cap RMB Shanghai B	Mkt cap RMB Shenzhen A	Mkt cap RMB Shenzhen B	Mkt cap HK$ H share Index
1990	1 234 326	NA	NA	NA	NA
1991	2 942 709	NA	7 965 250	NA	NA
1992	52 055 263	3 785 100	45 753 720	3 220 820	NA
1993	207 665 188	12 954 428	125 101 300	8 431 150	18 228 700
1994	248 353 740	11 659 240	103 249 720	5 798 980	19 981 320
1995	243 371 000	9 295 000	87 686 520	7 175 590	16 463 770
1996	531 613 000	16 168 000	413 242 650	23 214 700	31 530 630
1997	903 245 300	18 561 400	812 174 040	18 943 020	48 622 010
1998	1 052 538 400	10 053 900	877 391 000	10 581 700	33 532 660
3Q 99	1 585 397 070	15 955 710	1 310 399 102	16 826 271	54 403 370
US$	191 473 076	1 927 018	158 260 761	2 032 158	7 028 859

Source: Bloomberg; US$1 = RMB 8.28 and HK$ 7.75

Table 8.8: Trading Volume, SSE, SZSE and H-share Index (1990–3rd quarter 1999)

RMB (MM)	Shanghai		Shenzhen		Hong Kong
	A shares	B shares	A shares	B shares	H shares HK$
1990	1	NA	NA	NA	NA
1991	807	NM	3 530	NA	NA
1992	23 273	1 446	41 744	1 663	NA
1993	237 979	8 990	126 087	2 580	31 146
1994	562 673	10 835	237 635	1 620	33 073
1995	304 263	6 085	91 596	1 704	16 886
1996	902 024	9 457	1 203 205	18 530	24 890
1997	1 355 024	21 294	1 674 497	21 369	297 770
1998	1 230 423	8 188	1 111 349	4 465	73 539
3rd quarter 1999	1 480 259	12 785	1 240 540	11 504	39 973
Daily Volume	4 922	33	4 445	17 860	294
US$ Value (mm)	594	4	537	2	38

Source: Bloomberg; US$ 1 = RMB 8.28 and HK$ 7.75

market leaving it to the speculative retail element on both sides of the border. For comparison, the daily turnover of the New York Stock Exchange alone was US$29 billion. It should be noted, however, that there is a definite 'churning' element to Chinese trading statistics. The CSRC has recently enacted a regulation which interprets 'spot trading' as meaning that an investor cannot purchase and sell the same shares on the same day. This was done to inhibit overtrading of customer accounts by securities firms seeking to maximize fee revenues. While the latter is undoubtedly a concern, this measure, if persisted in, will make the markets more volatile than before.

8.5 Market volatility

Market watchers both domestically and internationally often talk about the extreme volatility that characterizes the Chinese equity markets and, indeed, there are many stories of extreme market moves, whether of individual stocks or of the index itself. These observations deserve a closer look. The results show, however, that the prevailing wisdom is somewhat incorrect. The data presented in Table 8.9 cover all major Chinese indices both domestic and international for three periods encompassing the past three years[3] and compares them against the US Dow Jones Industrials Index as a benchmark. Calculations are based on the 20 day average volatility over each of these three periods. Each index is ranked in the table in order of volatility over one year from high to low, although rankings may differ in the other periods. Calculations are based on the daily closing prices of each index.

Table 8.9: Comparative 1, 2 and 3 year market volatilities (1996–11 Dec. 1999)

	One year 20 day average	Two year 20 day average	Three year 20 day average
Shenzhen B	44.5%	37.6%	40.5%
Shanghai B	43.6%	40.5%	40.6%
HK H share Index	42.2%	49.6%	49.4%
HK Red Chip Index	38.4%	50.7%	51.2%
Shanghai Top 30[4]	26.7%	23.0%	28.9%
Shenzhen A	26.3%	23.5%	30.2%
Hang Seng Index	26.0%	33.9%	32.4%
Shanghai A	25.9%	22.3%	27.6%
Dow Jones Industrials	16.2%	17.0%	17.0%

Source: Bloomberg and Wind Information System

The results are somewhat surprising. There is no surprise in the fact that the Dow Jones has been the least volatile index over all time scales. The Dow represents the Blue Chip stocks of the world's largest economy. Excessive volatility in these stocks would be extremely worrying for the American economy as well as the global financial markets. Aside from this, the US capital markets are mature, appropriately supervised and characterized by a high degree of transparency. Their investor base is largely professional and extremely diverse. Given all this, a low level of volatility is to be expected.

The other indices can be grouped together into three 'listing classes': (1) A shares and B shares; (2) Red Chips and H shares; and (3) the Hang Seng Index. During the past year B shares have exhibited the most volatility over a 20 day period. This is a consequence of the extreme swings seen in this market during the 1999 summer rally and subsequent correction. In general, however, this result is to be expected due to the very poor liquidity in these stocks. Any significant buying or selling is amplified as volumes are small, the bid to offer spreads are wide and there is little market depth, that is, the investor base consists primarily of one investor class, retail.

The Red Chip and H share indices, although slightly less volatile than B shares over the last one year, have been the most volatile during the three years including 1999. These stocks, in particularly the Red Chips, saw huge swings through the Hong Kong handover and the Asian crisis. It is not uncommon for Red Chip or H share stocks to experience 10 per cent swings in a day for a number of days in a row. The third 'listing class' represents 'broad market' measures, Shanghai A shares as a whole, the top 30 Shanghai A shares[4] in terms of market capitalization, the Shenzhen A share Index and the Hang Seng Index. A comparison of these market indices shows that, except for the past year, it has been the Hong Kong, and not the mainland, market which has on average been the more volatile. This somewhat unexpected result is a reminder that Hong Kong is less developed than is usually thought. Because this result is somewhat surprising and perhaps even unsettling, it is worth seeking a clearer understanding of the forces driving the Hong Kong market.

There is no doubt that the Asian markets and, in particular, Hong Kong have had a very difficult past three years, but this does not fully account for the difference. While the closed system in which China's markets operate has insulated China from the extremes of 'hot' international money flows, there are two other factors that need to be taken

Table 8.10: Major constituents of the Hang Seng Index (as of 30 Nov. 1999)

Stock	Market capitalization %
HSBC Holdings	26.66
China Telecom (HK) Ltd.	15.93
Hutchison	11.37
Cable & Wireless (HK)	7.77
Cheung Kong	6.16
Total	67.89

Source: Bloomberg

into consideration. The first is that both Shanghai and Shenzhen impose 10 per cent up or down trading limits on a stock. This obviously limits the movement of individuals stocks and, therefore, the index. But it is also very seldom that the Hang Seng has ever moved more than 10 per cent in one day so this restriction has little impact on the comparison. The second, and more significant, factor lies in the structural composition of the two markets. The Hang Seng Index has historically been dominated by a handful of key stocks which in general have been very interest rate sensitive.[5] The shares of these five companies represent nearly 70 per cent of the total market capitalization of the Hang Seng Index and of these HSBC, Cheung Kong and a large part of Hutchison are either banking or property companies. The other part of Hutchison, China Telecom and Cable and Wireless are telecom companies which themselves have now become the darlings of the market. It is easy to understand how the 'broader' market may be driven by significant trading activity in these shares. This is a well known story. It has only been in the past few years that the composition of the Hong Kong market has been altered somewhat with the addition of the Chinese companies. But the contribution of H share and Red Chip companies still remains relatively limited.

In contrast, the Shanghai index is much more diversified and no single stock can drive the index to the same extent. The top five stocks by market capitalization shown in Table 8.11 represent a wide variety of business sectors: banking, property, airlines, energy and television manufacture. This is certainly not the limited market that is found in Hong Kong. The analysis above leads to a conclusion that Hong Kong is more volatile than Shenzhen, which in turn is more volatile than

Table 8.11: Largest Shanghai market constituents (as of 15 Nov. 1999)

Stock	Market capitalization %
Pudong Development Bank	4.49
Shenergy	2.37
Sichuan Changhong	1.93
China Eastern Airlines	1.38
Shanghai Liujiazui	1.16
Total	11.33

Source: Bloomberg

Shanghai. In terms of share types, Red Chips and H shares are more volatile than B shares which are more volatile than A shares.

This conclusion can be checked by going a step further in this analysis of volatility. Another way to look at volatility is to analyze how quickly different markets move over a given trend. Here a continuous trend is analyzed to arrive at the 'speed' of a market. For example, if the market rises for three consecutive days and moves a total of 4.5 per cent over this period, than the market's average speed was 1.5 per cent per day. This approach is taken for all up or down trends over the recent three years and a market speed is calculated for each trend as defined by its length in days, for example a two day trend. The maximum rising or falling speed is then shown in Table 8.12 for comparison across markets. The more stable the market, the smaller the moves and vice versa. A very speculative market should demonstrate very wild swings.

The results of this analysis are somewhat different from those reached previously. In terms of the broader markets, B shares are the most volatile on the upswing with Hong Kong and the A share markets roughly comparable. On the downturn, Shenzhen B shares stand out followed by Hong Kong, all Shanghai shares and then Shenzhen A shares. Setting aside the B share markets, Hong Kong remains the more volatile by this measure as compared with the A share markets. In terms of share classes the results here are the same: H shares and Red Chips are subject to the biggest moves followed by B shares and A shares. It is not surprising, for market watchers at least, that less developed markets can move much faster than more developed markets. The analysis above, like volatility itself, gives an easy measure of how violently different markets can react to news.

Table 8.12: Maximum index moves during up and down trends

Index	Maximum 'up' average change %	Index	Maximum 'down' average change %
H shares	4.4	Shenzhen B	3.7
Red Chips	3.8	H shares	3.4
Shenzhen B	3.3	Hang Seng	3.1
Shanghai B	2.8	Red Chips	3.0
Shenzhen A	1.9	Shanghai B	2.3
Hang Seng	1.8	Shanghai A	2.1
Shanghai A	1.7	Shenzhen A	1.7
Dow Jones	1.0	Dow Jones	1.1

Source: Bloomberg

8.6   A second look at market correlations

The conclusion of Section 8.1 was quite clear: China's markets operate in a closed system and, as a consequence, no significant correlation exists between the domestic A share markets and either of the New York or Hong Kong exchanges. On this broader level the finding holds, but a somewhat different picture emerges when the same question is asked about specific types of shares. An analysis of trading performance correlations between different types of Chinese shares round outs the discussion of volatility and also provides a clearer picture of how these markets function.

Table 8.13 indicates very high correlations between Red Chips and H shares (86 per cent) and both with the Hang Seng Index (74 per cent and 66 per cent respectively). A similar level of correlation exists between Red Chips and H shares, on the one hand, and B shares, on the other (55–65 per cent). This relationship suggests that most 'China stocks' are traded based on sentiment and at a country level, as opposed to a more detailed stock by stock, company by company approach.

The strong correlation between China shares and the overall Hang Seng on the face of it is a bit unexpected given the extremely different composition of the companies represented by each. The Hang Seng includes a few world class companies, for example HSBC Holdings, which contribute significant weight to the index as shown in Table 8.10. On top of this, the Hang Seng is often thought of as the premier exchange in non-Japan Asia. On the other hand, its trading is remarkably similar to the Red Chip index, which includes some of the most

Table 8.13: Correlation between Chinese share types

	Hang Seng %	Red Chip %	H Share %	Dow Jones %	SZ A %	SZ B %	SH A %	SH B %	SH 30 %
Hang Seng	100								
Red Chips	74	100							
H shares	66	86	100						
Dow Jones	60	41	29	100					
SZ A	0	13	16	−5	100				
SZ B	32	54	57	−2	40	100			
SH A	0	16	20	−4	93	44	100		
SH B	38	62	65	4	33	87	40	100	
SH 30	3	17	15	1	81	34	82	36	100

Source: Bloomberg. *Note*: SZ = Shenzhen; SH = Shanghai

poorly conceived and managed listed companies in Hong Kong. The answer to this seeming conundrum, however, is straightforward and unsurprising: aside from interest rates and telecom shares, the single largest other factor moving the Hang Seng Index is the Chinese economy or, more accurately, investor sentiment towards the Chinese economy. This fact also explains the relatively strong correlations (50–60 per cent) between the overseas listed Red Chips and H shares and the domestically listed B shares. As before, there is virtually no correlation with the A shares.

Among the domestic shares, there is a strong, but not perfect, correlation (93 per cent) between Shenzhen and Shanghai A shares. A similarly strong, but again not perfect, correlation (87 per cent) exists between the two B share markets. The slight difference between markets is not surprising since each market consists of a similar but also different mix of companies. The A and B share markets show correlations of around 40 per cent, which is suggestive as to a partially common investor base.

These patterns, of course, are no guide to future volatility or trading developments. China's participation in the WTO, which is expected in the year 2000, should open the domestic economy and its securities markets to increasing international capital flows leading inevitably to more volatility. This potential problem can best be offset by encouraging the rapid development of the domestic markets. With increased breadth and depth, the markets will be better able to absorb the shock which will come when the Renminbi becomes convertible on the capital account and as international banks are permitted to participate directly.

8.7 Dividends

The dividend payout is an aspect of stock market performance often forgotten in the scramble for capital gain. The Chinese markets tend to have a much lower cash dividend yield as compared with the international markets. In 1998 of the 400 listed companies in Shanghai only 137 paid a cash dividend with a similar picture seen in Shenzhen, 135 companies out of 425. Although cash dividends are paid by only one in every three companies, bonus and rights issues are very common corporate actions.[6]

In contrast, all Hang Seng stocks with the exception of China Telecom, paid a cash dividend in 1998. In 1999 China Telecom was joined in this non-payment by HK Shanghai Hotels and Guangdong Investment. Admittedly China Telecom, like many 'high tech' or other rapidly expanding companies, prefers to reinvest cash into development rather than pay cash out in the form of dividends. In general, investors welcome such a decision if results are, in fact, forthcoming.[7] In short, overall it appears far harder to get money out of a Chinese company, and especially a Shenzhen listed one, than to put it in.

Rights offerings are a frequent occurrence in the Chinese market and seem to be employed in lieu of cash dividends. Table 8.16 summarizes rights issues for the first three-quarters of 1999. Although significantly fewer than in 1998, such offerings have still raised over RMB20 billion. Rights issues are always offered at a substantial discount to the current market price to ensure subscription with the average discount being around 34 per cent for the first three quarters of 1999.

The dependence on bonus shares and rights issues in place of outright cash dividends is not surprising given the poor financial state of many of the listed companies.[8] Deeply discounted rights offering and bonus shares are seen by company management as a way to keep minority shareholders happy without affecting a company's cash position. They are also explained by the fact that Chinese companies have

Table 8.14: Comparative dividend yields (as of 17 Nov. 1999)

Index	Dividend yield %
Shanghai A shares	0.41
Shenzhen A shares	0.74
Hang Seng Index	2.67
Dow Jones Industrials	1.37

Source: Bloomberg

Table 8.15: A share dividend types

Dividend type	Shanghai A shares	%	Shenzhen A shares	%
Bonus shares	159	39.7	120	28.2
Rights offering	79	19.7	80	18.8
Cash dividend	137	34.3	135	31.8
None	25	6.2	90	21.2
Total Companies	400	100	425	100

Source: Shanghai and Shenzhen 1998 Fact Book

Table 8.16: A share rights offerings (RMB mm)

	Amount	Number	Discount %	Capital increase %
Shanghai	12 281	38	34.6	10.1
Shenzhen	8 836	39	35.0	10.2
Total	21 117	77	34.8	10.1

Source: Wind Information System

yet to develop, or even become aware of in most cases, the concept of cost of capital. The state, in one form of another, is the major shareholder and suffers from the same lack of awareness, finding a small dilution of its holdings preferable to cash going 'out the door'.

8.8 Comparative market performance

The graphic presentation of the performance of Chinese shares in Charts 8.6 and 8.7 presents much the same data in a more immediate form while bringing out the same basic points. Aside from an overview of the A share markets from their inception, all data have been rebased to July 1993, the listing date of Tsing Tao Brewery, the first H share IPO, thereby making individual market performances comparable. One way to think of this is that the charts show the consequence of an investment of US$100 made in each market in July 1993.

Chart 8.6 compares the market performance of H shares,[9] Red Chips and Shanghai A and B shares. The chart illustrates quite clearly the early popularity of H and B shares and the tremendous Red Chip binge investors went on in 1997. Clearer trends can be illustrated if Chart 8.6 is disaggregated into its comparable components.

Chart 8.6: All equity indexes rebased on the first H share IPO (July 1993)

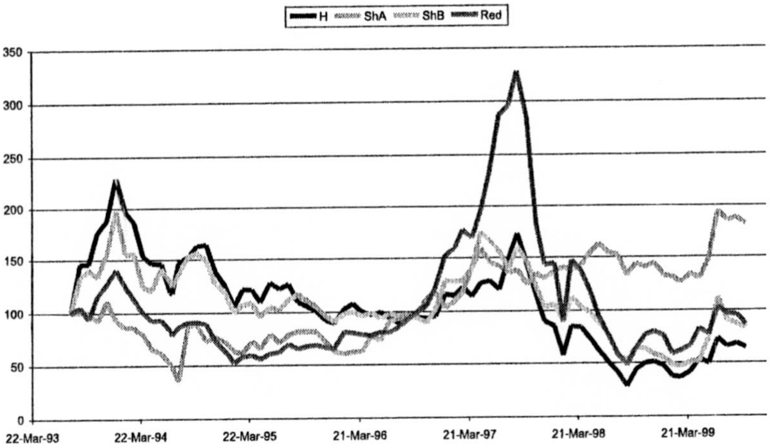

Source: Bloomberg

Shanghai and Shenzhen A and B shares

As noted above, despite different currencies and restrictions on domestic investors, the A and B shares are nonetheless comparable, particularly in the last few years, due to their largely common investor base: retail investors both non-Chinese and Chinese. In addition, they share the same market and regulatory environment and, to a similar extent, represent interests in companies which do not provide international standards of information disclosure. They differ only in terms of volatility which is largely a consequence of the shallow investor interest in the B shares. These are Chinese markets for Chinese and they move in reaction to Chinese events.

Chart 8.7 shows three clear periods: first, from May 1993 to March 1996 was a time of high counterinflationary interest rates and other administrative measures designed to cut inflation. High interest rates and a slowing economy drove these markets down. The second period began in March 1996 and ended in July 1997 when Thailand devalued the Baht and set off the Asian financial crisis. By early March 1996 inflation had been declining quickly for the past year and the PBOC cut interest rates for the first time since 1993. Both A and B share markets reacted strongly to the cut and to the return of confidence in

Chart 8.7: Performance of SSE and SZSE A and B shares (July 1993–June 1999)

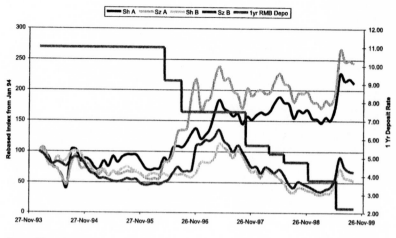

Source: Bloomberg

economic recovery. Strengthening this sentiment was the run up to the Hong Kong handover on 1 July 1997, which was well handled, leading to an outburst of enthusiasm. Unfortunately the party quickly ended soon after with the Baht's devaluation.

The third and current period shows the consequences of the Asian financial crisis on B shares and also underlines the degree to which China's true domestic markets, the A shares, are insulated from external economic events. In China, continued interest rate cuts have stimulated the A share markets as investors have little choice in investment products: either bank deposits or the stock market or under the bed. More recently, government measures and pronouncements on the health of the markets have driven the markets sky high. At the same time, however, no amount of interest rate cuts improved the outlook for the B share markets. The financial crisis drove all truly foreign money out of B shares and without that leavening the markets dried up. Recently, however, B shares have experienced a bounce based on government measures and announcements that non-state companies may be allowed to list B shares. By year end 1999 unsurprisingly that bounce had dribbled to an end.

H shares and Shanghai and Shenzhen B shares

The same three periods pertain to the H shares as well. What is of interest in Chart 8.8 is that B shares have, over time, performed better, and sometimes much better, than the H shares. From July 1993 until mid 1994, H shares were a new phenomenon on the SEHK and were met with enthusiasm to the detriment of the B shares. After 1994, however, H shares have generally lagged B shares due to poor company performance, anti-inflationary measures and the loss of confidence resulting from the Asian financial crisis in 1997. One would have thought that the B share companies would perform similarly, but they have not. The rise of the Shenzhen B share market in mid 1996 might explain why B shares have performed better. Although evidence remains scant, the liveliness of B shares may be due to the entry of funds from retail investors and mainland organizations in Hong Kong. The market is thin and can easily be manipulated which may provide the attraction. In contrast, Shanghai B shares have not enjoyed the same dynamism despite the ability of overseas investors to arbitrage between the two markets.

Red Chips, H shares and Shanghai A shares

The Red Chips were a phenomenon and are reminiscent of the more recent hi-tech craze. Touched off by Shanghai Industrial, listed in May 1996, they collapsed shortly after Beijing Enterprises completed its listing in May 1997. With the exception of profitless, track recordless and capital-less Chinese Internet companies, Red Chips are the purest China 'concept' stocks imaginable. Sponsored directly by governmental entities, packed with a mix of their 'best' assets and driven by wild

Chart 8.8: H shares and Shanghai and Shenzhen B shares

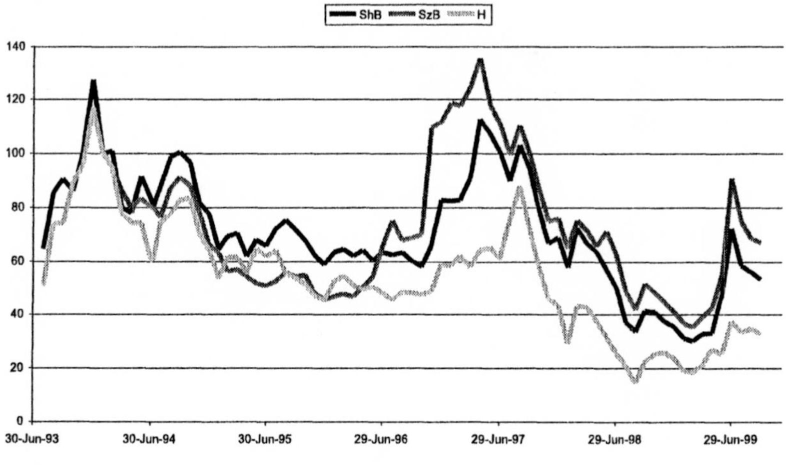

Source: Bloomberg

expectations of further 'asset injections', shares in Red Chip companies quadrupled in value in a one year period. But the realization quickly set in that most municipal or other governmental entities have little in the way of good assets or real management. The bubble was burst by the Asian financial crisis and the concept is now largely discredited. Their rise was only slightly less rapid than their fall as shown in Chart 8.9.

During the Red Chip boom, H shares continued to underperform significantly both the Red Chips and the Shanghai A shares. While the Red Chips were hot, they shared many things in common with Shanghai A shares. After the boom dried up and international investors retreated, local hot money was not sufficient to keep either market alive. Shanghai A shares, in contrast, continued to trade in a range around the peak they reached in mid 1997. This reflects the dearth of investment alternatives mentioned previously as well as the insulation of China's equity markets from the international markets.

Chart 8.9: Red Chips, H shares and Shanghai A shares

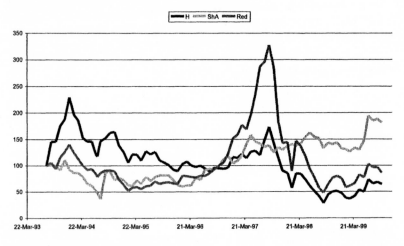

Source: Bloomberg

9
Summing Up and Looking Ahead

With the passage of the Securities Law in December 1998 and its effectiveness as of July 1999, the first stage of development of China's experiment with stocks and stock markets has come to an end. This eight-year period has witnessed an extremely vigorous effort to live up to Deng Xiaoping's January 1992 admonition to 'try out' stocks and securities markets 'in a determined fashion'. If success of the new is measured by how banal it comes to be seen, then stock markets in China have been very successful. At the turn of the century they have become part of the background noise of everyday Chinese life. Even someone as cautious as Jiang Zemin can state, 'The shareholding system is a form of capital organization of modern enterprises. It is beneficial for the separation of ownership rights and management authority, it is beneficial for raising the efficiency of an enterprise's use of capital. Capitalism can use this system, socialism also can use it.' Such an achievement should by no means be underestimated coming in a country as ideologically extreme as China was only a few short years ago. On the other hand, it is largely due to this previous ideology that China's stock markets have developed in a manner and a direction significantly different than stock markets in the West. This is not necessarily bad or good, but, markets being markets, no matter where they operate they are prone to distortion. Their heritage being what it is, it is no surprise that China's markets face the type and extent of challenges which they do. But this is only to be expected of any emerging market. What is unexpected is that they are no longer experimental – China's equity markets are a reality, having become a vital part of the nation's economic being.

China's companies and stock markets emerged in the 1980s out of an environment of radical state planning which over the previous

195

30 years had effectively eliminated the private sector of the economy. This extreme environment, however, was leavened, on the one hand, by a significant *de facto* decentralization of government authority due to technological limitations, and on the other, to the innate practicality of the Chinese people of whom it can truly be said, 'Where there's a will there's a way.' Thus, while it is true that there was only a state and no private sector at the start of the 1980s, by the end of that decade not only had a non-state sector begun to grow, the state sector itself had undergone a hollowing out as a result of the contract responsibility system and the company limited by shares experiment. Put more directly, those who directly controlled and operated assets on behalf of the state had become the true owners of such assets and direct beneficiaries of their production as such enterprises became independent of the state plan. The self-interest of this assortment of enterprise bosses, or '*laozong*', and local government officials could and did differ significantly from the interests of the central government or 'State'. In the absence of requisite institutions, laws and financial management systems, the shareholding system was tailor made for this set of economic players at the local operating levels for a variety of reasons, share financing not the least.

This point can be seen by summarizing the corporatization process as it took place in the 1980s. In order to reorganize to become a company limited by shares, the actual ownership of assets purchased with state funds or, like land, owned outright by the state, had to be documented and deeded over to the new corporate legal entity, the successor to the state. If legal documentation did not exist, which was frequently the case, proper documents were drawn up based on local standards. This process for the first time established a more or less clear legal boundary between the company and the state, something which did not exist (and did not need to exist) under the state planning system. Existing company management typically remained in charge of the new company, but reported to a Board of Directors and a Board of Supervisors whose membership was set by a General Shareholders Meeting, that is, the state. But what was the 'state'? The 'state' was that particular entity, whether a ministry, its local bureau or a local government, in charge of that particular enterprise or sector. In short, nothing had changed but the form of the arrangement with the key exception that the company, that is its management, now had outright legal possession of its own assets.

What would change if the company decided to sell shares representing an ownership interest? Arranging majority shareholder approval

Chart 9.1: Nationalization and its dilution (1949–99;Industrial Output)

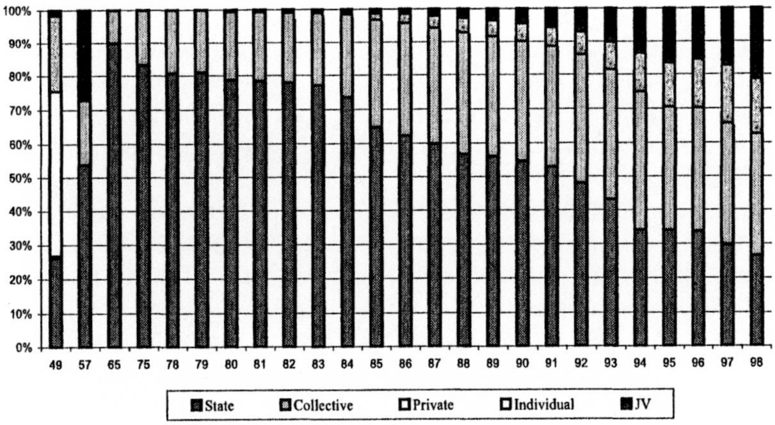

Source: China Statistical Yearbook 1985 and 1998

for an issue was easy since the company's directors, its major share-holder and the key local government approving agencies were all largely the same group of people who shared similar interests and who all, in one function or another, represented the 'state'. With 'state' approval the company sells shares and receives in return either additional assets or cash outright to do with what management and the Directors and Supervisors wish. The 'state' continues as the owner with an absolute majority in shares as well as unshakable control of the assets. But with this new self-financing capability the company (as well as its 'state' owner) has cut a further and even more critical tie with the larger state, becoming truly independent, particularly if it need not source supplies from or sell goods directly to the state. This situation works to the direct and personal benefit of all those members of what might be called the company's broader 'management team', which included the nominal regulator, the PBOC and local government agencies.

The share fever which broke out late in the 1980s played into the hands of this group since OTC counters could be set up, share transactions could be taxed and banks could earn transaction fees. Even social unrest worked to the advantage of the 'state'. Given its fear of instability, the political leadership of the true state with its planning mentality could see the wisdom of creating centralized and manageable securities exchanges. Its decision to establish formal stock exchanges in Shanghai and Shenzhen was not done to further enhance the independence or efficiency of companies, but in order to exert a controlling influence over individual investors while maintaining firm control over company shareholdings. This was a self-protective reflex. On the other hand, the 'owners' and managers of the exchanges, while nominally acting on behalf of the state, reserved the exchanges for the exclusive use of their own local companies. With company assets and a securities exchange, the local governments possessed a significant self-financing tool on which few restrictions or controls were imposed by the state at large.

Who knows where this situation would have led if the events of June 4 had not brought the ideological provenance of shares and stock markets into sharp relief as part of a broader discussion of China's future development. Even with this question favorably resolved by Deng himself, the potential of the cozy arrangements of the 1980s to pose a threat to the country's social stability was quickly demonstrated by the Shenzhen events of August 1992. The response was rapid. The central government, that is the state, would not permit these arrangements to continue without its direct oversight. The decade of the 1990s, therefore, has seen the central government bring control and discipline to China's local markets through the establishment of a relatively complete, if not entirely well co-ordinated, set of national laws and regulations governing the corporatization and listing process. The elevation of the CSRC to ministry status in mid 1998 and the formal passage of the Securities Law late the same year marked the successful completion of this effort.

But in the meantime, the entire program had shifted its focus somewhat from its original objective of improved production efficiencies to SOE recapitalization. In a way similar to the share fever among investors as they grasped the idea of equity value, SOEs, on seeing the financial benefits of selling what to them held little or no value, clamored to gain listing approvals or quotas in the early 1990s. Neither investors nor listed company managements as yet seem to have gotten over the excitement of what, at times, has seemed like free money by getting down to what used to be called 'making money the hard way'. No matter, the thrill of listing will drive market development as both investors and company management gain more experience. And the national effort to institutionalize the corporatization and listing program is the *sine qua non* if China's securities markets are to have the ability to truly develop into efficient national capital markets.

Against this background perhaps it is easier to understand why Chinese shares were defined as they were in the Standard Opinion. In the absence of effectively administered laws, had shares not been directly identified with the state and made nontradable, fraud and outright sales over the decade would without question have significantly reduced the state's ownership in at least certain industries and companies. This would have meant unacceptable economic losses as well – the recent example of the Chengdu Lianyi Group is most certainly not unique. From a political viewpoint also, any approach which did not make the state's ownership in the newly corporatized companies explicit and unshakable, would have been unacceptable.

Given the government's determination not to privatize coupled with weak control systems, this segmented share structure may have been the best compromise if the corporatization process was to proceed. The key point was to permit the process to go forward, not to get caught up in details which at some future point could be better addressed even if with difficulty. There were certainly many among the original promoters of the share system who fully understood that there was little point in adopting a shareholding system unless it was used to raise additional capital, that this could best be done through a developed marketplace and that such a market, once in existence, would lead to its own logical and inevitable consequences, one of which could possibly be stronger and more competitive companies.

The medium term consequence of this pathbreaking compromise, however, has been that the market itself has taken on the character of its accumulated corporate base: a massive overhang of nontradable shares has built up as part of the market's capitalization. This market overhang, representing nearly 70 per cent of total market capitalization, is perhaps the largest of all problems confronting China's markets at the turn of the century and relates directly to their proper valuation. Any announcement by the government of its intention to reduce the overhang by a large selldown would most certainly drive market valuations down, perhaps to as little as 20 per cent of current levels. This is most certainly unacceptable. The recent experiment designed to trickle out state shares also has demonstrated shortcomings: investors will rapidly learn that more shares means lower share valuations, all else remaining equal, and the end result may be the same: a collapse of market values. There seems no easy way to address this problem head on.

Relating to this problem is the issue of Renminbi non-convertibility on the capital account. As the trading levels of the 13 companies with both international and domestic listings illustrate, at present there is a significant valuation differential between domestic and international shares with domestic prices the higher. This differential amounts to more than five times for certain shares. What would be the impact of allowing full Renminbi convertibility? Full convertibility will come only when the Chinese government feels that it is dealing from a position of strength. This suggests the country's economy and, indeed, its markets will be far more developed than they are at present. In such circumstances, predicting the Renminbi impact on Chinese shares is nearly impossible. First of all, will the overseas shares of the 13 companies at such a time still be cheaper than their domestic shares? Second, local investors worldwide tend to invest in their home markets in companies with which they are familiar so the same should be expected of Chinese retail investors at a minimum. A third point is that while Asian markets crashed during the recent financial crisis, this was in large part because foreign capital had been allowed in and then had suddenly withdrawn. China's case is the opposite. So would shares fall? Perhaps if foreign capital can sell short the 'expensive' China market if, indeed, it is expensive at that time.

Any way out of this market overhang will have to involve as a first step a substantial reworking of the current market's relationship between the state and investors. This relationship can be broadly described as follows: individuals buy shares of largely commodity-like SOEs in exchange for the state's unspoken promise to price such shares cheaply and to maintain relative market stability. The consequences of this relationship include investor perception of a guarantee made by the state that the markets will operate in such a way as to ensure no one will lose money. Such reliance on the state means that if the markets do suffer for whatever reason, the government will most certainly take the blame. So the state should distance itself from the market, on the one hand and, on the other, listed companies should create true value. Economics drives share valuations and not the other way around.

The Securities Law marks a significant step forward in this regard. Under the law underwriters will assume responsibility for the quality of the companies issuing shares, the valuation and pricing of their shares and, as sponsors, for their disclosure to investors on an ongoing basis. Similarly, the CSRC will evolve into a more passive market regulator, only reviewing issuance documents presented to it to ensure compliance with the laws. Under the Securities Law the CSRC will no longer have full discretion over issuers and underwriters and in the future may even devolve listing approval authority to the two stock exchanges. In short, the next few years should witness a reversal of the centralizing trend of the 1990s as central authority is devolved onto specialist entities in the securities markets. This trend, if successfully pursued, will largely remove the state *per se* from its all too apparent center stage position as master of the markets. By the same token, investors will increasingly have to rely on their own judgement as to the merits of an investment as well as to the standards of the particular underwriter. Companies as well as IPOs must be allowed to fail before markets can further develop.

The second negative aspect of the current arrangement is a relative overemphasis on the primary to the disregard of the secondary markets. The state's historically cheap pricing of shares at issuance has almost guaranteed a quick return to investors in the primary market and, consequently, this is where people's minds are focused. The current market's huge rates of oversubscription and hundreds of millions of Renminbi in cash deposits to back up orders do not represent true demand for the shares of a given company. To the contrary, the company is largely of secondary importance, most important are the primary market shares and their quick profit potential.

This reality is clearly shown, for example, in the secondary market trading pattern of Konka's shares following its recent share offering. In a normal market the, by international standards, huge oversubscription of Konka's offering would suggest great interest in owning the company's shares at a given price. Konka enjoyed orders for nearly 584 million shares as against its offering of only 80 million shares. Such oversubscription, pricing at a level below market combined with only a fractional allocation of demand should have resulted in significant leftover demand for shares. In normal circumstances unsatisfied demand would have expressed itself as a bidding up of Konka's secondary market share price. In reality, following the start of trading on 6 November 1999, Konka's secondary market price trended slightly upward for a few days. This only indirectly reflected a certain amount of buying demand. But given the large subscription to the offering, stronger price appreciation in the shares should have been expected. More telling was the crash in share price after 9 November as investors dumped shares on realizing there would be no huge price gain on the offering.

Having made this point, it is true that China's secondary markets are liquid and quite active, but they have not yet been used as an instrument to value companies efficiently. The government easily manipulates the markets by floating new policy ideas and issuing new regulations: cut stamp duty here; announce consideration of private

Chart 9.2: Konka post-offering price performance

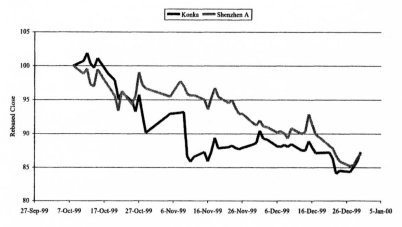

Source: Wind Information System

company access there. The markets trade only to a limited extent on fundamental company performance and prospects. Again, this is the aspect which is most in need of development. When the Ministry of Finance reports that 89 per cent of a sample of listed companies falsified their financial reports to show improved performance, what else can markets trade on?[1]

How then to create a better balance between primary and secondary markets? The best single answer to this is further market professionalization starting with the CSRC which must continue to beef up its market surveillance and corporate compliance functions to ensure greater market transparency. Its public support of minority shareholder interests would also be helpful. Professionalization also includes securities houses developing a strong equity research function and company managements learning about such issues as the cost of capital and investor relations. It should include allowing insurance companies and pension funds to participate directly in the markets in order to develop their own investment capabilities. And non-state sector enterprises of all ownership types, including private and foreign invested, should be allowed to access the markets as long as they meet the publicly available legal criteria.

In short, as its breadth and depth grow and its listed companies create value, China's equity markets will begin to function more properly as a capital valuation mechanism. With this function will come the capacity not only to absorb large chunks of state shares, but also to attract significant amounts of new domestic as well as foreign capital at the time when the Renminbi becomes fully convertible. The foundation for this second stage of development is already in place. During the course of 1999 much has been discussed which portends a bright future for China's domestic equity capital markets, it needs only further 'determined' implementation.

At the start of the 1990s the combination of China and stocks markets seemed to be a non-starter. It was something very few people even thought about. Ten years later with well developed exchanges, 1000 listed companies, 90 securities firms, 40 million equity investment accounts and a combined market capitalization of over US$300 billion, China's markets are well positioned to throw off their emerging status in the next decade. The present reach of China's markets was almost entirely unforeseen as recently as 1992. Now with accession to the WTO and the development of entire new industries from telecommunications to home electronics and the Internet, China's equity capital markets are positioned to provide a critical driving force behind the country's continued rapid blossoming as one of the world's major economic powers.

Appendices

Appendix 1: Shanghai shares: largest state and LP shareholders (30 Sept. 1999)

	A share code	Company name	% Holding	Total US$ market capitalization
1	600832	Oriental Pearl	93.97	1 955 986 207
2	600642	Shenergy	93.87	3 612 545 538
3	600633	PT Double Deer	91.32	153 336 254
4	600637	Guangdong Power	91.02	1 363 582 465
5	600627	Shanghai Electric	90.15	725 652 078
6	600605	Jinggong Machinery	88.58	370 628 406
7	600640	Guoyong Communications	88.31	762 375 690
8	600695	Dajiang Ltd.	87.31	754 802 679
9	600005	Wuhan Iron & Steel	87.04	1 393 653 333
10	600834	Lingqiao Ltd.	86.81	404 334 541
11	600817	Lianghua Industrial	86.38	146 001 019
12	600649	Yuanshui Ltd.	85.08	1 754 465 273
13	600098	Guangzhou Holdings	84.98	1 709 882 609
14	900945	Hainan Airlines B shares	84.93	39 334 000
15	600102	Benxi Iron and Steel	84.90	729 434 783
16	600665	Huchang Special Steel	84.69	700 099 265
17	600615	Fenghua Pearl	84.37	187 473 725
18	600638	New Huangpu	84.14	1 011 575 744
19	600863	Inner Mongolia Huadian	83.90	837 699 662
20	600809	Shanxi Fen Wine	83.48	397 369 977
21	600646	Guojia Industrial	83.09	519 812 969
22	600661	Nanyang Industrial	82.41	306 241 745
23	600096	Yuntianhua	82.40	803 551 797
24	600002	Qilu Petrochemical	82.06	1 224 637 681
25	600641	COSCO Development	82.05	544 246 153
26	600655	Yuyuan Department Store	81.38	476 306 589
27	900952	Jinzhou Port B share	80.56	53 058 000
28	600676	Jiaoyun Ltd.	80.33	201 143 235
29	600003	Northeast Expressway	80.22	955 321 739
30	600692	Asia Communications Ltd.	80.06	217 534 800

Appendix 2: Shenzhen shares: largest state and LP shareholders (30 Sept. 1999)

	A share code	Company name	% Holding	Total US$ market capitalization
1	0927	Tianjin Auto	87.74	1 243 493 143
2	0932	Hualing Pipeline	85.99	1 005 772 343
3	0050	Tianma Textiles	85.43	236 893 104
4	0866	Yangzi Petrochemical	84.98	1 252 234 300

Appendix 2: Shenzhen shares: largest state and LP shareholders *(30 Sept. 1999)*
(continued)

	A share code	Company name	% Holding	Total US$ market capitalization
5	0709	Tangshan Iron and Steel	84.88	1 069 055 979
6	0886	Hainan Expressway	84.43	1 104 669 296
7	0783	Shijiazhuang Refinery	83.35	751 304 348
8	0543	Anhui Electric Power	83.17	602 162 665
9	0817	Liaohe Oil Fields	81.82	777 173 913
10	0035	Zhongkejian	81.58	236 393 093
11	0896	Henan Power	81.42	473 623 188
12	0569	Sichuan Investment	81.31	386 190 104
13	0763	Jinzhou Petrochemical	80.98	526 902 174
14	0401	Eastern Hebei Cement	80.50	639 324 937
15	0033	Xindu Hotel	80.07	290 503 425
16	0937	Jiniu Energy	80.00	577 445 652
17	0038	Shenzhen Datong Ltd.	79.03	130 264 870
18	0828	Guangdong Fudi	78.74	872 106 017
19	0088	Xiantian Port	78.65	648 179 457
20	0751	Xinye Ltd	78.05	625 398 551
21	0835	Longyuan Industrial	77.50	192 130 435
22	0807	Yunnan Aluminum	76.77	273 683 575
23	0090	Shentianjian	76.62	460 544 460
24	0851	China Qiqiao	76.59	174 671 498
25	0065	Shenzhen Xilin	75.53	134 009 662
26	0681	Fareast Ltd.	75.15	222 342 995
27	0021	Shenzhen Scientific	75.15	2 575 884 558
28	0078	Haiwang Biology	75.11	382 553 623
29	0798	Zhongshuo Aquatics	75.07	317 130 435
30	0715	Zhongxing Commercial	75.05	204 289 855

Appendix 3: H share issuing A share companies *(30 Sept. 1999)*

A share code	H share code	Name
Shanghai A shares with H shares		
600600	168 HK	Tsingtao Beer
600688	338 HK	Shanghai Petrochechemical
600860	187 HK	Beiren Printing
600685	317 HK	Guangdong Shipping
600808	323 HK	Maanshan Iron and Steel
600806	300 HK	Kunming Machinery
600871	1033 HK	Yizheng Chemical Fiber
600874	1065 HK	Bohai Chemical
600875	1072 HK	Dongfang Electric

Appendix 3: H share issuing A share companies *(30 Sept. 1999) (continued)*

A share code	H share code	Name
600876	1108 HK	Luoyang Glass
600775	553 HK	Panda Electronics
600115	670 HK	China Eastern Airlines
600188	1171 HK	Yanzhou Coal
Shenzhen A shares with H shares		
0585	42 HK	Northeast Electric Power
0618	368 HK	Jilin Chemical
0666	350 HK	Jingwei Textile
0756	719 HK	Shandong Xinhua Pharmaceutical
0898	347 HK	Angang New Steel
0921	921 HK	Guangdong Kelon Electrical

Appendix 4: Shanghai A share companies with free float > 50% *(30 Sept. 1999)*

	A share code	Company name	Market capitalization US$
1	600602	Shanghai Vacuum Tube	899 897 281
2	600643	Aijian Ltd.	657 547 599
3	600653	Shenhua Industrial	628 480 761
4	600672	Yinghao Kejiao	582 843 189
5	600726	Heilongjiang Electric	575 436 936
6	600868	Meiying Ltd.	519 076 151
7	600664	Harbin Pharmaceutical	515 113 403
8	600654	Shanghai Feile Ltd.	507 392 059
9	600611	Dazhong Taxi	437 363 199
10	600816	Anshan Trust and Investment	419 347 008
11	600669	Anshan Synthetics	402 653 762
12	600872	Zhongshan Torch	394 614 275
13	600751	Tianjin Sea Transport	355 693 043
14	600604	Shanghai Erfangji	337 772 620
15	600601	Founder Scientific	328 507 826
16	600811	Dongfang Group	321 364 027
17	600603	Xingye Property	315 392 000
18	600054	Huangshan Tourism	306 150 000
19	600755	Xiamen International Trade	296 701 449
20	600667	Taiji Industrial	287 303 395
21	600652	Aishi Ltd.	286 416 000
22	600657	Qingdao Tianqiao	272 093 588
23	600651	Shanghai Feile Acoustics	254 979 362
24	600094	Huayuan Ltd.	252 206 812
25	600866	Xinghu Ltd.	249 505 970
26	600879	Wuhan Steel Cable	232 075 959
27	600875	Dongfang Power Equipment	225 217 391

Appendix 4: Shanghai A share companies with free float > 50% *(30 Sept. 1999)*
(continued)

	A share code	Company name	Market capitalization US$
28	600685	Guangzhou Shipyards Int'l	223 631 026
29	600612	First Pencil	203 214 035
30	600806	Kunming Machinery	203 051 826
31	600694	Dalian Department Store	201 030 925
32	600658	Beijing Tianlong	198 692 958
33	600066	Ningtong Passenger Cars	196 301 251
34	600671	Tianmu Pharmaceuticals	182 962 093
35	600689	Shanghai Sanmao	170 702 416
36	600827	Youyi Huaqiao	169 598 219
37	600801	Huaxin Cement	154 081 333
38	600644	Leshan Power	153 200 415
39	600738	Lanzhou People's Dept. Store	152 584 599
40	600803	Weiyuan Biological	151 238 287
41	600625	STShuishan	147 382 012
42	600670	STGaoqida	140 672 654
43	600898	STZhengzhou Dept. Store	134 584 922
44	600807	Jinan Department Store	132 953 545
45	600804	Gongyi Ltd.	122 807 930
46	600858	Bohai Group	122 519 152

Appendix 5: Shenzhen A share companies with free float > 50% *(30 Sept. 1999)*

	A share code	Company name	Market capitalization, US$
1	0001	Shenzhen Development Bank	4 365 038 499
2	0931	Zhongguancun Sci-tech	1 846 048 695
3	0921	Guangdong Kelon	1 363 192 658
4	0549	Hunan Torch	623 082 916
5	0002	Shenzhen Vanke	588 653 956
6	0527	Guangdong Meidi Electric	585 062 552
7	0039	Zhongji Group	549 121 836
8	0040	Zhenzhen Hongji	546 724 641
9	0009	STShenzhen Baoan	494 458 802
10	0509	Tiange Group	446 484 463
11	0550	Jiangling Motors	434 136 191
12	0520	Wuhan Fenghuang	418 846 296
13	0670	Tianjin Development	366 264 889
14	0541	Fuoshan Jiaoming	354 362 016
15	0055	Shenzhen Fangda	350 987 529
16	0573	Guangdong Hongyuan	337 917 869
17	0006	Shenzhen Chenye	337 815 905

Appendix 5: Shenzhen A share companies with free float > 50% *(30 Sept. 1999)*
(continued)

	A share code	Company name	Market capitalization, US$
18	0581	Suweifu	327 454 643
19	0507	STGuangdong Fuhua	324 580 906
20	0529	Guangdong Meiya	320 852 215
21	0561	Shaanxi Changling	294 882 536
22	0521	Meiling Electric	287 130 251
23	0688	Beiling Construction Tile	261 170 662
24	0530	Daling Ltd.	261 056 236
25	0423	Dongah Film	244 022 203
26	0564	Xian Minsheng	240 798 228
27	0513	Pretty Pearl Group	227 851 583
28	0017	STZhonghua	227 137 901
29	0553	Shalongda	218 025 561
30	0510	Jinlu Group	213 997 622
31	0406	Shiyou Daming	206 796 861
32	0554	Qilu Petrochemical	200 911 218
33	0003	Shenzhen Jintian	191 194 307
34	0056	Shenzhen Guoshang	184 887 242
35	0007	Shenzhen Dasheng	169 607 009
36	0759	Wuhan China Dept. Store	169 275 333
37	0506	STOemei	159 148 336
38	0511	Yinji Development	151 057 192
39	0545	Jilin Pharmaceutical	126 298 572
40	0416	Qingdai State Dept. Store	122 740 414
41	0518	PTSusanshan	103 860 342
42	0014	STShenzhen Huayuan	86 615 217
43	2726	Shandong Taishan	47 441 860

Appendix 6: The Stock Exchange of Hong Kong definition of Red Chips

Red Chips are Hong Kong-listed companies with significant equity controlled by entities in mainland China:

1. the company should have at least a 35% shareholding directly held by either:
    a. Mainland entities which are defined to include state-owned organizations, provincial or municipal authorities in mainland China; or
    b. listed or privately owned Hong Kong companies (Hong Kong or overseas incorporated) which are controlled by (a) above;

3. the company should have at least a 12-month trading record after having satisfied criterion (1) above;
4. the company should not have more than 20 trading days without turnover during the past 12 months, excluding days when the company was suspended from trading;
5. the company must not be a constituent stock of the Hang Seng China Enterprises Index (the H share Index).

See Appendix 7 for Red Chip or China-affiliated Corporations Index constituent stocks

Source: Hang Seng Services Ltd, www.hsi.com.hk

Appendix 7: Hang Seng China-affiliated Corporations Index *(31 August 1999)*

Code	Name
392 HK	Beijing Enterprises Ltd.
1185 HK	CASIL Telecommunications Holdings Ltd.
31 HK	China Aerospace International Holdings Ltd.
257 HK	China Everbright International Ltd.
165 HK	China Everbright Ltd.
256 HK	China Everbright Technology Ltd.
506 HK	China Foods Holdings Ltd.
144 HK	China Merchants Holdings (International) Co. Ltd.
688 HK	China Overseas Land & Investment Ltd.
1093 HK	China Pharmaceutical Enterprise & Investment Corporation Ltd
1109 HK	China Resources Beijing Land Ltd.
291 HK	China Resources Enterprise Ltd.
308 HK	China Travel International Investment Hong Kong Ltd.
560 HK	Chu Kong Shipping Development Co. Ltd.
183 HK	CITIC Ka Wah Bank Ltd.
135 HK	CNPC (Hong Kong) Ltd.
119 HK	Continental Mariner Investment Co. Ltd.
517 HK	COSCO International Holdings Ltd
1199 HK	COSCO Pacific Ltd.
203 HK	Denway Investment Ltd.
418 HK	Founder (Hong Kong) Ltd.
270 HK	Guangdong Brewery Holdings Ltd.
124 HK	Guangdong Investment Ltd.
1203 HK	Guangnan (Holdings) Ltd.
123 HK	Guangzhou Investment Co. Ltd.
1052 HK	GZI Transport Ltd.
535 HK	Hing Kong Holdings Ltd.

Appendix 7: Hang Seng China-affiliated Corporations Index *(31 August 1999)* *(continued)*

190 HK	Hong Kong Construction (Holdings) Ltd.
992 HK	Legend Holdings Ltd.
222 HK	Min Xin Holdings Ltd.
318 HK	Ng Fung Hong Ltd.
230 HK	ONFEM Holdings Ltd.
263 HK	Poly Investments Holdings Ltd.
363 HK	Shanghai Industrial Holdings Ltd.
152 HK	Shenzhen International Holdings Ltd.
697 HK	Shougang Concord International Enterprises Co. Ltd.
521 HK	Shougang Concord Technology Holdings Ltd.
604 HK	Shum Yip Investment Ltd.
409 HK	Stone Electronic Technology Ltd.
882 HK	Tianjin Development Holdings Ltd.
268 HK	Top Glory International Holdings Ltd.
349 HK	Union Bank of Hong Kong Ltd.

Appendix 8: Stock Exchange of Hong Kong definition of H share companies

The Stock Exchange of Hong Kong has compiled a Hang Seng China Enterprises Index. also known as the H share Index, with the objective of reflecting the stock price performance of companies listed in Hong Kong and incorporated in mainland China. The China Enterprises Index is a capitalization weighted index. Constituent stocks include all H share companies listed on the Stock Exchange of Hong Kong. See Appendix 10 for constituent stocks of the Hang Seng China Enterprises Index.

Source: Hang Seng Services Ltd, www.hsi.com.hk

Appendix 9: Stock Exchange of Hong Kong definition of Hang Seng Index

The Hang Seng Index is a capitalization weighted index and its constituent stocks grouped under the four sub-indices of commerce and industry, finance, properties and utilities. At present the Hang Seng Index comprises 33 stocks selected to be representative of the overall market. The selection process is systematic and rigorous. To be eligible for selection the company:

● should be among those constituting the top 90 per cent of the total market capitalization of all ordinary shares listed on the SEHK
● should be among those that constitute the top 90 per cent of the total turnover on the SEHK
● should have a listing history of 24 months; and
● should not be a foreign company as defined by the SEHK.

From among the eligible candidate companies final selections are based on: (1) company market capitalization; (2) the representation of the sub-sectors within the HSI must directly reflect that of the market; and (3) the financial performance of the company.

Source: Hang Seng Services Ltd, www.hsi.com.hk

Appendix 10: Hang Seng China Enterprises Index *(12 August 1999)*

Code	Name
347 HK	Angang New Steel Co. Ltd.
914 HK	Anhui Conch Cement Co. Ltd.
955 HK	Anhui Expressway Co. Ltd.
991 HK	Beijing Datang Power Generation Co. Ltd.
58 HK	Beijing North Star Co. Ltd.
325 HK	Beijing Yanhua Petrochemical Co. Ltd.
187 HK	Beiren Printing Machinery Holdings Ltd.
161 HK	CATIC Shenzhen Holdings Ltd.
1202 HK	Chengdu Telecommunications Cable Co. Ltd.
670 HK	China Eastern Airlines Corporation Ltd.
1138 HK	China Shipping Development Co. Ltd.
1055 HK	China Southern Airlines Co. Ltd.
1053 HK	Chongqing Iron & Steel Co. Ltd.
1072 HK	Dongfang Electrical Machinery Co. Ltd.
38 HK	First Tractor Co. Ltd.
74 HK	Great Wall Technology Co. Ltd.
921 HK	Guangdong Kelon Electrical Holdings Co. Ltd.
525 HK	Guangshen Railway Co. Ltd.
317 HK	Guangzhou Pharmaceutical Co. Ltd.
874 HK	Guangzhou Shipyard International Co. Ltd.
1133 HK	Harbin Power Equipment Co. Ltd.
902 HK	Huaneng Power International, Inc.
177 HK	Jiangsu Expressway Co. Ltd.
358 HK	Jiangxi Copper Co. Ltd.
368 HK	Jilin Chemical Industrial Co. Ltd.
350 HK	Jingwei Textile Machinery Co. Ltd.
300 HK	Kunming Machine Tool Co. Ltd.
1108 HK	Luoyang Glass Co. Ltd.
323 HK	Maanshan Iron & Steel Co. Ltd.
553 HK	Nanjing Panda Electronics Co. Ltd.
42 HK	Northeast Electrical Transmission & Transformation Machinery Manufacturing Co. Ltd.
1122 HK	Qingling Motors Co. Ltd.
1071 HK	Shandong International Power Development Co. Ltd.
719 HK	Shandong Xinhua Pharmaceutical Co. Ltd.
338 HK	Shanghai Petrochemical Co. Ltd.

Appendix 10: Hang Seng China Enterprises Index *(12 August 1999) (continued)*

Code	Name
548 HK	Shenzhen Expressway Co. Ltd.
107 HK	Sichuan Expressway Co. Ltd.
1065 HK	Tianjin Bohai Chemical Industry (Group) Co. Ltd.
168 HK	Tsingtao Brewery Co. Ltd.
1171 HK	Yanzhou Coal Mining Co. Ltd.
1033 HK	Yizheng Chemical Fibre Co. Ltd.
576 HK	Zhejiang Expressway Co. Ltd.
1128 HK	Zhenhai Refining & Chemical Co. Ltd.

Appendix 11: Top 20 Shanghai A shares by market capitalization *(30 Sept. 1999)*

	Code	Company name	Market capitalization, US$
1	600839	Sichuan Changhong Electronics	4 391 153 610
2	600642	Shenergy	3 612 545 538
3	600688	Shanghai Petrochemical	2 570 277 778
4	600663	Shanghai Lujiazui Property	2 261 833 135
5	600104	Shanghai Automobile	2 155 797 101
6	600009	Shanghai Hongqiao Airport	2 054 347 826
7	600115	China Eastern Airlines	2 004 710 145
8	600832	Oriental Pearl	1 955 986 207
9	600808	Maanshan Steel	1 864 993 949
10	600188	Yanzhou Coal	1 813 405 797
11	600649	Yuanshui	1 754 465 273
12	600098	Guangzhou Holdings	1 709 882 609
13	600871	Yizheng Chemical Fiber	1 698 792 271
14	600001	Handan Iron and Steel	1 584 846 961
15	600690	Tsingtao Beer	1 476 626 173
16	600005	Wuhan Iron and Steel	1 393 653 333
17	600171	Shanghai Belling	1 367 837 486
18	600637	Guangdong Power	1 363 582 465
19	600776	Eastern Communications	1 282 826 087
20	600002	Qilu Petrochemical	1 224 637 681

Note:
1. Capitalization is calculated based on A shares and nontradeable shares valued at the A share secondary market price.
2. Overseas listed shares including B and H shares are ignored in this measure.
3. The US$ is used as the unit of calculation for ease of comparison to international markets.

Appendix 12: Top 20 Shenzhen A shares by market capitalization *(30 Sept. 1999)*

	Code	Company name	Market capitalization, US$
1	0001	Shenzhen Development Bank	4 365 038 499
2	0021	Shenzhen Scientific	2 575 884 558
3	0618	Jilin Chemical	2 416 755 314
4	0682	Dongfang Electric	1 886 980 510
5	0931	ZhongGuanCun Sci-Tech Zone	1 846 048 695
6	0539	Guangdong Electric Power	1 618 248 667
7	0730	SEPEC	1 605 447 366
8	0048	Shenzhen Kondral	1 522 870 628
9	0063	Shenzhen Zhonxing Telecom	1 437 496 981
10	0839	CITIC Guoan Information Industry	1 415 942 029
11	0921	Guangdong Kelon Electrical	1 363 192 658
12	0800	First Auto Works Car Co.	1 311 041 667
13	0866	Yangzi Petrochemical	1 252 234 300
14	0927	Tianjin Auto	1 243 493 143
15	0858	Wuliangye Wine	1 213 140 097
16	0729	Yanjing Beer	1 115 142 533
17	0886	Hainan Expressway	1 104 669 296
18	0709	Tangshan Iron and Steel	1 069 055 979
19	0027	Shenzhen Energy Investment	1 029 250 282
20	0932	Hubei Hualing Pipe	1 005 772 343

Note:
1. Capitalization is calculated based on A Shares and nontradable shares valued at the A share secondary market price.
2. Overseas listed shares including B and H shares are ignored in this measure.
3. The US$ is used as the unit of calculation for ease of comparison to international markets.

Appendix 13: Shanghai Top 30 Index *(31 December 1999)*

	Code	Company name
1	600115	China Eastern Airlines
2	600776	Eastern Communications
3	600068	Gezhouba Hydroelectric
4	600868	Guangdong Meishan
5	600098	Guangzhou Development
6	600001	Handan Iron and Steel
7	600886	Hubei Xinghua
8	600887	Inner Mongolia Yili Industries
9	600072	Jiangnan Heavy Industries
10	600854	Jiangsu Chunlan Electric
11	600058	Minmetals Development
12	600812	North China Pharmaceutical

Appendix 13: Shanghai Top 30 Index *(31 December 1999) (continued)*

	Code	Company name
13	600811	Orient Group
14	600002	Qilu Petrochemical
15	600690	Haier Electric
16	600727	Shandong Lubei Group
17	600643	Shanghai Aijian Corporation
18	600104	Shanghai Auto Group
19	600009	Shanghai Hongqiao Airport
20	600663	Shanghai Lujiazui
21	600649	Shanghai Municipal Water
22	600631	Shanghai No.1 Department Store
23	600688	Shanghai Petrochemical
24	600642	Shenergy
25	600718	Shenyang New-Alpine
26	600839	Sichuan Changhong Electric
27	600702	Sichuan Top Enterprises
28	600736	Suzhou Hi-New Tech Industry Zone
29	600867	Dongda Er-pai
30	600100	Qinghua Dongfang

The Shanghai Top 30 Index consists of the 30 most representative A shares listed on the Shanghai exchange. Last updated on 6 July 1998, the Top 30 includes 15 industrials, one commerce, one property, six utilities and seven conglomerates.

Appendix 14: Chinese convertible bond issuers (*30 September 1999*)

Stock	Code/share type	Year issued	Notional amount (000)	Annual coupon %	Maturity
China Travel (HK)	308 HK/Red	1993	US$143 750	4.50	1998
Guangdong Investment	270 HK/Red	1993	US$102 000	4.50	1998 (called 1996)
China Textile	900906 CH/B	1993	CHF 35 000	1.00	1998
China Overseas Land	688 HK/Red	1993	US$150 000	5.25	2000 (called 1997)
Guangzhou Investment	123 HK/Red	1993	US$90 000	4.25	1998
Shougang Concord Int'l	697 HK/Red	1993	US$183 000	4.50	1998
Onfem	230 HK/Red	1994	US$28 000	5.13	1999
Ryoden Development	745 HK/Red	1994	US$50 000	3.00	1998
Shougang Concord Grand	730 HK/Red	1994	CHF100 000	1.50	1998
China Southern Glass	2012 HK/Red	1994	US$45 000	5.25	2000
China Resources Enterprise	291 HK/Red	1996	US$63 250	3.00	2005
Zhenhai Refinery	1128 HK/H	1996	US$200 000	3.00	2003
China Resources Beijing Land	1109 HK/Red	1997	US$172 500	2.00	2004
Guangdong Investment	270 HK/Red	1997	US$130 000	1.00	2002
Guangnan Enterprise	1203 HK/Red	1997	US$100 000	1.75	2000
Huaneng Power Int'l	902 HK/H	1997	US$230 000	1.75	2004
Qingling Motors	1122 HK/H	1997	US$100 000	3.50	2002
Shanghai Industrial	363 HK/Red	1997	US$250 000	1.00	2002
Guangdong Investment	270 HK/Red	1997	US$125 000	3.25	2003
Beijing Enterprises	392 HK/Red	1998	US$175 000	0.50	2003

Appendix 14: Chinese convertible bond issuers *(30 September 1999) (continued)*

Stock	Code/share type	Year issued	Notional amount (000)	Annual coupon %	Maturity
Nanning Chemical	Pre-IPO/A	1998	RMB150 000	1.00	2003
Wujiang Silk Co.	Pre-IPO/A	1998	RMB200 000	1.00	2003
COSCO Pacific	1199 HK/Red	1998	US$150 000	1.00	2003
Guangdong Investment	270 HK/Red	1998	US$125 000	3.25	2003
Shanghai Industrial	363 HK/Red	1998	US$150 000 000	1.00	2003
China Merchants	144 HK/Red	1999	US$60 000 000	7.00	2004
Maoming Refining	Pre-IPO/A	1999	RMB1 500 000	1.30	2004

Appendix 15: CSRC approved overseas listing candidates, 1992–99

First group	Second group	Special seven
October 1993	*January 1994*	*September 1994*
Shanghai Petrochemical*	Wuhan Iron & Steel	First Auto
Yizheng Chemical Fibre*	Second Auto (Dong Feng)	Legend Holdings*
Maanshan Iron & Steel*	Guangshen Railway*	Xinhua Pharamaceutical*
Tianjin Bohai Chemical*	Zhenhai Refining*	Guangdong Kelon*
Kunming Machinery*	China Eastern Airlines*	Guangzhou Pharmaceutical*
Tsingtao Beer*	China Southern Airlines*	Beida Founder*
Guangzhou Shipyard*	Shandong Huaneng Power*	Shenzhen Expressway*
Beiren Printing*	Huaneng International Power*	
Dongfang Electric*	Shandong International Power*	
	Tianjin Steel Pipe	
	Northeast Power Equipment*	
	Luoyang Glass*	
	Harbin Power*	
	Datang Power*	
	Qingling Auto*	
	Xian Aircraft	
	Jingwei Textile*	
	Chengdu Cable*	
	Nanjing Panda*	
	Jilin Chemical*	
	Haixing Shipping*	
	Guangdong Fuotao Ceramics	
9 of 9 listed	**17 of 22 listed**	**6 of 7 listed**

Note: * indicates listing completed.

Appendix 15: CSRC approved overseas listing candidates, 1992–99 *(continued)*

Fourth group	'Fourth $^1/_2$' and 5th group
December 1996	*December 1999*
Shanghai Power	Dalian Infrastructure
Wuhan Yangluo Power	Shenyang Infrastructure
Guizhou Wujiang Power	Heilongjiang Farms
Jilin Power	Ningbo Port
Guangxi Guiguan Power	Shandong Infrastructure
Anhui Xinji Coal	Wenzhou Infrastructure
Yanzhou Coal*	Beijing Airport*
China Aquatic	Hebei Highways
Jiangsu Ninghu Expressway*	Guangdong Agriculture
Chengyu Expressway*	
Angang New Steel*	
Panzhihua Steel	
Chongqing Steel*	
Jiangxi Copper*	
Qinghai Aluminum	
Yanshan Petrochemical*	
Panjin Ethylene	
Sichuan Chuanhua Group	
Jinan Ethylene	
Anhui Ningguo Cement*	
Hebei Taixing Cement	
First Tractor*	
Tianjin Auto	
Anyang CPT Glass	
Caihong Glass Tube	
Great Wall Computer*	
Aukman Refridgerator	
Jiangxi Huayi Compressor	
Huabei Pharmaceutical	
Harbin Pharmaceutical	
999 Pharmaceutical	
Anhui Expressway*	
China Trade Center	
Beijing Northern Group*	
China Huandao Group	
Yunnan Travel	
China Merchants Shekou Industrial Park	
China Aviation Technology M/X Corp.*	
Zhejiang Expressway*	
14 of 39 listed	**1 of 9 listed**

Note: * indicates listing completed.

Appendix 16: Twelve listed securities investment funds *(31 July 1999, RMB mm)*

Name	Size (mm)	Date	Issuing co-ordinator	Promoters	Fund manager
Kaiyuan	2 000	3/23/98	Southern Securities	Southern Sec; Guangxi TIC; Xiamen ITIC	Southern Securities
Puhui	2 000	12/30/98	Guoxin Securities	Guoxin Sec; Zhejiang Sec; Anshan City TIC; Anhui ITIC; Penghua FMC	Penghua FMC
Tongyi	2 000	4/2/99	CITIC Securities	CITIC Sec; Hubei Sec; Tianjin ITIC; Anhui TIC; Changsheng FMC	Changsheng FMC
Jinghong	2 000	4/27/99	Dapeng Securities	Guangda Sec; Dapeng Sec; China Eco Dev TIC; Guangdong Sec; Dacheng FMC	Dacheng FMC
Yulong	3 000	6/9/99	Guotong Securities	Great Wall TIC; Guangda Sec; Jinhua City TIC; Guotong Sec; Buoshi FMC	Buoshi FMC
Pufeng	3 000	7/8/99	Guoxin Securities	Guoxin Sec; Zhejiang Sec; Anshan City TIC; Anhui ITIC; Penghua FMC	Penghua FMC
Jintai	2 000		Guoxin Securities	Guotai Sec; China Power TIC; Sh'ghai Aijian TIC; Zhejiang ITIC	Guotai FMC
Taihe	2 000	4/1/99	Guangfa Securities	Guangfa Sec; Beijing Sec; Jilin TIC; China Coal TIC; Jiashi FMC	Jiahong FMC
Anxin	2 000	6/16/98	Guangfa Securities	Shanghai ITIC; Shandong Sec; Hua-an FMC	Hua-an FMC

Appendix 16: Twelve listed securities investment funds *(31 July 1999; RMB mm) (continued)*

Name	Size (mm)	Date	Issuing co-ordinator	Promoters	Fund manager
Hansheng	2 000	4/30/99	Haitong Securities	Haitong Sec; Shenyin Wangguo ; Jiangsu Sec; Fujian ITIC; Shandong ITIC; Fuguo FMC	Fuguo FMC
Yuyang	2 000	7/17/98	Guangda Securities	Great Wall TIC; Guangda Sec; Jinhua City TIC; Guoxin Sec; Buoshi FMC	Buoshi FMC
Xinghua	2 000	4/22/98	Huaxia Securities	Huaxia Sec; Beijing Sec; China Tech ITIC	Huaxia FMC
Anshun	3 000	6/09/99	Shanghai ITIC	Shanghai ITIC; Shandong Sec; Zhejiang Sec; Hua-an FMC	Huaxia FMC
Xinghe	3 000	7/08/99	Beijing Securities	Huaxia FMC; Beijing Sec; Huaxia Sec	Hua-an FMC

Source: Wind Information System

Appendix 17:   Glossary of English/Chinese securities industry terms

approval	*pizhun*
a shares	*A-gu*
asset appraisal	*zichan pinggu*
auction	*paimai*
audit	*shenji*
Blue Chips	*lanqiugu*
brokerage company	*quanshang*
B shares	*B-gu*
Chinese promoter shares	*Zhongguo farengu*
company limited by shares	*gufen youxian gongsi*
comprehensive securities companies	*zonghe quanshang*
conglomerate	*jituan gongsi*
contract responsibility system	*chengbaozhi*
convertible bond	*kehuan zhaiquan*
cyclicality	*zhouqixing*
directed offering (or fund raising) method	*dingxiang muji fangshi*
dividend	*guxi*
domestic legal person shares	*guonei farengu*
dual listing	*liangdi shangshi*
equity share	*gupiao*
examine and approve	*shenpi*
fixed income (or debt) security	*zhaiquan*
follow-on or secondary share offering	*zonggu*
foreign (capital) legal person shares	*waizi farengu*
foreign (or overseas) shares	*haiwaigu*
foreign promoter shares	*haiwai farengu*
fund	*jijin*
fund management company	*jijin guanli gongsi*
government bonds	*guojia zhaiquan (guozhai)*
H shares	*H-gu*
index	*zhishu*
individual (or employee) shares	*zhigonggu*
initial public offering	*shouci gupiao faxing*
institutional investor	*jigou touzizhe*
intermediary	*zhongjian jigou*
internal staff (or employee) shares	*neibuzhigonggu*
investor	*touzizhe*
investors	*gumin*
invisible seat	*wuxing xiwei*
issuing quota	*faxing e-du*
leftover rights offering shares	*zhuanpei yiliugu*
legal person	*faren*
legal person shares	*farengu*
limited liability company	*youxian zeren gongsi*
liquid shares (those being traded)	*liutonggu*
liquidity	*liutongxing*

listed company	*shangshi gongsi*
market capitalization	*shichang jiazhi (or shijia)*
market index	*shichang zhishu*
member of exchange	*jiaoyisuo huiyuan*
net asset value	*qingzichan jiazhi*
NYSE-listed shares	*N-gu*
on-line offering	*shangwang faxing*
ordinary shares	*putonggu*
over-the-counter trading	*guitai jiaoyi*
ownership right	*suoyouquan*
packaging (a company)	*baozhuang*
parent company	*mugongsi*
pension fund	*yanglao jijin*
pilot enterprises	*shidian qiye*
preferred shares	*youxuangu*
price/earnings ratio	*shiyinglu*
primary market	*yiji shichang*
private (i.e. non-Public) shares	*feigongyougu*
private placement	*zimu*
privatization	*siyouhua*
promoter	*faqiren*
promoter method	*faqi fangshi*
public (i.e., State) shares	*gongyougu*
public offering (or public fund raising)	*shehui muji fangshi*
quota	*e-du*
Red Chips	*hongqiugu*
restructuring (of assets)	*chungzu*
retail business office	*yingyebu*
retail investor	*sanhu (touzizhe)*
rights offering	*peigu*
roadshow	*luyan*
seat (eg., stock exchange seat)	*xiwei*
seat on the exchange floor	*youxing xiwei*
secondary market	*erji shichang*
securities exchange	*zhengquan jiaoyisuo*
securities investment fund	*zhengquantouzi jijin*
Securities Law	*Zhengquan Fa*
Securities repo	*zhengquan huigou*
security	*zhengquan*
share price	*gujia*
shareholding cooperative system	*gufen hozuo zhidu*
shareholding system	*gufenzhi*
shell company	*kongke gongsi*
social legal person shares	*shehui farengu*
special shares (i.e., B shares)	*tezhonggu*
Special Treatment shares	*ST-gu*
state shares	*guoyougu*
state-owned legal person shares	*guoyou farengu*
subscription	*muji*

subsidiary company	*zigongsi*
The Company Law	*Gongsi Fa*
The Standard Opinion	*Guifan yijian*
township and village enterprises	*xiangzhen qiye*
trading volume	*jiaoyiliang*
transfer (of ownership)	*zhuanrang*
treasury bonds	*guoku zhaiquan*
verify and approve	*hezhun*
volatility	*bodongxing*
work unit shares	*danweigu*

Notes

'To get rich is glorious!'

1. See, for example, Li Changjiang, *The History and Development of China's Securities Markets*, (Beijing: Zhongguo wuzi chubanshe, 1998), p. 86.
2. The primary market represents the value of all securities issued in a given year. In Chart 1.2 the proxy for this is the IPO market. The secondary market represents the value of all securities which can be traded based on their respective market prices at a given time. Market capitalization represents the total market value of all securities, listed or otherwise, of all listed companies and is shown in Chart 1.2 as 'Total A share cap'.
3. In this regard, China has never sold what are called primary shares in any of its companies, only secondary shares. This means, simply put, that the corporatized entity sold only new shares, thereby expanding the company's capital base and diluting the original shareholder's holding by proportion of total capital, but not in absolute terms. Privatization involves the state selling the shares which it owns – the primary shares – to non-state investors and thereby diluting its holdings both proportionally and in absolute terms.

2 Chinese equity securities

1. The history of the contract responsibility system's implementation and its effect of creating extremely autonomous 'feudal kingdoms' out of previously passive production units is a topic deserving further research. The original reform began in 1979 when the government permitted production units to retain a percentage of the profits which had heretofore been remitted entirely to the Ministry of Finance (MOF). With the tax reforms of 1983–84 this method was forced to change. The MOF depended largely on the collection of SOE profits to fund the budget while, at the same time, the new tax regime during its pilot implementation period had the effect of virtually eliminating the amounts of funds which could be retained by an enterprise. The enterprises fought against the tax and a compromise was reached whereby the enterprises guaranteed the payment of a certain amount of tax to the MOF and everything in excess of this amount was retained for their own use. The first contracts with enterprises were finalized in 1986 for a three-year period. The contracts were renewed in 1989 and 1992. This was the first approach to separating enterprises from government intervention and focusing enterprise management on profit rather than production volume alone and it ended with the passage of the Company Law in mid-1994. Just how great the financial impact this system had can be seen in the approximate 33 per cent share taken by Legal Person Shares in the market capitalization of the Shanghai and Shenzhen

exchanges. For a discussion see Cao Er-jie, *Research and Prospects for the Chinese Securities Markets*, (Beijing: Zhongguo caizheng jingji chubanshe, 1994), pp. 240–50.

2. SCRES, 'Standard opinion for companies limited by shares', 15 May 1992, in CSRC, *Zhengquan qihuo fagui huibian* (1992–93). (Beijing: Falu chubanshe: no date), pp. 79–101. There was later on a very brief and to the point clarification of the character of the Standard Opinion since it was unclear whether an 'opinion' was a 'law' or a temporary measure, SC, 'On the Implementation of the Standard Opinion', in CSRC, *Zhengquan qihuo fagui huibian* (1992–93), p. 69.

3. Other key regulations released simultaneously with the Standard Opinion included SCRES, SPC, MOF, PBOC, State Council Production Office Joint Release, 'Pilot method for shareholding enterprises', 15 May 1992, pp. 75–8; SCRES, 'Standard opinion for companies limited by shares', 15 May 1992, pp. 102–13; SPC and SCRES, 'Provisional regulations for the macro-administration of shareholding system pilot enterprises', 15 June 1992, pp. 114–18; and MOF and SCRES, 'Accounting system for shareholding system pilot enterprises', 23 May 1992, pp. 119–36, all in CSRC, *Zhengquan qihuo fagui huibian* (1992–93).

4. Following passage of the Company Law on 1 July 1994, companies which had previously been established under the Standard Opinion and other related regulations were permitted to continue to exist as they were, but were encouraged to bring themselves into accordance with the terms of the Company Law within a designated time frame. See Company Law, Art. 229, in Standing Committee, National People's Congress, 'PRC Company Law', 29 December 1993, in Shanghai Securities Administration Office. *Zhengquan fagui huibian*, (Shanghai: Xuexi dushu chuban gongsi, 1996), pp. 3–45.

5. State Council, 'Special decree on companies limited by shares offering shares and listing overseas', 4 August 1994, in CSRC, *Zhengquan qihuo fagui huibian* (1994), pp. 34–7.

6. The results of nearly a decade of experimentation were formalized in Ministry of Agriculture, 'Provisional regulations on farmer shareholding cooperative enterprises', 12 February 1990, in *Jinrong falu fagui quanshu*, Vol. 3 (Beijing: Sanxia Chubanshe, 1997), pp. 2826–30.

7. Background details can be found in Li Changjiang, pp. 53 ff.

8. Shenzhen Municipal People's Government, 'Provisional regulations on the pilot program for the transformation of state-owned enterprises into shareholding companies', 15 October 1986, *Jinrong falu fagui quanshu*, Vol. 3, pp. 2815–18.

9. Gao Shangquan and Ye Sen, *China Economic Systems Reform Yearbook 1990*, (Beijing: China Reform Publishing House, 1991), p. 88.

10. Li Changjiang, p. 55.

11. Gao Shangquan and Ye Sen, *China Economic Systems Reform Yearbook 1990*, p. 87.

12. Liu Hongru, 'Several issues regarding China's experiments with the shareholding structure', *Renmin Ribao*, 23 June 1992, p. 5. Statistics for this period are few and far between and are suggestive at best. But if Liu Hongru, the CSRC's renowned founding Chairman, and SCRES didn't know, then

no one did or does. Upon SCRES's disbandment in 1998 as part of the government's streamlining, all old S(RES libraries and files were apparently packed away somewhere, discarded or lost.

13. Liu's figure of 89 is in basic agreement with the figures shown in Table 6.1, which indicate that 97 is the correct number.

14. This office was later restructured, becoming the famous Shanghai Shenyin Securities Company or SISCO.

15. The discussion of 'stock fever' derives from Cao Er-jie, pp. 140 ff.

16. Shenzhen Municipal People's Government, 'Notice on strengthening the administration of the securities market and banning illegal trading', 28 May 1990, p. 2640; and Shenzhen Municipal People's Government, 'Notice on strictly prohibiting share or debt securities financing without authorization', 15 September 1990, p. 2641, both documents in *Jinrong falu fagui quanshu*, Vol. 3.

17. PBOC, 'Specialized banks must not directly carry out securities trading operations', 11 August 1990, *Jinrong falu fagui quanshu*, Vol. 3, p. 2640–1. The PBOC hereafter permitted the banks to carry out securities-related business through their subsidiary trust and investment companies. This created other problems which became all too clear at the end of the decade.

18. Gao Shangquan and Ye Sen, *China Economic Systems Reform Yearbook 1990*, p. 84.

19. SCRES, 'Opinion on strengthening the enterprise management undergoing restructuring', May 1990, as cited in Gao Shengquan and Ye Sen, *China Economic Systems Reform Yearbook 1991*, p. 71; and discussed in Li Changjiang, p. 60.

20. This whole problem of the financial management and accounting system and confusion as to what should be done was noted by SCRES in its 1990 summary report. See Gao Shangquan and Ye Sen, *China Economic Systems Reform Yearbook 1990*, p. 86.

21. Tong Yun Wei, Lynne Chow and Barry J. Cooper, *Accounting and Finance in China* (Hong Kong: Longman Group (Far East) Ltd., 1992), pp. 25 ff.

22. Company Law, Chap. 1, Art 4, in Shanghai Securities Administration Office, *Zhengquan fagui huibian*, p. 4.

23. Standard Opinion, Art 10, excludes Chinese private enterprises, 100 per cent foreign invested Chinese enterprises and Chinese natural persons from acting as a promoter. Sino-foreign JVs, however, can be a promoter, but can only represent less than one third of the total number of promoters of a new company, in CSRC, *Zhengquan qihuo fagui huibian* (1992–93), p. 80.

24. SAMB, 'Provisional measures on the determination of the boundary of state owned asset property rights and the resolution of property rights disputes', 21 December 1993, in China Securities Industry Training Center, *Zuixin Zhongguo zhengquan falu yu gongsi yunzuo guize* (Beijing: Zhongguo minzhu fazhi chubanshe: 1997), pp. 138–43.

25. Standard Opinion, Arts 19 and 20, in CSRC, *Zhengquan qihuo fagui huibian* (1992–93), pp. 82–3; Company Law, Arts 91–5, in Shanghai Securities Administration Office, *Zhengquan fagui huibian*, pp. 20–1; and Nicholas C. Howson, 'China's Company Law: One Step Forward, Two Steps Back?', *Columbia Journal of Asian Law*, 11:1, 1997, pp. 127–73.

26. But in order to accomplish a public listing, this company limited by shares must then transform itself into a '*shehui muji gongsi*', or a company limited by shares which can be offered to the public.
27. After an agonizing debate over a number of years, this practice was officially prohibited by the CSRC as of November 1998. This could stand as a chapter in itself.
28. This section summarizes Standard Opinion, Arts 10–21, in CSRC, *Zhengquan qihuo fagui huibian* (1992–93), pp. 80–3.
29. The use of this approach was terminated by SCRES in 1984, see SCRES, 'Notice on the immediate termination of approvals for shareholding companies established by direct offerings and the reaffirmation of the termination of approvals for the issue of shares to internal staff', 19 June 1994, in CSRC, *Zhengquan qihuo fagui huibian* (1992–93), p. 184.
30. The fact that SOEs own assets which the state itself does not directly own is a consequence of the contract responsibility system widely implemented during the 1980s which allowed SOEs to retain profits over a certain guaranteed level. These profits were then used to invest in assets which later became the basis for Legal Person shares of various types.
31. SAMB, Article 4.1, 'Implementing Opinion on the Administration of State Equity in Trial Shareholding Companies', 3 March 1994, in CSRC, *Zhengquan qihuo fagui huibian* (1994), pp. 170–1.
32. At the same time, in 1992, the government was probably not aware that a non-state Legal Person actually owned substantial assets. This seems to be borne out by the overwhelmed reaction of Deng Xiaoping during his Southern Excursion to Guangdong in early 1992. Beginning in early 1999 discussion began on permitting non-state sector companies to make use of China's capital markets and a very few Sino-foreign joint ventures have been permitted to list shares domestically, for example, the China World Trade Center. This is the start of a trend which should grow in strength.
33. Just how anomalous this has been can be seen in the long drawn out effort to prevent individual shares owned by a company's own employees from being freely traded. See Yao Chengxi, *Stock Market and Futures Market in the People's Republic of China*, (Oxford: Oxford University Press, 1998), pp. 10–11.
34. CSRC, 'Notice on several problems relating to the production of the 1996 listed companies annual reports', 22 January 1997, in CSRC, *Zhengquan qihuo fagui huibian* (1997), pp. 164–6.
35. Guo Qun, 'The classification of non-tradable share equity accounts is in dire need of standardization', *China Securities Daily*, 7 December 1999, p. 4.
36. Standard Opinion, Art. 30, in CSRC, *Zhengquan qihuo fagui huibian* (1992–93), p. 86.
37. For a discussion of this point see Cao Fengqi, *The Development, Standardization and Internationalization of China's Securities Markets*, (Beijing: Zhongguo jinrong chubanshe, 1998), pp. 118–20.
38. 'Lianyi Group discloses the inside story of its share transfer', *China Securities Daily*, 5 November 1999, p. 1
39. See Howson, pp. 158 ff.
40. Company Law, Art. 229, in Shanghai Securities Administration Office, *Zhengquan fagui huibian*, p. 45.

41. In July 1995 the State Council did issue a circular of all of three pages which basically permitted companies, and listed companies in particular, established prior to the Company Law to re-register in order to compaly with the Law. See SC, 'Circular on Initiating the Standardization of Original Limited Liability Companies and Companies Limited by Shares in accordance with the Company Law', 3 July 1995, in CSRC, *Zhengquan qihuo fagui huibian* (1995), pp. 92–3.

42. State Council Office of Trade and the Economy, 'Notice on several problems relating to The State Council Notice on conforming the original limited liability and shareholding companies with the Company Law', 29 December 1995, in CSRC, *Zhengquan qihuo fagui huibian* (1995), pp. 235–7.

43. Company Law, Art. 130, in Shanghai Securities Administration Office, *Zhengquan fagui huibian*, p. 27.

44. Howson, p. 160.

45. Company Law, Chap. 1, Art. 4, in Shanghai Securities Administration Office, *Zhengquan fagui huibian*, p. 4.

46. Company Law, Art. 74, in Shanghai Securities Administration Office, *Zhengquan fagui huibian*, p. 9.

47. SC, 'Special regulation on companies limited by shares offering shares and listing overseas (the 'Overseas Listing Rules')', 4 August 1994, in CSRC, *Zhengquan qihuo fagui huibian* (1994), pp. 34–7.

48. Company Law, Art. 147–8, in Shanghai Securities Administration Office, *Zhengquan fagui huibian*, p. 30.

49. SC, 'Provisions on the Listing of Foreign Investment Shares inside China by a Company Limited by Shares', No. 189, 25 December 1995, in CSRC, *Zhengquan qihuo fagui huibian* (1995), pp. 83–7.

50. The Overseas Listing Rules, like the Company Law, do not make mention of state and legal person shares.

51. B shares are similar in that those B shares listed on the Shenzhen Stock Exchange are denominated in Hong Kong dollars and pay dividends in Hong Kong dollars, while those listed on the Shanghai Stock Exchange are denominated in US dollars and pay dividends in US dollars.

52. This practice was incorporated in the Overseas Listing Rules, Art. 4 in CSRC, *Zhengquan qihuo fagui huibian* (1992–93), p. 34.

53. See SCRES, 'Supplementary Regulations for the Implementation of the "Standard Opinion" by Companies Listing in Hong Kong', 24 May 1993, in CSRC, *Zhengquan qihuo fagui huibian* (1992–93), pp. 270–4.

54. *Asia Wall Street Journal*, 23 July 1999 *Money & Investing*, p. 1.

55. National People's Congress, 'Securities Law', 29 December 1998, in CSRC, *Zhengquan qihuo fagui huibian* (1998), pp. 5–32. The Securities Law came into effect on 1 July 1999. For a commentary see Jackie Lo, 'New PRC Securities Law fails to fully unify regulation of securities issues in China', *China Law & Practice*, February 1999, pp. 21–4.

3   The impact of share and ownership structure

1. SCRES, 'Notice on the immediate halt to the approval of shareholding companies formed through private placements and a reiteration of a halt to

approval and issuance of internal employee shares', 19 June 1994, CSRC, *Zhengquan qihuo fagui huibian* (1994), p. 184.

2. 'Apparent' privatization since the authors were unable to detect by analyzing the trading and dividend performance of these shares any difference from typical state controlled A share companies. This would suggest that other variables might be more important in Chinese listed company performance than the shareholding structure *per se*.

3. Data for Shenzhen are not publicly available, although they can be purchased for an exorbitant sum from the exchange.

4. Chinese market capitalization numbers need to be approached carefully as even the Exchanges are confused over how to value certain types of shares, especially foreign shares listed overseas. The official Shanghai and Shenzhen exchange market capitalization figures are based on the following company valuation methodology: (1) companies with an A share listing and other non-tradable shares have their entire capital structure valued at the secondary market A share trading price; (2) companies with A, B or H share listings will value each listed share independently but will NOT include a value for non-tradable shares; (3) companies with a B share listing only will be valued at the B share market value with all non-tradable shares ignored; (4) for H share companies the SEHK follows the Chinese market practice, valuing only the H shares and ignoring all other shares in the mainland whether listed or non-tradable.

5. It should be noted that the Zhongguancun first share issuance in 1999 was not the entity's initial public offering. The company had been restructured, had new assets injected into it, and then offered shares again. This is not important to the argument at hand which focuses on the pricing of the transactions.

6. 17 October 1999. The official prefers to remain anonymous.

7. *China Securities Daily*, 15 October 1999, p. 1.

8. *China Securities Daily*, 29 November 1999, p. 1. Shares left unsold will be made available to the securities investment funds which will then enjoy a two-year lockup.

9. *China Securities Daily*, 2 December 1999, p. 1.

10. In the event, the first company to go to market with the sale failed miserably. The transaction, completed on 28 December 1999, was nearly 20 per cent undersubscribed forcing the underwriter to actually underwrite for a change! Market response to the second company was also exceedingly cold: only 76 per cent subscribed. The failure of these two experimental deals reflected people's expectations of much lower pricing. Although pricing was based on a 10 times P/E ratio, the calculation used the average of the past three years. The market felt that the consequent absolute price was still too high. Again, the real problem is the absence of value creation and the market's knowledge that there were plenty more state shares to come.

11. Yao, pp. 21–2.

12. Perhaps Yao is referring to the jump in share price at the time of the IPO as the 'latent transfer of value' in which case what should be argued for is a better pricing mechanism. See Section 3.3 for a discussion.

13. The simple appreciation of a company's assets is a matter of financial accounting, while the appreciation or depreciation of the same company's

shares is a matter of market forces which reflect a great many factors including supply and demand, industry outlook, macroeconomic outlook and politics among others. The point is there is no direct linkage between one and the other. In fact, an increase in assets may be the result of an investment decision which the market views negatively with the result that the share value falls. The suggestion that the government adopt a law to address the 'latent transfer of value from state ownership interests to the few individual shareholders caused by the government's self-imposed illiquidity' runs entirely contrary to the concept of markets. Such a law could only overcome the perceived difference in valuation by rigidly calculating share prices based on the audited value of a company's net assets. To push this a bit farther, since audited financial statements are done on a semi-annual basis in China, this would mean that share prices would be allowed to change only two times each year.

14. Special Treatment (ST) companies are defined by the SSE and SZSE as those listed companies with an abnormal financial situation or other special situations. Generally this means those companies showing losses over a consecutive two-year period. For such companies, the exchanges require special labeling and quarterly audited interim financial reports. In addition, a 5 per cent up and down trading band is imposed. There are also 'Particular Transfer (PT)' companies, which have shown losses for three years in a row. The trading of PT shares is basically suspended except for special transfer requests, which can be made each Friday. Any such transfer is also subject to the 5 per cent price band and is not included in the calculation of market trading statistics.

15. This is another indication that there is no 'latent transfer' of value from the state to the non-state investors.

16. The Price/Earnings, or 'P/E', ratio is calculated by taking the market price of a share and dividing it by the company's earnings per share. Comparing this with the P/E ratio of other companies in the same industrial sector gives the analyst a feel for comparative value. It should also be noted that high P/E ratios can also point to low or almost negligible earnings per share.

17. This restriction can be skirted by the use of the black market in foreign exchange, but this money flow is extremely small and can have no impact against the wall of money flowing from domestic retail investors.

4 China's stock exchanges

1. A good overview of the early Shenzhen experience can be found in Gao Shangquan and Ye Sen, *China Economic Systems Reform Yearbook* 1993, pp. 170–4; and 1992 edition, pp. 74–9.

2. Zhu Huayou, 'Development of the Shenzhen stock market and reflections it provokes', in Gao Shangquan and Chi Fulin, (eds), *The Chinese Securities Market*, (Beijing: Foreign Languages Press, 1996), pp. 50–62.

3. Li Changjiang, p. 64; and PBOC Shenzhen SEZ Branch, 'Notice on several issues regarding the administration of the transfer of securities between accounts in Shenzhen', 25 July 1989, *Jinrong falu fagui quanshu*, Vol. 3, p. 2635.

4. Shenzhen Municipal People's Government, 'Provisional regulations on collecting tax on the transfer of share ownership and individual income from shares', 28 June 1990, *Jinrong falu fagui quanshu*, Vol. 3. pp. 2470–1.
5. Li Changjiang, p. 64.
6. A good overview of Shanghai's experience in the 1980s can be found in Gao Shangquan and Ye Sen, *China Economic Systems Reform Yearbook* 1991, pp. 66–73; and Zhu Huayou, 'Retrospect and policies for future development of the Shanghai Stock Exchange', in Gao Shangquan and Chi Fulin, (eds), *The Chinese Securities Market*, pp. 30–50.
7. Beginning in 1988 the PBOC initiated an effort to bring such infringements on its authority under the control of its local branches. But, as will be discussed in greater detail in Chapter 5, the local branches of the PBOC have always been close partners of local governments rather than part of a strong centralized organization. PBOC, 'Notice on the requirement of approval by the PBOC for the establishment of securities companies or similar institutions', 15 July 1988, *Jinrong falu fagui quanshu*, Vol. 3, p. 2751.
8. SCRES, 'Opinion on strengthening the management of enterprises undergoing restructuring', May 1990, cited in Gao Shangquan and Ye Sen, *China Economic Systems Reform Yearbook* 1991, p. 71.
9. The fact that the Shanghai Securities Exchange later on unilaterally changed its name in English to the 'Shanghai Stock Exchange' is an indication of its efforts at establishing an independent identity. Later Shenzhen followed this practice.
10. PBOC Shanghai Branch, 'Shanghai Securities Exchange Articles of Incorporation', August 1990, *Jinrong falu fagui quanshu*, Vol. 3, pp. 2756–8; and PBOC Shenzhen Branch, 'Shenzhen Securities Exchange Articles of Incorporation', 1 January 1991, *Jinrong falu fagui quanshu*, Vol. 3, p. 2746.
11. The earliest form of these commissions was seen in Shenzhen. Shenzhen Municipal People's Government, chap. 6, 'Shenzhen SEZ provisional regulations on the restructuring of SOEs into companies limited by shares', 15 October 1986, *Jinrong falu fagui quanshu*, Vol. 3, p. 2818.
12. SCSC, 'Provisional regulations for the management of securities exchange', 7 July 1993, Shanghai Municipal Securities Administration Office, *Zhengquan fagui huibian*, pp. 204–14.
13. 'Shenzhen Securities Exchange Articles of Incorporation (Revised)', 20 May 1993, Chun Hong, Zhou Shengye and Wu Shaoqiu, *Zhongguo zhengquan fagui zonghui*, Vol. 8, (Beijing: Zhongguo renmin daxue chubanshe, 1998), pp. 866–73.
14. Article 7.4, 'Shanghai Securities Exchange Articles of Incorporation', Revised March 1993, Chun *et al.*, *Zhongguo zhengquan fagui zonghui*, Vol. 8, pp. 858–63. The SSE's operating regulations, however, specified the SCSC and the CSRC as its 'supervisory organization', Art. 5, 'Shanghai securities exchange market operating regulations', January 1993, Chun *et al.*, *Zhongguo zhengquan fagui zonghui*, Vol. 8, pp. 840.
15. Zhu Huayou, 'Retrospect and policies for future development of the Shanghai Stock Exchange', in Gao Shangquan and Chi Fulin, *The Chinese Securities Market*, pp. 45–7.
16. SCSC, 'Regulations on the Administration of Stock Exchanges', 21 August 1996, CSRC, *Zhengquan qihuo fagui huibian* (1996), pp. 50–66.

17. Securities Law, Chapter 5.
18. CGBs must be bought and owned outright as no securities borrowing facilities are permitted. Each individual CGB issue has a conversion ratio indicating the amount of the loan which can be borrowed against it. For example, CGB 9905 has a conversion ratio of 100 meaning that RMB 100 can be borrowed against it. Other bonds have different ratios. Repo maturities have standard maturities of 3, 7, 14, 28, 91 or 182 days, but the market is deepest for the 3 and 7 day repos. The minimum market trade is 100 *shou* or RMB100 000.
19. The SSE and SZSE market statistics fully capture the trading volume conducted through the trading centers.
20. CSRC, 'Notice on several problems on further restructuring the securities trading centers', 8 December 1998, in CSRC, *Zhengquan qihuo fagui huibian* (1998), p. 95.
21. See Stock Exchange Executive Council, 'The National Security Trading Automated Quotation System', in Gao Shangquan and Ye Sen, *China Economic Systems Reform Yearbook* 1991, pp. 106–10.
22. Gao Shangquan and Ye Sen, *China Economic Systems Reform Yearbook* 1993, p. 63.
23. 'Articles of Incorporation of STAQ', *STAQ Annual Manual* (1995) (Beijing: Internal Publication, 1995), p. 1.
24. PBOC, 'China Securities Trading System Corp. Ltd. Operating Regulations', 1 January 1991, *Jinrong falu fagui quanshu*, Vol. 3, pp. 2764–74.
25. PBOC, 'Articles of Incorporation of China Securities Trading System Co. Ltd.', 8 March 1993, *Jinrong falu fagui quanshu*, Vol. 3, pp. 2800–2.

5   Market regulatory structure

1. Brilliance China Automotive listed on the NYSE on 7 October 1992, about one week prior to the announcement of the CSRC's formation. At the time this was considered a kind of black project as it marked an end around other simultaneous efforts which went on to become the principal direction of policy. Nonetheless, it was accepted at last as China's first international issue if only by SCRES. For a review see, Gao Sangquan and, Ye Sen, *China Economic Systems Reform Yearbook* 1993, pp. 92–4.
2. SC, 'PRC provisional regulations on the administration of banks'; 7 January 1986, *Jinrong falu fagui quanshu*, Vol. 2, pp. 2085–9.
3. PBOC, 'Notice that the establishment of securities companies or similar financial entities must be approved by the PBOC', 15 July 1988, *Jinrong falu fagui quanshu*, Vol. 3, p. 2751; and the State Council document is quoted in PBOC, 'The PBOC forwards the State Council's Minutes of the meeting on researching problems associated with cleaning up and restructuring government securities intermediary organizations', 7 August 1990, *Jinrong falu fagui quanshu*, Vol. 3, p. 2754.
4. SC, 'Notice on strengthening the administration of share and debt securities', 28 March 1987, *Jinrong falu fagui quanshu*, Vol. 3, p. 2633.
5. PBOC Shenzhen SEZ Branch, 'Principles for the review and approval of the issuance of enterprise shares', 1989, *Jinrong falu fagui quanshu*, Vol. 3, pp. 2467–8.

6. SCRES, 'Opinion on strengthening the management of enterprises undergoing restructuring', May 1990, Gao Sangquan and Ye Sen, *China Economic Systems Reform Yearbook* 1991, p. 71.

7. PBOC, 'Specialized banks must not manage directly or carry out securities trading operations', 11 August 1990, *Jinrong falu fagui quanshu*, Vol. 3, p. 2640.

8. PBOC, 'Provisional methods for the administration of securities companies', 12 October 1990, pp. 2758–60; 'Notice on several problems relating to the establishment of securities trading agency arrangements', 19 October 1990, p. 2761; and 'Provisional methods on the administration of securities trading business offices', 22 November 1990, pp. 2761–4, all in *Jinrong falu fagui quanshu*, Vol. 3.

9. PBOC, 'Provisional measures for the administration of inter-regional securities trading', 19 October 1990, *Jinrong guizhang zhidu xuanbian* 1990, Vol. 1, (Beijing, Jinrong chubanshe, 1991), pp. 115–18.

10. As referenced in SCRES, PBOC, SAMB, 'Notice on the resubmission for review and approval by pilot shareholding enterprises issuing shares to the public', 9 May 1991, *Jinrong guizhang zhidu xuanbian* 1991, Vol. 1, pp. 40–2.

11. Song Guoliang, 'The trial divisions of function in China's securities administration system and their characteristics', unpublished paper, Beijing, undated.

12. State Council, 'Circular on the Establishment of the SCSC (Establishment Circular)' 12 October 1992.

13. The functions of the SCSC and the CSRC were clarified in the famous State Council Document 68, 'Notice on further strengthening the macro-administration of the securities markets', No. 68, 17 December 1992, in CSRC, *Zhengquan qihuo fagui huibian* (1992–93), pp. 61–4.

14. State Council, 'Notice on further strengthening the macro-administration of the securities markets', No. 68, 17 December 1992, in CSRC, *Zhengquan qihuo fagui huibian* (1992–93), pp. 61–4.

15. To get a flavor for how these local securities administration offices worked, read a selection of work reports in Chinese Securities Yearbook Editorial Board, *China Securities Yearbook* 1998, pp. 164–98.

16. For full details of this incident see Yao, Chap. 4.

17. Liu Hongru has written extensively about this and was the Chief Editor of an important book on the topic of overseas listings, Liu Hongru, *A Review of and the Prospects for Overseas Listings by Chinese Enterprises*, (Beijing: Zhongguo caizheng jingji chubanshe, 1998).

18. For example see, 'Power Struggle Blocks HK Listings', *Window*, 8 January 1993, p. 59, which describes the CSRC's fight with PBOC.

19. This section is based on an extended article by Liu Hongru, the first Chairman of the CSRC, 'Capital Markets and the Use of Foreign Capital', *Capital Markets*, March 1997, and can also be found in Liu Hongru, Chief Editor, *A Review of and the Prospects for Overseas Listings by Chinese Enterprises*, pp. 25–9.

20. SCSC, 'Notice on the authorization of the CSRC to investigate and enforce violations of securities laws and statutes', in CSRC, *Zhengquan qihuo fagui huibian* (1992–93), p. 212. The SCSC was authorized by the State Council to

enforce securities laws in State Council, 'Provisional measures for share issuance and trading', 22 April 1993, in CSRC, *Zhengquan qihuo fagui huibian* (1992–93), pp. 39–55.

21. Ministry of Justice, CSRC, 'Provisional measures for determining the qualifications for lawyers and law offices conducting securities business', 12 January 1993, pp. 251–2; MOF, CSRC, 'Regulation on determining the qualifications of CPAs and accounting firms conducting securities business', 23 February 1993, pp. 253–6; SAMB, CSRC, 'Regulations on determining the qualifications of asset appraisal companies conducting securities business', 20 March 1993, pp. 257–9, Audit Office, CSRC, 'Notice on several problems regarding determining the qualifications of auditing companies conducting securities business', 23 March 1993, p. 260, all in CSRC, *Zhengquan qihuo fagui huibian* (1992–93).

22. State Council, 'Notice on resolutely prohibiting the blind development of the futures markets', 4 November 1993, in CSRC, *Zhengquan qihuo fagui huibian* (1992–93), pp. 70–1. Chairman Liu have wished that futures had not been given the CSRC since the Shenyin Securities fiasco on 1995 was the presumed reason for his removal from office.

23. SCSC, 'Regulations on Securities Exchanges', 21 August 1996, in CSRC, *Zhengquan qihuo fagui huibian* (1996), pp. 50–66.

24. Securities Law, Chap. 10.

25. Securities Law, Art. 19.

26. For a thorough discussion of the Listing Committee see CSRC, *Securities Issuance and Underwriting*, (Beijing: Shanghai caijing daxue chubanshe, 1999), pp. 125–7.

6 The issuers and the listing process

1. The most successful Chinese IPO of all time, China Telecom (HK) Limited, raised US$4.2 billion in October 1997, but the company is a technical anomaly since its parent in located in the British Virgin Islands for tax purposes. While absolutely the same as a Red Chip, it is not included in the Hang Seng Red Chip Index.

2. The sectors included and excluded in various state policy proclamations. For example, SCRES, SPC, MOF, PBOC and SC, Art. 1, 'Trial measures on the shareholding system', 15 May 1992, in CSRC, *Zhengquan qihuo fagui huibian* (1992–93), p. 75; and CSRC, Art. 1, 'Circular on certain issues relating to share issuance', 26 December 1996, in CSRC, *Zhengquan qihuo fagui huibian* (1996), p. 166. The trend has been to broaden the scope open to investors for a variety of reasons including greater government familiarity with the implications of public listings as well as the need to raise project funding. Similarly, the quota system described in this section was done away with in 1998.

3. At the National People's Congress in March 1999, China's Constitution was revised to give the non-state sector the same legal recognition as the state sector. Following this there has been much talk of providing bank financing as well as opening the capital markets to the non-state sector. One trial balloon, which boosted the B share markets briefly, was to allow private companies to issue B shares.

4. See SPC and SCRES, 'Regulations on the macro-administration of pilot shareholding enterprises', 15 June 1992, CSRC, *Zhengquan qihuo fagui huibian* (1992–93), pp. 114–16.

5. The various conditions which must be met and materials presented are detailed in State Council, 'Provisional regulations on the administration of the issuing and trading of shares', 22 April 1993, CSRC, *Zhengquan qihuo fagui huibian* (1992–93), pp. 39–55; and CSRC, 'Circular on the application materials for enterprises publicly offering shares', 5 September 1995, CSRC, *Zhengquan qihuo fagui huibian* (1995), pp. 195–7.

6. Article 45, Securities Law. B shares continued to be governed by the 1995 Regulations.

7. Article 46, Securities Law. This marks a major departure from past practice which required an approval (*pizhun*) from the CSRC and is in line with the effort to shift such responsibility to the company and its intermediaries.

8. CSRC, 'Circular on the form and content of listing public notices', 6 January 1997, CSRC, *Zhengquan qihuo fagui huibian* (1997), pp. 137–42. Of course, a glance at any day's copy of the *China Securities Daily* will provide plenty of actual examples.

9. For example, see SSE, 'Shanghai Securities Exchange securities listing administration procedures', January 1993, Shanghai Securities Administration Office, *Zhengquan fagui huibian*, pp. 715–21.

10. Articles 10–12, 1995 Provisions.

11. There is an extensive Chinese 'how to' literature for aspiring SOE managers. The following book is a good example and contains the restructuring proposals of each variety of listing company, Jiang Xinwen, Chief Editor, *Guide to Shareholding Enterprise Restructuring and Actual Examples*, (Beijing: Zhongguo jingji chubanshe, 1997).

12. This only became apparent after the China Haixing Shipping listing in 1994. In that case the company was not attractive enough to enjoy a blowout in a market which, anyhow, was just going South. See Business Section, *South China Morning Post*, 30 July 1994, p. 2, quoting the *Shanghai Securities News*.

13. SC, 'Provisional measures on the management of share issuance and trading', 22 April 1993, CSRC, *Zhengquan qihuo fagui huibian* (1992–93), pp. 39–55.

14. For example, see SCRES, 'Supplementary Regulations on Companies Implementing the "Standard Opinion" and Listing in Hong Kong', 24 May 1993, CSRC, *Zhengquan qihuo fagui huibian* (1992–93), pp. 270–4.

15. For a discussion of this practice see Cao Fengqi, (ed.) *Zhongguo Zhengjuan Shichang, Fazhan, Guifan yu Guojihua*, pp. 120 ff.

16. CSRC, 'Notice on doing a good job carrying out equity issuance in 1997', 10 September 1997, downloaded from the CSRC website.

17. CSRC, 'Circular on Further Improving the Method of Issuing Shares', 28 July 1999, *China Securities Daily*, 29 July 1999, p. 1.

18. *Focus*, No. 89, 6 November 1999, pp. 12–13.

7 Investors and other market participants

1. *China Insurance Daily*, 16 September 1999, p. 1.

2. *China Securities Daily*, 27 October 1999, p. 1.

3. An excellent discussion of investment funds and the problems associated with them in the years prior to the standardizing legislation of 1997 can be found in Cao Fengqi, Chapter 7.
4. CSRC, 'Provisional measures for administering securities investment funds', 5 November 1997, CSRC, *Zhengquan qihuo fagui huibian* 1997, pp. 89–97.
5. For example, a procedure was set establishing fund management companies, CSRC, 'Notice on problems related to the establishment of fund management companies', 12 December 1997, pp. 200–2; and CSRC, 'Notice on the standards for implementing Provisional measures for administering securities investment funds', 12 December 1997, pp. 206–43, in CSRC, *Zhengquan qihuo fagui huibian* 1997.
6. PBOC, MOF, 'Circular mandating severance of PBOC local branches from economic entities managed by them', 4 September 1993, *Jinrong falu fagui quanshu*, Vol. 2, p. 2060.
7. SC, 'Decision on Financial System Reform', 25 December 1993, *Jinrong falu fagui quanshu*, Vol. 2, pp. 2098–102, which states 'The securities industry shall be operated and managed as a separate industry independent of the banking, trust and the insurance industries. Securities companies shall be established independent of banks, trust institutions and insurance companies.'
8. Article 6, Securities Law.
9. Applications were initiated early in 1999 and largely followed the rules set out in PBOC, 'Provisional regulations relating to the administration of securities firms', 12 October 1990, *Jinrong falu fagui quanshu*, Vol. 3, p. 2758–60. The procedure should be the same, since that part of the PBOC Financial Institutions Department dealing with securities firms was transferred *en masse* to the CSRC in early 1999.
10. By mid August the CSRC had initiated the process based on a 5 July document with completion expected before the end of September.
11. *Da Gong Bao*, 18 January 1999.
12. The 1990 Regulations required a minimum level of registered capital of only RMB10 million.
13. On 6 August 1999, the CSRC approved the merger of J&A Securities with Guotai Securities creating the largest firm in the industry with US$360 million in capital. This was the first such merger among industry participants approved and was spurred by a major scandal involving the senior management of J&A.
14. 'Support the development of the capital markets, expand the space for securities companies to finance', *China Securities Daily*, 20 October 1999, p. 1.
15. Hang Seng Services Ltd, www.hsi.com.uk.

8 Market trends and performance

1. The figures are based on the average 50 trading day price return correlations.
2. This is a reflection of both pricing strategy by investment banks as well as the SEHK's market capacity.
3. The three periods are: 15 November 1996 to 12 November 1999, 15 November 1997 to 12 November 1999 and 15 November 1998 to 12 November 1999.

4. The Shanghai 30 Index is an index of the top thirty stocks listed in the Shanghai exchange. See Appendices for constituent stocks.
5. This has held true historically up until the end of 1999 when the fever for Internet and Internet-related stocks hit Hong Kong much like the Red Chip craze in 1997. The performance of what remain concept stocks has over-shadowed the traditional heavyweights, but it remains to be seen whether this will persist.
6. Bonus Issues are similar to stock dividends. The company offers existing investors (including all investor types) as of a specified ex-rights date a divi-dend which is paid in new shares. A rights issue is an offering wherein existing investors are given the right to subscribe to new shares being issued by the company priced at a discount to market.
7. China Telecom investors, in any event, should certainly be happy. The stock is up over 200 per cent since its IPO in October 1997.
8. As of 30 September 1999 there were 64 'special treatment' companies with a market capitalization of over RMB11 billion listed domestically. Such 'ST' companies are those which have not recorded a profit for the previous two calendar years and are in danger of being delisted.
9. The Charts 8.6 and 8.7 use the H share index as defined by Hong Kong exchange regulations as follows: to reflect the stock price performance of companies listed in Hong Kong and incorporated in mainland China all H share companies listed on the SEHK are included in the Hang Seng China Enterprises Index (HSCEI). The Red Chip index is similarly defined by the SEHK as noted previously and also carried in the Appendices.

9 Summing up and looking ahead

1. *China Securities Daily*, 23 December 1999, p. 1.

Select Bibliography

Newspapers

Asian Wall Street Journal
China Securities Daily
Da Gong Bao
People's Daily (Remin ribao)
South China Morning Post

Electronic information systems

Bloomberg
Wind (*'Wande'*) Information System

Websites

China Securities Daily	www.cs.com.cn
Chinese bonds	www.chinabond.com.cn
CSRC	www.csrc.gov.cn
Hang Seng Services Ltd.	www.hsi.hk.com
Homeway	www.homeway.com.cn
HK Securites and Futures Commission	www.hksfc.org
Shanghai Securities Daily	www.stocknews.com.cn
Shanghai Stock Exchange	www.sse.com.cn
Shenzhen Stock Exchange	www.sse.org.cn
South China Morning Post/Homeway	www.chinaweb.com
Stock Exchange of Hong Kong	www.sehk.com.hk
Wind Information System	www.wind.com.cn

Publications

Cao Er-jie, *Research and Prospects for the Chinese Securities Markets*, (Beijing: Zhongguo Caizheng jingji chubanshe, 1994).

Cao Fengqi, *The Development, Standardization and Internationalization of China's Securities Markets*, (Beijing: Zhongguo jinrong chubanshe, 1998).

China Chengxin Securities Rating Service Ltd., ed., *China Listed Companies Reports 1998*, (Beijing: Bingqi gongye chubanshe, 1998).

China Securities Industry Training Center, ed., *Zuixin Zhongguo zhengquan falu yu gongsi yunzuo guize* (Beijing: Zhongguo minzhu fazhi chubanshe: 1997).

China Securities Regulatory Commission, ed., *Zhengquan qihuo fagui huibian* (1992–98), (Beijing: Falu chubanshe: undated), annual.

China Securities Regulatory Commission, *Securities Issuance and Underwriting*, (Beijing: Shanghai caijing daxue chubanshe, 1999).

China Securities Yearbook 1998 (Beijing: Zhongguo jingji chubanshe, 1998).

Chun Hong, Zhou Shengye and Wu Shaoqiu, eds, *Zhongguo zhengquan fagui zonghui*, Vol. 8 (Beijing: Zhongguo renmin daxue chubanshe, 1998).

Gao Shangquan and Chi Fulin, eds, *The Chinese Securities Market*, (Beijing: Foreign Languages Press, 1996).

Gui Minjie, ed., *Shenzhen Securities Market Exchange Statistics*, (Shenzhen: Southwest Finance University Publishing House, monthly.)

Gao Shangquan and Ye Sen, eds, *China Economic Systems Reform Yearbook 1990*, (Beijing: China Reform Publishing House, 1991), annual.

Howson, Nicholas C., 'China's Company Law: One Step Forward, Two Steps Back?', *Columbia Journal of Asian Law*, 11:1, 1997, pp. 127–73.

Jiang Ping, advisor, *Jinrong falu fagui quanshu*, (Beijing: Sanxia chubanshe, 1997), three volumes.

Jiang Xinwen, chief editor, *Guide to Shareholding Enterprise Restructuring and Actual Examples*, (Beijing: Zhongguo jingji chubanshe, 1997)

Li Changjiang, *The History and Development of China's Securities Markets*, (Beijing: Zhongguo wuzi chubanshe, 1998).

Liu Hongru, chief editor, *A Review of and the Prospects for Overseas Listings by Chinese Enterprises*, (Beijing: Zhongguo caizheng jingji chubanshe, 1998).

Liu Hongru, 'Several issues regarding China's experiments with the shareholding structure', *Renmin Ribao*, 23 June 1992, p. 5.

Lo, Jackie, 'New PRC Securities Law fails to fully unify regulation of securities issues in China', *China Law & Practice*, February 1999, pp. 21–4.

People's Bank of China, *Jinrong guizhang zhidu xuanbian* 1989–1991 (Beijing: Jinrong chubanshe, 1991), annual.

Shanghai Securities Administration Office, ed., *Zhengquan fagui huibian*, (Shanghai: Xuexi dushu chuban gongsi, 1996).

Shanghai Stock Exchange Fact Book 1998, (Shanghai: Shanghai Stock Exchange, 1999), annual.

Shenzhen Securities Exchange Fact Book (1994–98), (Shenzhen: China Capital Publishing House).

Shanghai Stock Exchange Statistics Annual (1990–99), (Shanghai: Shanghai People's Publishing House).

Song Guoliang, 'The trial divisions of function in China's securities administration system and their characteristics', unpublished paper undated, Beijing.

Stock Exchange Executive Council, *STAQ Annual Manual* (1995), (Beijing: Internal Publication, 1995).

Tang Yun Wei, Lynne Chow and Barry J. Cooper, *Accounting and Finance in China* (Hong Kong: Longman Group (Far East) Ltd., 1992).

Tu Guangshao, ed., *Shanghai Stock Exchange Monthly Statistics*, (Shanghai: Shanghai Securities News Issuing Co.)

Yao Chengxi, *Stock Market and Futures Market in the People's Republic of China*, (Oxford: Oxford University Press, 1998).

Index

Printed in the United States
56783LVS00009B/1